ROOTS OF THE RIGHT
READINGS IN FASCIST, RACIST AND ELITIST IDEOLOGY

General Editor: GEORGE STEINER
Fellow of Churchill College, Cambridge

MAX STIRNER:
THE EGO AND HIS OWN

MAX STIRNER:

THE EGO AND HIS OWN

Edited and Introduced by
JOHN CARROLL

1817

HARPER & ROW, PUBLISHERS
New York, Evanston, San Francisco, London

First published 1845 under the title *Der Einzige und sein Eigenthum*. English translation by Steven T. Byington first published 1907. This edition revised, selected and annotated by John Carroll, 1971.

FIRST U.S. EDITION

STANDARD BOOK NUMBER: 06-014131-X

LIBRARY OF CONGRESS CATALOG CARD NUMBER: 70-156573

GENERAL EDITOR'S PREFACE

Reliable estimates put at about seventy million the figure
of those dead through war, revolution and famine in
Europe and Russia between 1914 and 1945. To all but a
few visionaries and pessimistic thinkers of the nineteenth
century the image of such an apocalypse, of a return to
barbarism, torture and mass extermination in the heart-
lands of civilized life, would have seemed a macabre
fantasy. Much of the crisis of identity and society that has
overshadowed twentieth-century history comes from an
impulse towards totalitarian politics. The theory of man as
a rational animal, entitled to a wide exercise of political
and economic decision, of man as a being equally endowed
whatever his race, has been attacked at its religious, moral
and philosophic roots. The most 'radical' attack — 'radical'
in that it demands a total revaluation of man's place in
society and of the status of different races in the general
scheme of power and human dignity — has come from the
Right.

Using the concept of the Fall of Man, of man as an
instinctual savage requiring total leadership and repeated
blood-letting, a number of elitist, racist and totalitarian
dreamers and publicists have offered an alternative statement of the human condition. Fascism, Nazism, the programme of the Falange or the *Croix de Feu*, represent
different variants of a related vision. Although this vision
is often lunatic and nakedly barbaric, it can provide
acute, tragic insights into the myths and taboos that
underlie democracy.

Because the political and philosophical programme of

the Right has come so near to destroying our civilization and is so alive still, it must be studied. Hence this series of source-readings in elitist, racist and fascist theory as it was articulated in France, Germany, Italy, Spain and other national communities between the 1860s and the Second World War. These 'black books' fill an almost complete gap in the source material available to any serious student of modern history, psychology, politics and sociology (most of the texts have never been available in English and several have all but disappeared in their original language). But these books also touch on the intractable puzzle of the co-existence in the same mind of profound inhumanity and obvious philosophic and literary importance.

GEORGE STEINER

CONTENTS

INTRODUCTION

The Ego and His Own is an extremist document. We are faced immediately on reading it by the question of where to place it politically; its ideas do not slot neatly into any one category. Moreover, an examination of the influence it has had presents no specific answer.

Stirner's philosophy of individualist anarchism involves an uncompromising rejection of all authority beyond the reach of the individual, which, at a first glance, places it to the left of Marx. It unleashes one of the most savage and penetrating attacks ever written on liberal democracy. 'I do not want the liberty of men, nor their equality,' Stirner writes; 'I want only *my* power over them, I want to make them my property, *material for enjoyment.*' But Stirner is no more sympathetic towards socialism and communism; he sees them permeated with the same ineffectual liberal ethos—their revolution will merely substitute one repressive set of institutions for another.

The isolating of liberalism and socialism as the twin vehicles of all that is degenerate and poisoning in political life is one of the distinguishing marks of fascist ideology. The above quotation concludes: 'I do not renounce, from any access of humility, even the power over life and death.' The tenor, and sometimes the argument, of Stirner's philosophy were to be heard again, in the twentieth century, from the mouths of Mussolini and Hitler. The common enemy was contained in the idea of a politics which, in the name of stability and equality, would usher in a drab society of petty officials and financiers, in which passion was stifled by morality and virtue made of half-heartedness and mediocrity.

Although Stirner has been generally regarded as the most radical of the Left Hegelians gathered in Berlin in the early eighteen forties, his philosophical extremism is pursued with such rigour that it becomes detached from any of the bases of political action which are traditionally accepted as being viable. This is manifest in the ease with which its threads can be twisted to match fascist ideology, as Hans Helms has taken six hundred pages to demonstrate.[1] The ideal of a free economy, the picture of society as a battleground where only the boldest and fittest survive, the emphasis on a healthy and virile youth, on action oriented towards the central value of self-exaltation, and an ahistorical and thus, at least to a Marxist, disinherited and uncritical consciousness, are themes which grouped together form a highly charged field whose centre of motion is easily deflected from its individualist-anarchist path towards totalitarian ends. Stirner's romanticist emphasis on self-realization and the individual's striving to create his own glory, once projected into the political arena, tends towards militant nationalism.

Stirner argues that action at the level of the large group or society can only be justified by appeal to some abstraction. Values with a concrete reality are only found in the circle of the individual and his friends; beyond are god, fetish, and ideal. Here Stirner is in key with the general anarchist principle of rejecting political action *en bloc* in favour of socio-economic change. He admired Christ for his indifference to Caesar, his independence from politics. However, as Thomas Mann pointed out, such a position is profoundly political, in the twentieth century at least.

[1] Hans G. Helms, *Die Ideologie der anonymen Gesellschaft* (M. Du Mont Schauberg, Köln, 1966).

In essence, Stirner's case is not much different from that of the German intellectual who, prior to Hitler's rise to power, claimed to stand aloof from politics—this independence implied, in the terms of the political reality, a complicity with *whatever* was to follow. The Left, which is committed to political action, and to using efficacious means—large-scale organization and violence—has some right to say: 'He who is not with us is against us.' It is unnecessary to detail the cases in which fragmentation of the Left in a time of crisis has facilitated a Rightist seizure of power. In an age of 'mass politics', and the centralization of power in the bureaucratic State, the choice to be apolitical is not available; in such an arena Stirner has by default Rightist tendencies.

The suggestion that Stirner played an important role in the rise of European fascism needs careful clarification. We must look at the men the ideas have influenced as well as the ideas themselves. But are we to accept the view that theory contains within itself its own praxis, in the sense that the way it is used represents a part of its own inner reality? Is the manner in which an idea is interpreted, and that interpretation realized, essential to its ontological nature? Does the fact that Mussolini was enthusiastic about his work make Stirner in any way responsible for the atrocities of Italian fascism? There is clearly no simple answer; all we can do here is report that influence.

Mussolini wrote from prison in 1911 of his flights over the intellectual peaks of Europe: 'And these summits of the spirit are called Stirner, Nietzsche, Goethe, Schiller, Montaigne, Cervantes, etc.' It must be remembered that Mussolini's notorious exhibitionism made him less a passionate follower of ideas than an intellectual opportunist, freely swapping them to suit the cause of the moment. Nevertheless, Stirner would have fed his ambition. In

1919 Mussolini wrote: 'Leave the way free for the elemental power of the individual; for there is no other human reality than the individual! Why shouldn't *Stirner* become significant again?'

In Germany, Stirner's influence on fascism was much more obscure than Nietzsche's. Indeed, his importance in this context can be largely reduced to the degree that he influenced Nietzsche, whose work was much better known. Dietrich Eckart, however, who helped Hitler financially in the vital early years following 1918 in Munich, knew Stirner's book. Although Helms shows that he borrowed ideas from it, it is clear that he was far from an enthusiastic Stirnerian; he was more profoundly affected by the parallel individualism of Ibsen's *Peer Gynt*. It is unlikely that Hitler ever heard of Stirner.

There is another reason for differentiating Stirner from the Left. The most significant response to his book came from Marx and Engels; *The German Ideology* was begun in 1845 but in spite of their efforts was not published in full until 1932. Their critique of German philosophy and socialism, as the book is subtitled, allots seventy pages to Feuerbach, a meagre twenty to Bruno Bauer, and three hundred and eighty, in the section headed 'Saint Max', to Stirner — two-thirds of the entire manuscript. Its composition and style suggest that in 1845 they considered Stirner to be their most dangerous adversary. The relentless, often vicious, ridiculing of him in this book cannot be passed off as merely the product of Marx's choleric temperament. 'Saint Max' is the work of a mind under stress. Karl Löwith, in summing up this period, wrote: 'The only thing radical enough to be compared to Marx is the converse programme of Stirner ... ' Feuerbach had written of Stirner in a letter dated late in 1844 as 'the most gifted and freest writer it has been given me to know'. Recently the Polish Marxist Leszek Kolakowski wrote: 'Stirner's grounds are irrefutable ... Even Nietzsche seems inconsequential in comparison to him.'[1]

It would be naive to deny a place on the left of the political spectrum to all philosophies with which Marx had a serious confrontation. Nevertheless, a fundamental polarization emerges from the Stirner-Marx debate. For Stirner, the condition of man is to be improved through the individual; a healthy society is an association of healthy egoists, each having emancipated himself from the social environment which formed him. Marx, on the contrary, argued that socio-economic change is a necessary prerequisite for a better individual life, and regarded Stirner as the philosopher for the petty bourgeoisie—for schoolmasters and shopkeepers. Looking at the dichotomy from the Marxist standpoint, as Helms does, Stirner becomes the first ideologist of the middle class and one of the precursors of fascism. However, he is blatantly misrepresented by this interpretation and its determination to search out the economic class to which some of his ideas seem most appropriate. It disregards the most important aspects of his work—his psychology, his analysis of morality, and his critique of Christianity and liberalism. Helms, in his Marxist attempt to place Stirner in the 'roots of the Right', had to strain possible associations to the extent of referring to 'the existentialist wave of sublimated fascism'.

In the end we have to admit that the case for including Stirner in the 'roots of the Right' is not watertight. *The Ego and His Own* is important for a number of reasons, one

[1] Finally, after a long period in which the ever-expanding corpus of secondary literature on Marx has virtually neglected these facts, notice has been taken of the importance of Stirner in the development of Marx's thought, by David McLellan in his book *The Young Hegelians and Karl Marx* (Macmillan, London, 1969).

of them being that many of its themes form a vital component of fascist ideology—the others will be discussed below. The appeal of German fascism can only be understood with reference to the tradition of romantic individualism which matured through the nineteenth century. Stirner was a key figure in this development, the one in a line including Goethe, Wagner and Nietzsche who went the furthest in exploring a philosophy of the glorification of the ego in the context of political and socio-economic ideas. It is primarily for this reason that he presents himself as an important contributor to the growth of European fascism. At the same time, to be fair to him, we accept that his work is categorically anti-authoritarian, that there is no suggestion of racism, and that he had nothing but contempt for German nationalism; in Dostoevsky's terms his anarchism stands with Christ against the Grand Inquisitor. Moreover, on the question of influence the scales may finally balance; there have been a number of men more introspective than Mussolini who have paid Stirner homage and who in their quiet way may have exerted just as profound a sway on the development of Western thought and behaviour. As for the author's responsibility for what posterity has done with his work, we must allow Stirner the final word: 'Do I write out of love for men? No, I write because I want to procure for *my* thoughts an existence in the world; and, even if I foresaw that these thoughts would deprive you of your rest and your peace, even if I saw the bloodiest wars and the fall of many generations springing up from this seed of thought—I would nevertheless scatter it. Do with it what you will and can, that is your affair and does not trouble me.'

Stirner is one of the men who defy political classification; the orthodox categories break down. The same can be said of Nietzsche. In one sense the ends of the political spectrum here meet. The extreme Left begins to look like the extreme Right if the many try collectively to put its ideas into practice. In America Malcolm X, and Eldridge Cleaver in *Soul on Ice*, search for a way out of a prevailingly racist social morality that would not lead to its being replaced by another, equally repressive one; each, through his own example, pointed to the individual finding a personal dignity. Yet it was finally the militant, exclusive Black Panthers who translated their ideas into political action.

The life Stirner wrote about and the life he lived were in marked contrast. A drab and inconsequential reality was compensated for by an assertive philosophy concerned with limitless human possibility. However, there is too much trenchant psychology in *The Ego and His Own* to identify its author as a day-dreamer escaping from a society with whose practicalities he could not cope.

Stirner was born on October 26th, 1806, in a house overlooking the marketplace in Bayreuth.[1] His father, Albert Christian Heinrich Schmidt, a flute-maker, died when the young boy, christened Johann Caspar, was only six months old. Two years later the widow married a fifty-year-old apothecary's assistant called Ballerstedt, who soon afterwards bought a pharmacy in Kulm in East Prussia.

At the age of twelve the boy was sent back to the town of his birth and the care of his childless uncle and god-father, Johann Caspar Martin Sticht. He stayed with him and his wife for eight years while he completed his secondary schooling, with distinction but not brilliance.

[1] Nearly all of the sparse evidence we have about Stirner's life is a result of the research of John Henry Mackay, and is recorded in his biography, *Max Stirner. Sein Leben und sein Werk* (Schuster und Loeffler, Berlin, 1898).

His unusually high forehead gained him the nickname of *Stirner* at school, and, with his individualist fancy tickled and his romantic ambitions stirred by the allusion to the stars (*Stirn* = forehead, *Gestirn* = star), the plebeian name of Schmidt was abandoned.

And so in 1826 it was 'Max Stirner' who became a student at Berlin University, where for two years he was to have his philosophical consciousness awakened by the one man he may ever have recognized as a master— Hegel. Whatever else it achieved, this period seems to have induced a great restlessness: he spent one term in Erlangen in 1828, then registered in Kant's old fief, Königsberg, but rushed off before he had attended one lecture to nurse his increasingly mentally unbalanced mother. He was back in Berlin by October 1832, struggling for an academic qualification. By the middle of 1834 he thought himself ready to take his examinations, but must have quickly changed his mind, a decision well understandable in the light of the subsequent assessment of his Latin examiner: 'His exposition was feeble and tedious.' Finally he completed his orals in the following April. The report of the examiners emphasized two major failings: lack of precise knowledge of anything but the Bible, and the possession of an extremely rigorous logical mind which tended to stifle his thought. He was awarded a limited *facultas docendi*, permitting him to teach in a Prussian Gymnasium but ending ambitions of further academic glory. Of singular interest in this period is the essay Stirner wrote for his examination, published eventually in 1920: *Über Schulgesetze* (1834). Although it was written much more obviously under the influence of Hegel than his major work ten years later, it already displayed some striking originality.

Meanwhile he had taken up residence in the house of a

midwife. Under the same roof were Caroline Friederike Burtz and her illegitimate daughter, Agnes Clara Kunigunde Burtz. For a year and a half Stirner worked as an unpaid teacher at the Königliche Realschule in Berlin, and he seems to have become resigned to the Prussian Government's refusal to give him a salaried post. His stepfather died in 1837 leaving him little if any inheritance. His mother was by now incurably insane and entered a nursing home in Berlin. The year had a less morbid side to it, for on December 12th Caspar Schmidt married Kunigunde Burtz. However, the passionate advocate-to-be of sensual love was later to confess that sexual happiness had not been a part of their married life. Perhaps Max Stirner was only capable of consummating a relationship with ideas? We know too little to say. We do know that in August of the following year the youthful wife of twenty-two died in childbirth.

In October 1839 his luck changed and he began teaching at Madame Gropius's educational institute for young ladies. He was to remain there for five years before resigning, when the imminent publication of his book must have awakened images of the carefree life of a fêted philosopher.

Mackay's researches have left us something of a portrait of Stirner. He was of slightly less than medium height, well proportioned, slender, and always dressed with care, though without pretension. He wore steel-rimmed spectacles which heightened his pedagogic appearance. His hair was blond, his blue eyes were gentle, neither dreamy nor penetrating. His thin lips in later years usually wore a sarcastic, yet never bitter, smile. He had a strong chin, but the most distinctive of his features were his hands—slim, white and well tended. In short, his appearance was sympathetic, although not striking. The

portrait is cast in a different light by the researches of
Rolf Engert,[1] who received a pencil drawing of 'Joh.
Kasp. Schmidt' from a Berlin worker who claimed that his
grandfather had known Stirner. It is a romantic sketch of
a signally handsome young man, in the style of Byron:
large intense eyes, long fluted nose, pursed sensual lips
giving a slightly haughty and very determined air, matched
by the square-set jaw and the long hair casually brushed
back from a high, aristocratic brow.

In spite of a spark of unrecognized promise in 1834,
Max Stirner, an unremarkable student of obscure origins,
seemed by the age of thirty-five destined to the humble
life of a school-teacher. The question of how he developed
into the incisive author of the revolutionary *The Ego and
His Own* immediately arises. How did Caspar Schmidt's
adolescent dream of an *alter ego*, Max Stirner, turn into a
reality? The catalyst for the transformation was to be
found in Hippel's Weinstube on Friedrichstrasse, which
Stirner began to frequent late in 1841. He joined the group
of Young Hegelians who met there to debate the master's
ideas, and who, vaguely under the leadership of Bruno
Bauer, called themselves *Die Freien* (The Free Ones). The
extravagant spirit of this group, which had at times
attracted such guests as Marx and the poet Georg
Herwegh, has been immortalized by Engels in a pencil
sketch he made of a meeting in the Walburg'sche Weinstube on November 10th, 1842. The guests were Arnold
Ruge, Marx's early socialist colleague, and Otto Wigand,
who published much of the radical neo-Hegelian work of
the time, including Stirner's book. Ruge—massive, pot-
bellied and pompous—trying to interest the local Berliners
in setting up a 'free university', is shown preparing

[1] Rolf Engert, *Das Bildnis Max Stirners* (Verlag des dritten Reiches,
Dresden, 1921).

to defend himself from the blows of an enraged Bruno Bauer. Edgar Bauer is about to slam his fist down on a table cluttered with teetering bottles and glasses. Ludwig Buhl, short and emaciated, cuts a ridiculous figure as he stands in front of the towering, lanky, full-bearded Karl Nauwerk. Karl Friedrich Köppen, in a lieutenant's uniform and sporting a sword, is slouched drunkenly over the table, firmly clutching a wine-glass. To one side lounges a high-browed, bespectacled figure, indifferent to the proceedings, taciturnly puffing a cigar. It is Stirner —calm, ironical, self-contained, and distant from the raucous confusion of his philosophical brethren. The drawing reinforces the impression of solitariness which echoes through the pages of his work. In *Die Freien* he must have gained the confidence that he had something uniquely valuable to tell the world, and although the meetings would have provided him with a lively forum in which to test his ideas they can have had little direct influence on the substance of his philosophy. (Mackay records that he seldom participated in the passionate discussions, preferring to talk quietly with his neighbour while he smoked a cigar, his only luxury.)

In addition to his book, whose first copies were distributed late in 1844, Stirner wrote a number of newspaper and journal articles between 1842 and 1848; Karl Marx published two of the better ones in his *Rheinische Zeitung* in 1842. They read as patchy, confused and incomplete meditations, brilliantly original in places.

One of the frequenters of Hippel's in the early 'forties was Marie Dähnhardt, a slight, graceful apothecary's daughter, who had been attracted away from her native village by the free life of Berlin. She wore her heavy blonde hair in ringlets, smoked cigars and dressed in male attire, presumably to win favour with *Die Freien* and to prove the desirability of having an emancipated woman among 'free-thinking' males (there is no indication that the relationships went beyond intellectual comradeship). She was attractive for her natural freshness and liveliness rather than her intelligence or physical appearance. The sensitive, lonely Stirner, searching for everything his first marriage had not been, fell for her glamour; they were married on October 21st, 1843. The marriage ceremony is one of the rare events in his life that history has recorded; the local newspaper found the antics of these queer philosophers worthy of public attention.

The officiating clergyman, a certain Marot, reputedly of liberal views, arrived at Stirner's apartment to find the bride absent and the groom casually filling in time with a game of cards with his shirt-sleeved friends. Finally the bride arrived—clad in her everyday clothes. The bewildered Marot sought for a Bible but one was not to be found. He had to suggest that Buhl put his coat on. The guests stared out of the window during the 'dry and sober' proceedings; indeed, order reigned until the clergyman asked for the rings. Of course, no one had thought of such embellishments; however, Bruno Bauer saved the day by removing the brass rings from his purse fastener. They were hastily blessed, the two pronounced one, and Marot fled in spite of an invitation to stay for dinner.

The marriage lasted little more than three years before Marie left for London and later Australia. She had been with Stirner most of the time he was writing his book without showing any appreciation for the work whose first page was to bear the dedication *Meinem Liebchen Marie Dähnhardt* in larger type than Max Stirner's name appeared on the title page. Lauterbach, the editor of the Reclam edition of the book, rededicated it with the Spanish proverb: 'God gives almonds to those who have no teeth.'

Stirner should not have all our sympathy in this affair. Although the fact that he could dedicate his book so warmly to her one year after they had been married indicates that he, for his part, was far from indifferent, all that Marie would say of him, fifty years later when Mackay managed to contact her in London, was that he was 'very sly', 'too selfish', and that she had neither loved nor respected him. It appears that the only time he spent with her was at night when they met with their friends at Hippel's. Moreover, he was not endowed with much practical intelligence. After leaving Madame Gropius's institute he translated some of the writings of the economists J. B. Say and Adam Smith, but must have found this a tedious way of earning a living. Theodor Fontane[1] describes the adventures of the 'seven wise men of Hippel's Cellar', such 'an interesting group (*Die Freien*) as Berlin has seldom seen', and the disastrous entry into business of the first of their circle who dared venture into marriage, 'the subsequently famous Stirner'.

His wife had some money, which, the wisdom of the 'seven wise men' reasoned, ought to be immediately invested in a collective enterprise. It was decided to set up a *dairy* ... The 'seven' toured the surrounding villages—I should have liked to be present when, for example, St Paul [Prussian army-officer, friend of Fontane's and sometime drinking companion of *Die Freien*, 1842 censor of the *Rheinische Zeitung* in Cologne] negotiated with a young milkmaid in a cowshed—and settled with innumerable farmers a contract for milk delivery. From a certain day on each had to deliver so many quarts. The office and

[1] See Theodor Fontane (1819–98), *Von Zwanzig bis Dreißig*, (Fontane & Co., Berlin, 1898). Fontane was a German writer, best known for his novel, *Effi Briest*.

the cellars, magnificent in style, were established in Bernburgerstrasse. Indeed, the milk came, but buyers stayed away, and eventually after a certain tang of sour milk had passed through the Bernburgerstrasse air for several days, the necessity was seen one night to let the whole stock flow down the then still blooming Berlin gutters [*die damals noch in Blüte stehenden Berliner Rinnen*].

To complete the record, we must add that Stirner published in 1852 two turgid and unoriginal volumes entitled *Die Geschichte der Reaction*. Of his latter years virtually nothing is known. As early as the summer of 1846 he advertised for a loan, using his reputation as collateral. He is recorded in 1853–4 as having spent two spells in a debtors' prison, together totalling eight weeks. The most telling summary of the obscurity, the incoherence and the despair of a life that wrote itself into the history of Western thought in one short flash of clarity, is in the circumstance of his death. Mackay relates him succumbing on June 25th, 1856, to the bite of a poisonous fly. Ludwig Buhl, Bruno Bauer and a few others attended the miserably cheap funeral.

When we look at the Stirner legacy and the men on whose consciousnesses it has impinged, the names of Marx and Mussolini are not the only ones to stand out; just as significant historically was the probable influence on Friedrich Nietzsche. The bounds of coincidence are strained by the degree to which Stirner anticipates Nietzsche both in ideas and prose style; too many of their central concerns are parallel, they have too many key concepts in common—Antichrist, immoralism, priest-morality, irrationalism, and superman/egoist. Stirner also wrote about the 'death of God', the enervating curse of democracy, and the State as the new idol; he also developed a psychology implicitly founded on a notion of the 'unconscious'. (His book first appeared within days of Nietzsche's birth.)

However, the association is not definite. According to Peter Gast, Nietzsche did not once mention the name of Stirner in his published writings, in his notebooks, or in private conversation. Nevertheless, C. A. Bernoulli, in a book on Nietzsche and his friend Franz Overbeck, wrote of the few positive contributions he had discovered to the debate that flourished in the decade following 1892, when the question of this influence seems to have been first broached. Overbeck related the testimony of another of Nietzsche's friends, Adolf Baumgartner, to the effect that during a semester at Basle in 1874, which he had spent in the philosopher's most intimate company, he 'became acquainted with Stirner's work at Nietzsche's warmest recommendation'. It has been confirmed that Baumgartner, but not Nietzsche, borrowed *The Ego and His Own* from the Basle library, on July 14th of the same year. There are a number of sources from which Nietzsche could have obtained the book, most likely in the late eighteen sixties. Overbeck's final conclusion after finding more quite persuasive, but circumstantial, evidence was that Nietzsche had read Stirner, was impressed, and worried that he should be confused with him. It is true that Nietzsche showed a virtually obsessive concern for originality.

The fortunes of *The Ego and His Own* were little more auspicious than that of its author until the last decade of the century, when a series of disparate factors converged to resurrect from oblivion what the Reclam edition of 1893 referred to as this 'philosophical comet' — a striking claim for a man whose identity at that time was a complete mystery.

Otto Wigand had published a second edition in 1882; the timing was premature and the book sold badly. It was not until April 1889, when John Henry Mackay advertised for information about Stirner, that the renaissance began. However, of much greater significance was a speech of March 28th, 1892, with which the celebrated conductor of the Berlin Philharmonic Orchestra, Hans von Bülow — the first husband of Richard Wagner's second wife Cosima (further links with Nietzsche) — announced his resignation. 'Mankind is essentially an abstraction,' the speech went, 'a phantom, and finally mankind has become a pantheistic straw puppet, which a German philosopher, unfortunately unknown in his own time and forgotten by posterity, has pulled to shreds for us; the philosopher was Max Stirner, who died in 1856.' Von Bülow concluded by comparing Prince Bismarck and Beethoven (the concert had included the *Eroica*) as Germany's greatest brothers. The occasion created a sensation in the newspapers, which immediately linked the name of Stirner, now hailed as one of the prophets of the German Reich, with that of Bismarck.

We know of two other factors which helped to raise interest in *The Ego and His Own*. In the 'nineties the rapidly growing fame of Nietzsche led to a search for his philosophical ancestors — Stirner was obviously one of the main contenders. Secondly, the anarchist movement gained momentum in this decade, both in Europe and America, and again a search for precursors and founding fathers led to Stirner. Plekhanov wrote in 1894: 'Max Stirner has a legitimate right to the title of the father of anarchism.' As early as the late eighteen eighties the leading American anarchist, Benjamin R. Tucker, began to publish literature on Stirner in his weekly journal *Liberty*; its pages soon took a strong Stirnerian line.

Two French translations appeared in 1900, followed by one in Spanish in 1901, Italian and Danish translations in 1902, a second Spanish one in 1905, and two Russian translations in 1906. Finally in 1907 Benjamin R. Tucker published the first English edition. Although at least four editions were to appear in England alone between 1912 and 1921 the secondary writing on Stirner in English even today stands surprisingly at no more than a couple of short articles and odd references.

It is not possible to form a clear picture of the influence of Stirner's ideas since their acceptance in the eighteen nineties as an important chapter in the history of radical thought. There are two distinct ways in which ideas influence men. Taken up as slogans, they serve as symbols of unity and common purpose, channelling their adherents' diffuse frustrations and longings into a standpoint for action. Alternatively, ideas can be approached with caution, lived with, and slowly reinterpreted in the unique terms of the receiver. Where new conceptual associations have been absorbed into a world-view, which in the process gains new contours, the links between consciousness and behaviour are not generally made explicit in catch-phrases or slogans. Stirner's introspective psychology demands to be approached in the second way, and, as a consequence, the breadth of its influence is hard to trace. We can, at least, list some of the more important figures who have paid him direct homage in their writing; they are men of many political allegiances.

Eduard Bernstein wrote in 1891: 'All his preachers and followers could only create something that falsified Stirner, removed him ... What Bakunin offered, and what Mackay offers, are only bastard Stirnerian ideas.'

Rudolf Steiner, the father of anthroposophy, wrote in an eulogy titled *Voilà un homme*: 'A conqueror without equal is Max Stirner.' George Brandes, the first man to lecture on Nietzsche, considered Stirner important enough to include him suddenly, in 1907, in a series of expositions on the most important literary figures for the time.

However, in the latter half of the nineteenth century it was in the hotbed of revolutionary thought and action, Russia, that Stirner's ideas were seized upon with the greatest enthusiasm. There they formed an important component of the egoist-nihilist-anarchist complex of doctrines. The only convincingly documented reference relates to the great critic, V. G. Belinsky, widely regarded as the father of the Russian intelligentsia. Pavel V. Annenkov, in his literary memoirs of that 'extraordinary decade' which began in 1839, describes Belinsky in the last six months of his life losing his enthusiasm for literary feuds. Now a solitary figure even in his own party, he turned to meditate on the emerging definitions of man's social responsibility. It was then that he read Stirner, whom Annenkov reports as 'creating a sensation' at the time. The problem Stirner raised held the critic's attention, he returned to it again and again; it forced a final alteration in the moral credo he had developed throughout his life. This credo became egoism, a superlatively cultivated egoism which, through sensitivity to the external world, gains a sense of moral purpose.

Thomas Masaryk suggests in his history of Russia that Herzen, Pisarev and perhaps even Chernyshevsky borrowed from Stirner; later, summing up the situation at the turn of the century, he writes: 'Especially influential in Russia have been, in addition to the works of Tolstoy, those of Nietzsche, Stirner, and Ibsen.' Finally, Nicolas Berdyaev, writing in exile, admitted that his philosophy of 'personalism' had essentials in common with Stirner's.

Stirner's contribution to anarchist action is even more elusive and tenuous than his part in the development of fascism. Ivo Andrić, in his Nobel-Prize-winning novel, *The Bridge on the Drina*, pointed out that Stirner's ideas were influential just prior to 1914 in the Sarajevo school, one of the centres of the 'anarcho-nationalists'. In the Soviet Republic which was declared in Munich in April 1919, but which only managed to survive one month, two of the nine ministers borrowed from Stirner's ideas.

For the most part Stirner's influence has been restricted to those who were great individualists themselves. The German painter Max Ernst was oriented throughout his youth by Stirner; the tie, almost identification, was life-long. Martin Buber wrote an essay on Stirner and Kierkegaard. Albert Camus devoted a section of *L'Homme révolté* to Stirner, one which is significantly omitted from the English translation. Herbert Read made numerous references in his many writings to Stirner; he opened his essay *The Creative Nature of Humanism* thus: 'One book that I read in my youth I have never wholly forgotten. To say that it had a great influence on me would not be correct, for influences are absorbed and become part of one's mind. This book refused to be digested—to use our vivid English metaphor: it stuck in the gizzard, and has been in that uncomfortable position ever since.' The book was *The Ego and His Own*, where, he suggested elsewhere, Sartre's philosophy originated. In *The Contrary Experience* Read confessed that, having renounced a supernaturally sanctioned morality, he was faced with the alternative— either Stirner's egoism or a pragmatic attachment to the needs of the community—strongly drawn to the former and its freedom, he nevertheless hedged, fearful of the despair which he saw its hedonism producing.

There are a number of reasons for reappraising Stirner's work; it has a peculiarly modern relevance. Today individualist-anarchist themes are forming an increasingly visible nucleus of the critical offensive, in theory and praxis, against advanced industrial society and its moral perspectives.[1] Have we other testimonies of the social malaise of the nineteen sixties to match the intensity and the poignancy of Malcolm X's autobiography or the deeds of the Paris students in their May insurrection, when many followed the *drapeau noir*? These witnesses to the precariousness of liberation at least found the question 'From what?' readily answerable, in terms of racial inequality or a dark vision of man enclosed by a massive, bureaucratic social order. However, to recognize the enemy is not necessarily to see the means to his defeat. The question 'Liberation, where to?' posed a dilemma for the students in particular, marked by the silence which has met Lenin's perennial demand: 'What is to be done?'

As a candidate for an ideology of hope and liberation, Marxism has suffered from the dated content of some of its hypotheses, the living examples of its application, and, above all, the emphasis it places on central organization and the necessary movement of large-scale socio-economic forces in history. Stirner's philosophy developed from the same intellectual roots as Marxism, yet pointed to an entirely different structure of liberation. It gives us a philosophical framework for understanding some of the main currents of revolt in the last decade in the advanced industrial societies. In addition, it could provide at least a coherent basis for action, a tenable response to the 'Liberation, where to?' for a generation disillusioned with

[1] Noam Chomsky, for example, in his *American Power and the New Mandarins* (1969) considers that the 'revival of anarchist thinking in the "New Left" and the attempts to put it into effect are the most promising development of the past years'.

parliamentary democracy and political liberalism. In fact, Stirner is the first critic of liberalism as we know it today; he rejects the idea of liberty as merely the hollow end of a negative process of 'freeing from' or getting 'rid of'—stripping away all external constraint leads not to self-expression and fulfilment but to the void and nihilism. He substitutes the value of 'ownness', the result of taking possession and realizing one's own.

In this context it is important to realize that the German title of his book, *Der Einzige und sein Eigenthum*, cannot be fully rendered in English. '*Ein/eigen*', which translates as 'one/unique/proper', forms the root of both '*Einzige*' and '*Eigenthum*'. Thus the impression is conveyed of the unique one and the uniqueness of his property. The English translator's choice of *The Ego and His Own* has the virtues of being concise, striking, and yet reasonably accurate.

Stirner's philosophy evolved during a time of hesitancy in the great period of German philosophy from Kant to Nietzsche and Freud. Viewed from our distant point in time it appears as if the thought of Kant, Fichte and Hegel had become heavy and unmalleable by the eighteen forties; the idealist movement, encumbered by its abstractions, had lost its momentum. Stirner, like his most outstanding contemporaries, Feuerbach and Marx, knew that he had to escape from the towering Hegelian legacy that had nurtured him. Unlike the latter two, who developed materialist philosophy, he set off in a quite different direction. It was to lead, at a tangent to social-revolutionary thought, on to Nietzsche and Freud; although rarely accredited, Stirner was one of the seminal minds in this tradition. At a few significant points his movement is parallel to that of Schopenhauer, whose main work he would not have known in spite of its being published as early as 1819.

I feel, additionally, the need to question the orthodox treatment of Stirner as one moment in the erratic anarchist tradition, and, at the same time, to point to the uniqueness, and perhaps centrality, of his anarchism. Anarchism is not primarily a historical movement, nor is it a catchword to relate a group of thinkers with common ground; to weave the picture of a coherent intellectual movement from the strands of the diverse and idiosyncratic individuals in history who have warred against authority often implies a contradiction in their own terms. Moreover, to identify anarchism with the sum of common ideas and traits so derived is to devalue it. Stirner's work offers us the key to an entirely different approach to intellectual history. His anarchism is a philosophy of life here-and-now, anti-teleological, and self-contained as a model of individual behaviour. *The Ego and His Own* is an exploration in self-meaning, a theoretical building up of the anarchist identity, and indeed a direct challenge to any reader who seeks to divine its message; unless he himself is willing to join Stirner on a voyage charting his own identity, questioning where he questions, he will gain no understanding of the essence of the book. At the best he will be excited by a few striking aphorisms.

Stirner himself gives the clue to how to approach his work in his egoistic command, 'Realize Yourself!' Ego antecedes essence, essence being what one realizes. A dynamic principle is posited, defining a *modus vivendi*, not a descriptive characterization of a style of life. One of Stirner's main concerns is to show the vacuity of such general qualities or essences as 'love' or 'reasonableness', either as explanatory terms or as guidelines for living. They are used as rationalizations of prior action and have little to do with its roots. His command is closely akin to Nietzsche's 'Become who you are!' in sharp contrast, for example, to the command, 'Become just!' As in the sense later taken up by existentialist philosophy, the content is to be realized, it is unique in each man. Indeed, Stirner is often most appropriately placed at the beginning of the existentialist tradition. To take but one case, we note that he heads his preface with Goethe's 'I have founded my affair on nothing'; the following line of the poem is just as central: 'And to me belongs the entire world.'

Stirner writes with no end in view, he does not proselytize, and as far as we know he sought no following. He likens himself to the singer in the heights of his song. He sings for his own sake, not for that of anyone else, not even for the truth's sake; the enjoyment of singing justifies itself and if others enjoy the song that is a bonus. Self-sufficiency of this nature constitutes the most threatening of anarchist stances, independence from the social and moral law, indeed indifference towards it. Nietzsche also believed that in music, in particular in the dance, the inner harmonies of the soul gained consummate expression; Rilke wrote: 'Song is existence.'

Surely anarchism, it will be countered, like Marxism, is about praxis, changing the institutional structures of society? To answer this question would first require a close acquaintance with Stirner's own praxis, insurrection, and his reservations about the efficacy of so-called revolutionary action. However, it is worth noting in passing that intellectual studies of anarchism have tended to exhibit a deep hostility to the philosopher of the self. Perhaps such an uncompromising examination of one's identity is liable to creep under the skin, especially of intellectuals with a latent commitment to changing social institutions; the fear of nihilism in another's philosophy is a projection of the fear of the same phenomenon in oneself, an insight drawn from Stirner's analysis of the revolutionary's psyche.

Max Stirner found his own identity, and, what is synonymous, his independence, through his book. His personal praxis was philosophy, the act of thinking one's being. Through wrestling with his angel for five hundred pages he sustained, for at least a short period, a life which at every turn threatened to lapse into incoherence; at the same time he gave content, in Hegel's language, to the universal concept 'self'. *The Ego and His Own* was Max Stirner; of the man behind the nom de plume, that is, of Johann Caspar Schmidt, we know very little.

Stirner's uncompromising advocacy of self-realization sets him far apart from other anarchist philosophers, especially Proudhon and Kropotkin. He would have regarded their scrupulous plans and their halcyon dreams of the anarchist paradise as abstract and religious in the extreme, not far removed in spirit from the millenarian vision of William Morris's *News from Nowhere*. Stirner's own prolonged introspection gave him a psychological perceptivity which was too down to earth to permit Orphic musings—it is this 'realism' that makes his brand of anarchism the one most congruent to today's situation.

A concentrated study of Stirner as the prototypal anarchist would satisfy the doubts about the orthodox approach to the study of anarchism. In the first place, Stirner is the only writer to develop fully the implications of a total rejection of external authority. In his book the anarcho-egoist stands before us in full view. The problems that his existence poses for society are likely to render the notorious conflicts between anarchists over modes of social organization peripheral to the discussion. Secondly, we may sense from the tone of *The Ego and His Own*, its persistence in searching out every facet of a theme, its vigour, and its peculiarly undulating intensity, the presence of a man face to face with his inner world, feeling his way out of deep personal necessity through the labyrinths of meaning. This style, I have suggested, filters to the very core of anarchism, evoking what it can mean to live it.

I have used Steven T. Byington's excellent translation, with minor alterations, in my selection. Short sections from three of Stirner's earlier articles, translated by myself, have been added. My major concern has been to eliminate the repetitiveness which mars *The Ego and His Own* while preserving both its central themes and, what is essential to them, the author's style, the sustained, cyclically progressing monologue which develops its own inner logic. I have not tried to impose any external structure on this curiously unsystematic work; the original format remains more or less intact, except in the long second part to Chapter V where I have added sub-headings.

Most of the footnotes are my own. I have retained a number of Byington's annotations where Stirner's keen usage of etymological association has been lost in translation. In addition, James J. Martin, the editor of the 1963 Libertarian Book Club edition, has kindly allowed me to use a number of his biographical annotations to figures referred to in the text. In the few cases where the footnotes are Stirner's own they are indicated with asterisks or daggers.

The text is referenced throughout, to the 1912 edition of *The Ego and His Own* (*Ego*) and the 1914 edition of Stirner's *Kleinere Schriften* (*K.S.*).

The selected bibliography is designed to span the more important areas of Stirner's work and its influence, and is in no other way comprehensive. Wherever available, the

English edition of a work is the one quoted. In spite of the widespread influence Stirner has raised since 1844 there is still nothing that measures up to a definitive interpretation of his philosophy and its significance.

JOHN CARROLL

THE EGO AND HIS OWN

PREFACE

'I HAVE FOUNDED MY AFFAIR
ON NOTHING'[1]

What is not supposed to be my concern![2] First and foremost, the Good Cause,[3] then God's cause, the cause of
mankind, of truth, of freedom, of humanity, of justice;
further, the cause of my people, my prince, my fatherland; finally, even the cause of Mind, and a thousand
other causes. Only *my* cause is never to be my concern.
'Shame on the egoist who thinks only of himself!'

Let us look and see, then, how they manage *their* concerns—they for whose cause we are to labour, devote
ourselves, and grow enthusiastic.

You have much profound information to give about
God, and have for thousands of years 'searched the depths
of the Godhead', and looked into its heart, so that you
can doubtless tell us how God himself attends to 'God's
cause', which we are called to serve. And you do not
conceal the Lord's doings, either. Now, what is his cause?
Has he, as is demanded of us, made an alien cause, the
cause of truth or love, his own? You are shocked by this
misunderstanding, and you instruct us that God's cause
is indeed the cause of truth and love, but that this cause
cannot be called alien to him, because God is himself
truth and love; you are shocked by the assumption that
God could be like us poor worms in furthering an alien
cause as his own. 'Should God take up the cause of truth

[1] '*Ich hab' Mein' Sach' auf Nichts gestellt,*' first line of Goethe's poem,
Vanitas! Vanitatum Vanitas!

[2] *Sache.*

[3] *Sache.*

39

if he were not himself truth?' He cares only for *his* cause, but, because he is all in all, therefore all is *his* cause! But we, we are not all in all, and our cause is altogether little and contemptible; therefore we must 'serve a higher cause'.—Now it is clear, God cares only for what is his, busies himself only with himself, thinks only of himself, and has only himself before his eyes; woe to all that is not well-pleasing to him! He serves no higher person, and satisfies only himself. His cause is—a purely egoistic cause.

How is it with mankind, whose cause we are to make our own? Is its cause that of another, and does mankind serve a higher cause? No, mankind looks only at itself, mankind will promote the interests of mankind only, mankind is its own cause. That it may develop, it causes nations and individuals to wear themselves out in its service, and, when they have accomplished what mankind needs, it throws them on the dung-heap of history in gratitude. Is not mankind's cause—a purely egoistic cause?

I have no need to take up each thing that wants to throw its cause on us and show that it is occupied only with itself, not with us, only with its good, not with ours. Look at the rest for yourselves. Do truth, freedom, humanity, justice, desire anything else than that you grow enthusiastic and serve them?

They all have an admirable time of it when they receive zealous homage. Just observe the nation that is defended by devoted patriots. The patriots fall in bloody battle or in the fight with hunger and want; what does the nation care for that? By the manure of their corpses the nation comes to 'its bloom'! The individuals have died 'for the great cause of the nation', and the nation sends some words of thanks after them and—has the profit of it. I call that a paying kind of egoism.

But only look at that Sultan who cares so lovingly for his people. Is he not pure unselfishness itself, and does he not hourly sacrifice himself for his people? Oh, yes, for 'his people'. Just try it; show yourself not as his, but as your own; for breaking away from his egoism you will take a trip to jail. The Sultan has set his cause on nothing but himself; he is to himself all in all, he is to himself the only one, and tolerates nobody who would dare not be one of 'his people'.

And will you not learn by these brilliant examples that the egoist gets on best? I for my part take a lesson from them, and propose, instead of further unselfishly serving those great egoists, rather to be the egoist myself.

God and mankind have concerned themselves for nothing, for nothing but themselves. Let me then likewise concern myself for *myself*, who am equally with God the nothing of all others, who am my all, who am the unique one.

If God, if mankind, as you affirm, have substance enough in themselves to be all in all to themselves, then I feel that *I* shall still less lack that, and that I shall have no complaint to make of my 'emptiness'. I am not nothing in the sense of emptiness, but I am the creative nothing, the nothing out of which I myself as creator create everything.

Away, then, with every concern that is not altogether my concern! You think at least the 'good cause' must be my concern? What's good, what's bad? Why, I myself am my concern, and I am neither good nor bad. Neither has meaning for me.

The divine is God's concern; the human, man's. My concern is neither the divine nor the human, not the true, good, just, free, etc., but solely what is *mine*, and it is not a general one, but is—unique, as I am unique.

Nothing is more to me than myself!

PART ONE · MAN

Man is to man the supreme being, says Feuerbach.
Man has just been discovered, says Bruno Bauer.
Then let us take a more careful look at this
supreme being and this new discovery.

I. A HUMAN LIFE

From the moment when he catches sight of the light of
the world a man seeks to find and prove *himself* in the
midst of the confusion, in which he, with everything else,
is tossed about.

But everything that comes in contact with the child
defends itself in turn against his attacks, and asserts its
own persistence.

Accordingly, because each thing *cares for itself* and at
the same time comes into constant collision with other
things, the *combat* of self-assertion is unavoidable.

Victory or defeat — between the two alternatives the fate of
the combat wavers. The victor becomes the *lord*, the
vanquished one the *subject*: the former exercises *supremacy*
and 'rights of supremacy', the latter fulfils in awe and
deference the 'duties of a subject'.

But both remain *enemies*, and always lie in wait: they
watch for each other's *weaknesses* — children for those of
their parents and parents for those of their children (their
fear, for example); either the stick conquers the man, or
the man conquers the stick.

In childhood liberation takes the direction of trying to

get to the bottom of things, to get at what is 'behind' things; therefore we spy out the weak points of everybody, for which, it is well known, children have a sure instinct; therefore we like to smash things, like to rummage through hidden corners, pry after what is covered up or out of the way, and try what we can do with everything. When we once get at what is behind things, we know we are safe; when we have got at the fact that the rod is too weak against our obduracy, then we no longer fear it, 'have outgrown it'.

Behind the rod, mightier than it, stands our—obduracy, our obdurate courage. By degrees we get at what is behind everything that was mysterious and uncanny to us, the mysteriously dreaded might of the rod, the father's stern look, etc., and behind all we find our ataraxia—our imperturbability, intrepidity, our counter forces, our odds of strength, our invincibility. Before that which formerly inspired in us fear and deference we no longer retreat shyly, but take *courage*. Behind everything we find our *courage*, our superiority; behind the sharp command of parents and authorities stands, after all, our courageous choice or our outwitting shrewdness. And the more we feel ourselves, the smaller appears that which before seemed invincible. And what is our trickery, shrewdness, courage, obduracy? What else but—*mind*![1]

Through a considerable time we are spared a fight that is so exhausting later—the fight against *reason*. The fairest part of childhood passes without the necessity of coming to blows with reason. We care nothing at all about it, do not meddle with it, admit no reason. We are not to be persuaded to anything by *conviction*, and are deaf to good arguments and principles; on the other hand, coaxing,

[1] *Geist*. This word will be translated sometimes by 'mind' and sometimes by 'spirit' in the following pages.

punishment, and the like are hard for us to resist. This stern life-and-death combat with *reason* enters later, and begins a new phase; in childhood we scamper about without racking our brains much.

Mind is the name of the *first* self-discovery, the first undeification of the divine: that is, of the uncanny, the spooks, the 'powers above'. Our fresh feeling of youth, this feeling of self, now defers to nothing; the world is discredited, for we are above it, we are *mind*. Now for the first time we see that hitherto we have not looked at the world *intelligently* at all, but only stared at it.

We exercise the beginnings of our strength on *natural powers*. We defer to parents as a natural power; later we say: Father and mother are to be forsaken, all natural power to be counted as riven. They are vanquished. For the rational, the 'intellectual' man, there is no family as a natural power; a renunciation of parents, brothers, etc., makes its appearance. If these are 'born again' as *intellectual, rational powers*, they are no longer at all what they were before.

And not only parents, but *men in general*, are conquered by the young man; they are no hindrance to him, and are no longer regarded; for now he says: One must obey God rather than men.

From this high standpoint everything '*earthly*' recedes into contemptible remoteness; for the standpoint is—the *heavenly*.

The attitude is now altogether reversed; the youth takes up an *intellectual* position, while the boy, who did not yet feel himself as mind, grew up on mindless learning. The former does not try to get hold of *things* (for instance, to get into his head the *data* of history), but of the *thoughts* that lie hidden in things, and so, therefore, of the *spirit* of history. On the other hand, the boy understands *connections*, no doubt, but not ideas, the spirit; therefore he strings together whatever can be learned, without proceeding *a priori* and theoretically, without looking for ideas.

As in childhood one had to overcome the resistance of the *laws of the world*, so now in everything that he proposes he is met by an objection of the mind, of reason, of his *own conscience*. 'That is unreasonable, unchristian, unpatriotic', and the like, cries conscience to us, and—frightens us away from it. Not the might of the avenging Eumenides, not Poseidon's wrath, not God, far as he sees the hidden, not the father's rod of punishment, do we fear, but—*conscience*.

We 'track our thoughts' now, and follow their commands just as before we followed parental, human ones. Our course of action is determined by our thoughts (ideas, conceptions, *faith*) as it is in childhood by the commands of our parents.

For all that, we were already thinking when we were children, only our thoughts were not fleshless, abstract, *absolute*, that is, **nothing but thoughts**, a heaven in themselves, a pure world of thought, *logical* thoughts.

On the contrary, they had been only thoughts that we had about a *thing*; we thought of the thing so or so. Thus we may have thought 'God made the world that we see there', but we did not think of ('search') the 'depths of the Godhead itself'; we may have thought 'that is the truth about the matter', but we do not think of Truth itself, nor unite into one sentence 'God is truth.' The 'depths of the Godhead, who is truth' we did not touch. Over such purely logical (theological) questions as 'What is truth?' Pilate does not stop, though he does not therefore hesitate to ascertain in an individual case 'what truth there is in the thing', whether the *thing* is true.

Any thought bound to a *thing* is not yet *nothing but a thought*, absolute thought.

To bring to light the *pure thought*, or to be of its party, is the delight of youth; and all the shapes of light in the world of thought, like truth, freedom, humanity, Man, illumine and inspire the youthful soul.

But, when the spirit is recognized as the essential thing, it still makes a difference whether the spirit is poor or rich, and therefore one seeks to become rich in spirit; the spirit wants to spread out so as to found its empire—an empire that is not of this world, the world just conquered. Thus, then, it longs to become all in all to itself; for, although I am spirit, I am not yet *perfected* spirit, and must first seek the complete spirit.

But with that I, who had just now found myself as spirit, lose myself again at once, bowing before the complete spirit as one not my own but *supernal*, and feeling my emptiness.

Spirit is the essential point for everything, to be sure; but then is every spirit the 'right' spirit? The right and true spirit is the ideal of spirit, the 'Holy Spirit'. It is not my or your spirit, but just—an ideal, supernal one, it is 'God'. 'God is spirit.' And this supernal 'Father in heaven gives it to those that pray to him'.*

The man is distinguished from the youth by the fact that he takes the world as it is, instead of everywhere fancying it amiss and wanting to improve it, model it after his ideal; in him the view that one must deal with the world according to his *interest*, not according to his *ideals*, becomes confirmed.

So long as one knows himself only as *spirit*, and feels that all the value of his existence consists in being spirit (it becomes easy for the youth to give his life, the 'bodily

* Luke xi 13.

life', for a nothing, for the silliest point of honour), so long as it is only *thoughts* that one has, ideas that he hopes to be able to realize some day when he has found a sphere of action; thus one has meanwhile only *ideals*, unexecuted ideas or thoughts.

Not till one has fallen in love with his *corporeal* self, and takes a pleasure in himself as a living flesh-and-blood person—but it is in mature years, in the man, that we find it so—not till then has one a personal or *egoistic* interest, an interest not only in our spirit, for instance, but in total satisfaction, satisfaction of the whole chap, a *selfish* interest. Just compare a man with a youth, and see if he will not appear to you harder, less magnanimous, more selfish. Is he therefore worse? No, you say; he has only become more definite, or, as you also call it, more 'practical'. But the main point is this, that he makes *himself* more the centre than does the youth, who is infatuated about other things, for example, God, fatherland, and so on.

Therefore the man shows a *second* self-discovery. The youth found himself as *spirit* and lost himself again in the *general* spirit, the complete, holy spirit, Man, mankind—in short, all ideals; the man finds himself as *embodied* spirit.

Boys had only *unintellectual* interests (those interests devoid of thoughts and ideas), youths only *intellectual* ones; the man has bodily, personal, egoistic interests.

If the child has not an *object* that it can occupy itself with, it feels boredom; for it does not yet know how to occupy itself with *itself*. The youth, on the contrary, throws the object aside, because for him *thoughts* arose out of the object; he occupies himself with his *thoughts*, his dreams, occupies himself intellectually, or 'his mind is occupied.'

The young man includes everything not intellectual

under the contemptuous name of 'externalities'. If he
nevertheless sticks to the most trivial externalities (such
as the customs of students' clubs and other formalities),
it is because, and when, he discovers *spirit* in them, when
they are *symbols* to him.

As I find myself behind things, and that as mind, so I
must later find *myself* also behind *thoughts* — to wit, as their
creator and *owner*. In the time of spirits thoughts grew till
they overtopped my head, whose offspring they yet were;
they hovered about me and convulsed me like fever-
phantasies — an awful power. The thoughts had become
corporeal on their own account, were ghosts, such as God,
Emperor, Pope, Fatherland, etc. If I destroy their
corporeity, then I take them back into mine, and say:
'I alone am corporeal.' And now I take the world as what
it is to me, as *mine*, as my property; I refer all to myself.

If as spirit I had thrust away the world in the deepest
contempt, so as owner I thrust spirits or ideas away into
their 'vanity'. They have no longer any power over me,
as no 'earthly might' has power over the spirit.

The child was realistic, taken up with the things of
this world, till little by little he succeeded in getting at
what was behind these very things; the youth was idealistic, inspired by thoughts, till he worked his way up to
where he became the man, the egoistic man, who deals
with things and thoughts according to his heart's pleasure,
and sets his personal interest above everything. Finally,
the old man? When I become one, there will still be time
enough to speak of that.

(*Ego* 9–16)

II. THE MODERNS

A.—THE SPIRIT

If somebody told you you were altogether spirit, you would take hold of your body and not believe him, but answer: 'I *have* a spirit, no doubt, but do not exist only as spirit, but as a man with a body.' You would still distinguish *yourself* from 'your spirit'. 'But', replies he, 'it is your destiny, even though now you are yet going about in the fetters of the body, to be one day a "blessed spirit", and, however you may conceive of the future aspect of your spirit, so much is yet certain, that in death you will put off this body and yet keep yourself, your spirit, for all eternity; accordingly your spirit is the eternal and true in you, the body only a dwelling here below, which you may leave and perhaps exchange for another.'

Now you believe him! For the present, indeed, *you* are not spirit only; but, when you emigrate from the mortal body, as one day you must, then you will have to help yourself without the body, and therefore it is needful that you be prudent and care in time for your proper self. 'What should it profit a man if he gained the whole world and yet suffered damage in his soul?'

But, even granted that doubts, raised in the course of time against the tenets of the Christian faith, have long since robbed you of faith in the immortality of your spirit, you have nevertheless left one tenet undisturbed, and still ingenuously adhere to the one truth, that the spirit is your better part, and that the spiritual has greater claims on you than anything else. Despite all your atheism, in zeal against *egoism* you concur with the believers in immortality.

But whom do you think of under the name of egoist? A man who, instead of living to an idea, that is, a spiritual thing, and sacrificing to it his personal advantage, serves the latter. A good patriot brings his sacrifice to the altar of the fatherland; but it cannot be disputed that the fatherland is an idea, since for beasts incapable of mind, or children as yet without mind, there is no fatherland and no patriotism. Now, if any one does not approve himself as a good patriot, he betrays his egoism with reference to the fatherland. And so the matter stands in innumerable other cases: he who in human society takes the benefit of a prerogative sins egoistically against the idea of equality; he who exercises dominion is blamed as an egoist against the idea of liberty, and so on.

You despise the egoist because he puts the spiritual in the background as compared with the personal, and has his eyes on himself where you would like to see him act to favour an idea. The distinction between you is that he makes himself the central point, but you the spirit; or that you cut your identity in two and exalt your 'proper self', the spirit, to be ruler of the paltrier remainder, while he will hear nothing of this cutting in two, and pursues spiritual and material interests just *as he pleases*. You think, to be sure, that you are falling foul of those only who enter into no spiritual interest at all, but in fact you curse at everybody who does not look on the spiritual interest as his 'true and highest' interest. You carry your knightly service for this beauty so far that you affirm her to be the only beauty of the world. You live not to *yourself*, but to your *spirit* and to what is the spirit's, that is, ideas.

(*Ego* 36–8)

Let us, in brief, set Feuerbach's theological view and our

contradiction over against each other![1] 'The essence of man is man's supreme being;[2] now by religion, to be sure, the *supreme being* is called *God* and regarded as an objective essence, but in truth it is only man's own essence; and therefore the turning point of the world's history is that henceforth no longer *God*, but man, is to appear to man as God.'*

To this we reply: The supreme being is indeed the essence of man, but, just because it is his *essence* and not he himself, it remains quite immaterial whether we see it outside him and view it as 'God', or find it in him and call it 'Essence of Man' or 'Man'. I am neither God nor *Man*, neither the supreme essence nor my essence, and therefore it is all one in the main whether I think of the essence as in me or outside me. In fact, we really do always think of the supreme being as in both kinds of otherworldliness, the inward and outward, at once; for the 'Spirit of God' is, according to the Christian view, also 'our spirit', and 'dwells in us'.† It dwells in heaven and dwells in us; we poor things are just its 'dwelling',

[1] At the time of its publication the stir that *The Ego and His Own* caused was largely due to the critique it contained of Feuerbach. In his *The Essence of Christianity* (1841) Feuerbach attacked Christianity for recognizing the supernatural power, God, before which all mortal man could do was to bow down and efface himself. In addition he criticized Hegel for a similar degradation of the human, his God being 'absolute thinking' or 'reason'. Feuerbach put man at the centre of his universe and posited his essential qualities, in particular love, as the source of ultimate value and humanity. This new view of religious alienation was regarded as the first major philosophical breakthrough since Hegel. Stirner's critique of Feuerbach, whom he identifies with liberalist humanism, is taken up again and again throughout the book and the few specific passages included here give but the barest outline of the case.

[2] Or 'highest essence'. The word *Wesen* translates as either 'essence' or 'being'.

* Cf, e.g., Ludwig Feuerbach, *The Essence of Christianity* (second edn, Wigand, Leipzig, 1843), p. 402.

† E.g. Rom. viii 9; 1 Cor. iii 16; John xx 22; and numerous other passages.

and, if Feuerbach goes on to destroy its heavenly dwelling
and force it to move to us bag and baggage, then we, its
earthly apartments, will be badly overcrowded.

(*Ego* 41–2)

To God, who is spirit, Feuerbach gives the name 'Our
Essence'. Can we put up with this, that 'Our Essence' is
brought into opposition to *us*—that we are split into an
essential and an unessential self? Do we not therewith go
back into the dreary misery of seeing ourselves banished
out of ourselves?

(*Ego* 40)

Nothing at all is justified by *essence*. What is thought of *is*
as well as what is not thought of; the stone in the street
is, and my notion of it *is* too. Both are only in different
spaces, the former in airy space, the latter in my head, in
me; for I am space like the street.

(*Ego* 455)

After the annihilation of faith Feuerbach thinks to put in
to the supposedly safe harbour of *love*. 'The first and
highest law must be the love of man to man. *Homo
homini Deus est*—this is the supreme practical maxim, this
is the turning point of the world's history.'* But, properly
speaking, only the god is changed—the *deus*; love has
remained: there love to the superhuman God, here love
to the human God, to *homo* as *Deus*. Therefore man is to
me—sacred. And everything 'truly human' is to me—
sacred! 'Marriage is sacred of itself. And so it is with all
moral relations. Friendship is and must be *sacred* for you,
and property, and marriage, and the good of every man,

---

* *The Essence of Christianity*, second German edn, p. 402 ('Man is God to
man—').

but sacred *in and of itself*.'* Haven't we the priest again
there? Who is his God? Man with a capital M! What is
the divine? The human! Then the predicate has indeed
only been changed into the subject, and, instead of the
sentence 'God is love', they say 'love is divine'; instead of
'God has become man', 'Man has become God', etc. It
is nothing more or less than a new — *religion*. 'All moral
relations are ethical, are cultivated with a moral mind,
only where of themselves (without religious consecration
by the priest's blessing) they are counted *religious*.' Feuerbach's proposition, 'Theology is anthropology,' means
only 'religion must be ethics, ethics alone is religion.'[1]

Altogether Feuerbach accomplishes only a transposi-
tion of subject and predicate, a giving of preference to the
latter. But, since he himself says, 'Love is not (and has
never been considered by men) sacred through being a
predicate of God, but it is a predicate of God because it
is divine in and of itself,' he might judge that the fight
against the predicates themselves, against love and all
sanctities, must be commenced. How could he hope to
turn men away from God when he left them the divine?
And if, as Feuerbach says, God himself has never been the
main thing to them, but only his predicates, then he might
have gone on leaving them the tinsel longer yet, since the
doll, the real kernel, was left at any rate. He recognizes,
too, that with him it is 'only a matter of annihilating an
illusion';† he thinks, however, that the effect of the
illusion on men is 'downright ruinous, since even love,

[1] The crux of Stirner's argument is that Feuerbach has not achieved any
radical detheologizing, for he has substituted the new humanist gods,
'Man' and 'love', for the old Christian God and for Hegel's god 'Reason'.
Man is just as tied to the alienating abstraction or fixed idea, only now it
takes the form of ethical commands: 'Thou shalt ... ' or 'Thou shalt
not ... '

* Op. cit., p. 403.
† Op. cit., p. 408.

in itself the truest, most inward sentiment, becomes an obscure, illusory one through religiousness, since religious love loves man only for God's sake, therefore loves man only apparently, but in truth God only'. Is this different with moral love? Does it love the man, *this* man for *this* man's sake, or for morality's sake, and so—for *homo homini Deus*—for God's sake?

(*Ego* 74-5)

How natural is the supposition that *man* and *ego* mean the same! And yet one sees, as by Feuerbach, that the expression 'man' is to designate the absolute ego, the *species*, not the transitory, individual ego. Egoism and humanity (humaneness) ought to mean the same, but according to Feuerbach the individual can 'only lift himself above the limits of his individuality, but not above the laws, the positive ordinances, of his species'.* But the species is nothing, and, if the individual lifts himself above the limits of his individuality, this is rather his very self as an individual; he exists only in raising himself, he exists only in not remaining what he is; otherwise he would be done, dead. Man with a capital M is only an ideal, the species only something thought of. To be a man is not to realize the ideal of *Man*, but to present *oneself*, the individual. It is not how I realize the *generally human* that needs to be my task, but how I satisfy myself. *I* am my species, am without norm, without law, without model, and the like. It is possible that I can make very little out of myself; but this little is everything, and is better than what I allow to be made out of me by the might of others, by the training of custom, religion, the laws, the State. Better—if the talk is to be of better at all —better an unmannerly child than an old head on young

* Op. cit., p. 401.

shoulders, better a mulish man than a man compliant in everything. The unmannerly and mulish fellow is still on the way to form himself according to his own will; the prematurely knowing and compliant one is determined by the 'species', the general demands—the species is law to him. He is *determined* by it; for what else is the species to him but his 'destiny', his 'calling'? Whether I look to 'humanity', the species, in order to strive toward this ideal, or to God and Christ with like endeavour, where is the essential dissimilarity? At most the former is more washed-out than the latter. As the individual is the whole of nature, so he is the whole of the species too.

(*Ego* 237–8)

B.—THE POSSESSED

THE SPOOK

To know and acknowledge essences alone and nothing but essences, that is religion; its realm is a realm of essences, spooks, and ghosts.

The longing to make the spook comprehensible, or to realize *non-sense*, has brought about a *corporeal ghost*, a ghost or spirit with a real body, an embodied ghost. How the strongest and most talented Christians have tortured themselves to get a conception of this ghostly apparition! But there always remained the contradiction of two natures, the divine and human, the ghostly and sensual; there remained the most wondrous spook, a thing that was not a thing. Never yet was a ghost more soul-torturing, and no shaman, who pricks himself to raving fury and nerve-lacerating cramps to conjure a ghost, can endure such soul-torment as Christians suffered from that most incomprehensible ghost.

But through Christ the truth of the matter had at the same time come to light, that the veritable spirit or ghost is—man. The *corporeal* or embodied spirit is just man; he himself is the ghostly being and at the same time the being's appearance and existence. Henceforth man no longer, in typical cases, shudders at ghosts *outside* him, but at himself; he is terrified at himself. In the depth of his breast dwells the *spirit of sin*; even the faintest thought (and this is itself a spirit, you know) may be a *devil*, etc.— The ghost has put on a body, God has become man, but now man is himself the gruesome spook which he seeks to get behind, to exorcize, to fathom, to bring to reality and to speech; man is—*spirit*. What matter if the body wither, if only the spirit is saved? Everything rests on the spirit, and the spirit's or 'soul's' welfare becomes the exclusive goal. Man has become to himself a ghost, an uncanny spook, to which there is even assigned a distinct seat in the body (dispute over the seat of the soul, whether in the head, etc.).

You are not to me, and I am not to you, a higher essence. Nevertheless a higher essence may be hidden in each of us, and call forth a mutual reverence. To take at once the most general, Man lives in you and me. If I did not see Man in you, what occasion should I have to respect you? To be sure, you are not Man and his true and adequate form, but only a mortal veil of his, from which he can withdraw without himself ceasing; but yet for the present this general and higher essence is housed in you, and you present before me (because an imperishable spirit has in you assumed a perishable body, so that really your form is only an 'assumed' one) a spirit that appears, appears in you, without being bound to your body and to this particular mode of appearance—therefore a spook. Hence I do not regard you as a higher essence, but only respect that higher essence which 'walks' in you; I 'respect Man in you'. The ancients did not observe anything of this sort in their slaves, and the higher essence 'Man' found as yet little response. To make up for this, they saw in each other ghosts of another sort. The People is a higher essence than an individual, and, like Man or the Spirit of Man, a spirit haunting the individual—the Spirit of the People. For this reason they revered this spirit, and only so far as he served this or else a spirit related to it (as in the Spirit of the Family) could the individual appear significant; only for the sake of the higher essence, the People, was consideration allowed to the 'member of the people'. As you are hallowed to us by 'Man' who haunts you, so at every time men have been hallowed by some higher essence or other, like People, Family, and such. Only for the sake of a higher essence has any one been honoured from of old, only as a ghost has he been regarded in the light of a hallowed, a protected and recognized person. If I cherish you because I hold you dear, because in you my heart finds nourishment, my need satisfaction, then it is not done for the sake of a higher essence whose hallowed body you are, not on account of my beholding in you a ghost, an appearing spirit, but from egoistic pleasure; you yourself with *your* essence are valuable to me, for your essence is not a higher one, is not higher and more general than you, is unique like you yourself, because it is you.

(*Ego* 51–4)

BATS IN THE BELFRY

Man, your head is haunted; you have bats in your belfry! You imagine great things, and depict to yourself

a whole world of gods that has an existence for you, a
spirit-realm to which you suppose yourself to be called,
an ideal that beckons to you. You have a fixed idea!

Do not think that I am jesting or speaking figuratively
when I regard those persons who cling to the Higher,
and (because the vast majority belongs under this head)
almost the whole world of men, as veritable fools, fools
in a madhouse. What is it, then, that is called a 'fixed
idea'? An idea that has subjected the man to itself. When
you recognize, with regard to such a fixed idea, that it is
a folly, you shut its slave up in an asylum. And is the
truth of the faith, say, which we are not to doubt; the
majesty of the people, which we are not to strike at (he
who does is guilty of—lese-majesty); virtue, against
which the censor is not to let a word pass, that morality
may be kept pure;—are these not 'fixed ideas'? Is not all
the stupid chatter of most of our newspapers the babble
of fools who suffer from the fixed idea of morality,
legality, Christianity, and so forth, and only seem to go
about free because the madhouse in which they walk
takes in so broad a space? Touch the fixed idea of such a
fool, and you will at once have to guard your back against
the lunatic's stealthy malice. For these great lunatics are
like the little so-called lunatics in this point too—that
they assail by stealth him who touches their fixed idea.
They first steal his weapon, steal free speech from him,
and then they fall upon him with their nails. Every
day now lays bare the cowardice and vindictiveness of
these maniacs, and the stupid populace hurrahs for their
crazy measures. One must read the journals of this
period, and must hear the Philistines talk, to get the
horrible conviction that one is shut up in a house with
fools. 'Thou shalt not call thy brother a fool; if thou
dost—etc.' But I do not fear the curse, and I say, my

brothers are arch-fools. Whether a poor fool of the insane asylum is possessed by the fancy that he is God the Father, Emperor of Japan, the Holy Spirit, or whatnot, or whether a citizen in comfortable circumstances conceives that it is his mission to be a good Christian, a faithful Protestant, a loyal citizen, a virtuous man—both these are one and the same 'fixed idea'. He who has never tried and dared not to be a good Christian, a faithful Protestant, a virtuous man, and the like, is *possessed* and prepossessed[1] by faith, virtuousness, etc. Just as the schoolmen philosophized only *inside* the belief of the Church; as Pope Benedict XIV[2] wrote fat books *inside* the papist superstition, without ever throwing a doubt upon this belief; as authors fill whole folios on the State without calling in question the fixed idea of the State itself; as our newspapers are crammed with politics because they are conjured into the fancy that man was created to be a *zoon politicon*—so also subjects vegetate in subjection, virtuous people in virtue, liberals in humanity, without ever putting to these fixed ideas of theirs the searching knife of criticism. Undislodgeable, like a madman's delusion, those thoughts stand on a firm footing, and he who doubts them—lays hands on the *sacred*! Yes, the 'fixed idea', that is the truly sacred!

Is it perchance only people possessed by the devil that meet us, or do we as often come upon people *possessed* in the contrary way—possessed by 'the good', by virtue, morality, the law, or some 'principle' or other? Possessions of the devil are not the only ones. God works on us, and the devil does; the former 'workings of grace', the latter

---

[1] *Gefangen und befangen*, literally 'imprisoned and prepossessed'.

[2] Prospero Lambertini (1675–1758), Pope Benedict XIV from 1740 to 1758, a very learned, intellectual and many-sided pope who came under the influence of the Enlightenment.

'workings of the devil'. Possessed people[1] are set[2] in their opinions.

If the word 'possession' displeases you, then call it pre-possession; yes, since the spirit possesses you, and all 'inspirations' come from it, call it—inspiration and enthusiasm. I add that complete enthusiasm—for we cannot stop with the sluggish, half-way kind—is called fanaticism.

It is precisely among cultured people that *fanaticism* is at home; for man is cultured in so far as he takes an interest in spiritual things, and interest in spiritual things, when it is alive, is and must be *fanaticism*; it is a fanatical interest in the sacred (*fanum*). Observe our liberals, look into the *Sächsische Vaterlandsblätter*,[3] hear what Schlosser says:[4] 'Holbach's company constituted a regular plot against the traditional doctrine and the existing system, and its members were as fanatical on behalf of their unbelief as monks and priests, Jesuits and Pietists, Methodists, missionary and Bible societies, commonly are for mechanical worship and orthodoxy.'

Take notice how a 'moral man' behaves, who today often thinks he is through with God and throws off Christianity as a bygone thing. If you ask him whether he has ever doubted that the copulation of brother and sister is incest, that monogamy is the truth of marriage, that filial piety is a sacred duty, then a moral shudder will come over him at the conception of one's being allowed to touch his sister as wife also. And whence this shudder?

---

[1] *Besessene.*

[2] *versessen.*

[3] A weekly published in Dresden, beginning in 1841.

[4] Stirner cited page 519 from the second volume of *Geschichte des achtzenten Jahrhunderts* of Friedrich Christoph Schlosser (1776–1861), historian and professor at Heidelberg, whose book was published in that city in 1823. The reference is to the rationalists and the writers of the Enlightenment, Holbach, d'Alembert, Diderot and others, and their part in undermining the beliefs of the period prior to the French Revolution.

Because he *believes* in those moral commandments. This moral *faith* is deeply rooted in his breast. Much as he rages against the *pious* Christians, he himself has nevertheless as thoroughly remained a Christian—to wit, a *moral* Christian. In the form of morality Christianity holds him a prisoner, and a prisoner under *faith*. Monogamy is to be something sacred, and he who may live in bigamy is punished as a *criminal*; he who commits incest suffers as a *criminal*. Those who are always crying that religion is not to be regarded in the State, and the Jew is to be a citizen equally with the Christian, show themselves in accord with this. Is not this of incest and monogamy a *dogma of faith*?[1] Touch it, and you will learn by experience how this moral man is a *hero of faith* too, not less than Krummacher,[2] not less than Philip II. These fight for the faith of the Church, he for the faith of the State, or the moral laws of the State; for articles of faith, both condemn him who acts otherwise than *their faith* will allow. The brand of 'crime' is stamped upon him, and he may languish in reformatories, in jails. Moral faith is as fanatical as religious faith! They call that 'liberty of faith', then, when

---

[1] The choice of these deeply held moral laws is deliberate; Stirner stresses that all values, however fundamental they appear to the viability of society, must be put in question. Why cannot bigamy, why not incest, be valid self-expressions? Indeed, there is the suggestion in Stirner's writings that the man who overcomes the primal taboo of incest, or in Freud's language breaks the Oedipal complex, the ultimate immoralist, thereby moves closest to the well-springs of feeling and sensibility—a theme which returned in the nineteenth century in the lives and works of the romantic poets (Byron, Wordsworth, Shelley, for example), and received its most complete statement in Wagner's *Ring*, where all love that is not brother-sister is seen as betrayal.

[2] It is not clear from the context which member of this formidable family of fierce defenders of orthodox German Protestantism Stirner is referring to; Friedrich Adolf Krummacher (1768–1845), his brother Gottfried Daniel (1774–1837) and his son Friedrich Wilhelm (1796–1868) all had reputations as theologians. The last-named's strong attacks on rationalists in various books suggest that he is the referent.

brother and sister, on account of a relation that they should have settled with their 'conscience', are thrown into prison. 'But they set a pernicious example.' Yes, indeed: others might have taken the notion that the State had no business to meddle with their relation, and thereupon 'purity of morals' would go to ruin. So then the religious heroes of faith are zealous for the 'sacred God', the moral ones for the 'sacred good'.

Those who are zealous for something sacred often look very little like each other. How the strictly orthodox or old-style believers differ from the fighters for 'truth, light, and justice', from the Philalethes, the Friends of Light, the Rationalists, and others. And yet, how utterly unessential is this difference! If one buffets single traditional truths (miracles, unlimited power of princes), then the Rationalists buffet them too, and only the old-style believers wail. But, if one buffets truth itself, he immediately has both, as *believers*, for opponents. So with moralities; the strict believers are relentless, the clearer heads are more tolerant. But he who attacks morality itself gets both to deal with. 'Truth, morality, justice, light, etc.' are to be and remain 'sacred'. What any one finds to censure in Christianity is simply supposed to be 'unchristian' according to the view of these rationalists; but Christianity must remain a 'fixture', to buffet it is outrageous, 'an outrage'. To be sure, the heretic against pure faith no longer exposes himself to the earlier fury of persecution, but so much the more does it now fall upon the heretic against pure morals.

*   *   *

Piety has for a century received so many blows, and had to hear its superhuman essence reviled as an 'inhuman' one so often, that one cannot feel tempted to draw the sword against it again. And yet it has almost always been only moral opponents that have appeared in the arena, to assail the supreme essence in favour of—another supreme essence. So Proudhon, unabashed, says: 'Man is destined to live without religion, but the moral law is eternal and absolute. Who would dare today to attack morality?'* Moral people skimmed off the best fat from religion, ate it themselves, and are now having a tough job to get rid of the resulting scrofula. If, therefore, we point out that religion has not by any means been hurt in its inmost part so long as people reproach it only with its superhuman essence, and that it takes its final appeal to the 'spirit' alone (for God is spirit), then we have sufficiently indicated its final accord with morality, and can leave its stubborn conflict with the latter lying behind us. It is a question of a supreme essence with both, and whether this is a superhuman or a human one can make (since it is in any case an essence over me, a super-mine one, so to speak) but little difference to me. In the end the relation to the human essence, or to 'Man', as soon as ever it has shed the snake-skin of the old religion, will yet wear a religious snake-skin again.

(*Ego* 54–60)

From a certain standpoint of morality people reason something like this: Either man is led by his sensuality, and is, following it, *immoral*, or he is led by the good, which, taken up into the will, is called moral sentiment (sentiment and prepossession in favour of the good); then he shows himself *moral*. From this point of view how, for instance, can Sand's act against Kotzebue be called

* Pierre Joseph Proudhon, *De la Création de l'ordre dans l'humanité, ou principes d'organisation politique* (Paris, 1843), p. 36.

immoral?[1] What is commonly understood by unselfish it certainly was, in the same measure as (among other things) St Crispin's[2] thieveries in favour of the poor. 'He should not have murdered, for it stands written, Thou shalt not murder!' Then to serve the good, the welfare of the people, as Sand at least intended, or the welfare of the poor, like Crispin—is moral; but murder and theft are immoral; the purpose moral, the means immoral. Why? 'Because murder, assassination, is something absolutely bad.' When the Guerrillas[3] enticed the enemies of the country into ravines and shot them down unseen from the bushes, do you suppose that was assassination? According to the principle of morality, which commands us to serve the good, you could really ask only whether murder could never in any case be a realization of the good, and would have to endorse that murder which realized the good. You cannot condemn Sand's deed at all; it was moral, because in the service of the good, because unselfish; it was an act of punishment, which the individual inflicted, an— *execution* inflicted at the risk of the executioner's life. What else had his scheme been, after all, but that he wanted to suppress writings by brute force? Are you not acquainted with the same procedure as a 'legal' and sanctioned one? And what can be objected against it from your principle of morality?—'But it was an illegal execution.' So the immoral thing in it was the illegality, the disobedience to law? Then you admit that the good is nothing else than —law, morality nothing else than *loyalty*. And to this

[1] The assassination of August Friedrich Ferdinand von Kotzebue (1761–1819) by Karl-Ludwig Sand (1795–1820). Kotzebue, a defender of the older political order, ridiculed the new German nationalism which grew out of the struggle against Napoleon. He was called a 'traitor' and was stabbed to death by Sand, an extremely zealous younger exponent of this sentiment.

[2] The patron saint of shoemakers.

[3] A reference to the irregular forces fighting in Spain against Napoleon during the Peninsular Wars, 1808–14.

externality of 'loyalty' your morality must sink, to this righteousness of works in the fulfilment of the law, only that the latter is at once more tyrannical and more revolting than the old-time righteousness of works. For in the latter only the *act* is needed, but you require the *disposition* too; one must carry *in himself* the law, the statute; and he who is most legally disposed is the most moral. Even the last vestige of cheerfulness in Catholic life must perish in this Protestant legality. Here at last the domination of the law is for the first time complete. 'Not I live, but the law lives in me.' Thus I have really come so far to be only the 'vessel of its glory'. 'Every Prussian carries his *gendarme* in his breast,' says a high Prussian officer.[1]

Why do certain *opposition parties* fail to flourish? Solely for the reason that they refuse to forsake the path of morality or legality. Hence the measureless hypocrisy of devotion, love, etc., from whose repulsiveness one may daily get the most thorough nausea at this rotten and hypocritical relation of a 'lawful opposition'. — In the *moral* relation of love and fidelity a divided or opposed will cannot have place; the beautiful relation is disturbed if the one wills this and the other the reverse. But now, according to the practice hitherto and the old prejudice of the opposition, the moral relation is to be preserved above

[1] Stirner has a much stronger claim than Nietzsche (e.g. in *Ecce Homo*) to be the first *immoralist*. To schematize what is perhaps the major axis in nineteenth-century German thought we can regard Stirner as having turned Hegel's master-slave dialectic (*The Phenomenology of Mind*, 1807) on its head, taking the slave to be subservient through *morality* to his own dictatorial conscience (Marx developed Hegel's idea, that the slave is forced to labour for his master, into the materialist theory of *economic* exploitation). For Stirner the slave (cleric) was condemned, and all hopes for liberation resided with the master (egoist), whereas for Marx, as for Hegel, the seeds of liberation lie latent within the slave class and its labour. Nietzsche's superman (*Übermensch*)–ascetic priest dichotomy mirrors Stirner's egoist–cleric one at most points, and notably does so in its central assumption — that modern man's malaise results from moral rather than socio–economic or political repression.

all. What is then left to the opposition? Perhaps the will
to take a liberty, if the beloved one sees fit to deny it? Not
a bit! It may not *will* to have the freedom, it can only
wish for it, 'petition' for it, lisp a 'Please, please!' What
would come of it, if the opposition really *willed*, willed
with the full energy of the will? No, it must renounce *will*
in order to live to *love*, renounce liberty—for love of
morality. It may never 'claim as a right' what it is permitted only to 'beg as a favour'. Love, devotion, etc.,
demand with undeviating definiteness that there be only
one will to which the others devote themselves, which they
serve, follow, love. Whether this will is regarded as reasonable or as unreasonable, in both cases one acts morally when
one follows it, and immorally when one breaks away from
it. The will that commands the censorship seems to many
unreasonable; but he who in a land of censorship evades
the censoring of his book acts immorally, and he who sub-
mits it to the censorship acts morally. If some one let his
moral judgment go, and set up a secret press, one would
have to call him immoral, and imprudent into the bargain
if he let himself be caught; but will such a man lay claim
to a value in the eyes of the 'moral'? Perhaps!—That is,
if he fancied he was serving a 'higher morality'.

The web of the hypocrisy of today hangs on the frontiers
of two domains, between which our time swings back and
forth, attaching its fine threads of deception and self-
deception. No longer vigorous enough to serve *morality*
without doubt or weakening, not yet reckless enough to
live wholly to egoism, it trembles now towards the one and
now towards the other in the spider-web of hypocrisy, and,
crippled by the curse of *halfness*, catches only miserable,
stupid flies. If one has once dared to make a 'free' motion,
immediately one waters it again with assurances of love,
and—*shams resignation*; if, on the other side, they have had

the face to reject the free motion with *moral* appeals to confidence, immediately the moral courage also sinks, and they assure one how they hear the free words with special pleasure; they — *sham approval*. In short, people would like to have the one, but not go without the other; they would like to have a *free* will, but not for their lives lack the *moral will*. Just come in contact with a servile loyalist, you Liberals. You will sweeten every word of freedom with a look of the most loyal confidence, and he will clothe his servilism in the most flattering phrases of freedom. Then you go apart, and he, like you, thinks 'I know you, fox!' He scents the devil in you as much as you do the dark old Lord God in him.

A Nero is a 'bad' man only in the eyes of the 'good'; in mine he is nothing but a *possessed* man, as are the good too. The good see in him an arch-villain, and relegate him to hell. Why did nothing hinder him in his arbitrary course? Why did people put up with so much? Do you suppose the tame Romans, who let all their will be bound by such a tyrant, were a hair the better? In old Rome they would have put him to death instantly, would never have been his slaves. But the contemporary 'good' among the Romans opposed to him only moral demands, not their *will*; they sighed that their emperor did not do homage to morality, like them; they themselves remained 'moral subjects', till at last one found courage to give up 'moral, obedient subjection'. And then the same 'good Romans' who, as 'obedient subjects', had borne all the ignominy of having no will, hurrahed over the nefarious, immoral act of the rebel. Where then in the 'good' was the courage for the *revolution*, that courage which they now praised, after another had mustered it up? The good could not have this courage, for a revolution, and an insurrection into the bargain, is always something 'immoral', which one can resolve upon only when one ceases to be 'good' and becomes either 'bad' or—neither of the two. Nero was no viler than his time, in which one could only be one of the two, good or bad. The judgment of his time on him had to be that he was bad, and this in the highest degree: not a milksop, but an arch-scoundrel. All moral people can pronounce only this judgment on him. Rascals such as he was are still living here and there today in the midst of the moral. It is not convenient to live among them, certainly, as one is not sure of his life for a moment; but can you say that it is more convenient to live among the moral? One is just as little sure of his life there, only that one is hanged 'in the way of justice', but least of all is one sure of his honour, and the national cockade is gone before you can say Jack Robinson. The hard fist of morality treats the noble nature of egoism altogether without compassion.

'But surely one cannot put a rascal and an honest man on the same level!' Now no human being does that oftener than you judges of morals; yes, still more than that, you imprison as a criminal an honest man who speaks openly against the existing constitution, against the hallowed institutions, and you entrust portfolios and still more important things to a crafty rascal. So *in praxi* you have nothing to reproach me with. 'But in theory!' Now there I do put both on the same level, as two opposite poles—to wit, both on the level of the moral law. Both have meaning only in the 'moral' world, just as in the pre-Christian time a Jew who kept the law and one who broke it had meaning and significance only in respect to the Jewish law; before Jesus Christ, on the contrary, the Pharisee was no more than the 'sinner and publican'. So before self-ownership the moral Pharisee amounts to as much as the immoral sinner.

Nero became very inconvenient by his possessedness.

But a self-owning man would not sillily oppose to him the 'sacred', and whine if the tyrant does not regard the sacred; he would oppose to him his will. How often the sacredness of the inalienable rights of man has been held up to their foes, and some liberty or other shown and demonstrated to be a 'sacred right of man'! Those who do that deserve to be laughed out of court—as they actually are—were it not that in truth they do, even though unconsciously, take the road that leads to the goal. They have a presentiment that, if only the majority is once won for that liberty, it will also will the liberty, and will then take what it *will* have. The sacredness of the liberty, and all possible proofs of this sacredness, will never procure it; lamenting and petitioning only shows beggars.

The moral man is necessarily narrow in that he knows no other enemy than the 'immoral' man. 'He who is not moral is immoral!' and accordingly reprobate, despicable, etc. Therefore the moral man can never comprehend the egoist. Is not unwedded cohabitation an immorality? The moral man may turn as he pleases, he will have to stand by this verdict; Emilia Galotti[1] gave up her life for this moral truth. And it is true, it is an immorality. A virtuous girl may become an old maid; a virtuous man may pass the time in fighting his natural impulses till he has perhaps dulled them, he may castrate himself for the sake of virtue as St Origen[2] did for the sake of heaven: he thereby honours sacred wedlock, sacred chastity, as inviolable; he is—moral. Unchastity can never become a moral act. However indulgently the moral man may judge and excuse him who committed it, it remains a transgression, a sin against a moral commandment; there clings to it an in-

[1] The heroine of the play of the same name by Gotthold Ephraim Lessing (1729–81).

[2] One of the Fathers and Doctors of the Christian Church, resident of Alexandria, A.D. *c.* 185–*c.* 254.

delible stain. As chastity once belonged to the monastic vow, so it does to moral conduct. Chastity is a—good.— For the egoist, on the contrary, even chastity is not a good without which he could not get along; he cares nothing at all about it.

(Ego 64–71)

* * *

Now do you suppose unselfishness is unreal and nowhere extant? On the contrary, nothing is more ordinary! One may even call it an article of fashion in the civilized world, which is considered so indispensable that, if it costs too much in solid material, people at least adorn themselves with its tinsel counterfeit and feign it. Where does unselfishness begin? Right where an end ceases to be *our* end and our *property*, which we, as owners, can dispose of at pleasure; where it becomes a fixed end or a—fixed idea; where it begins to inspire, enthuse, fanaticize us; in short, where it passes into our *stubbornness* and becomes our— master. One is not unselfish so long as he retains the end in his power; one becomes so only at that 'Here I stand, I cannot do otherwise,' the fundamental maxim of all the possessed; one becomes so in the case of a *sacred* end, through the corresponding sacred zeal.

I am not unselfish so long as the end remains my *own*, and I, instead of giving myself up to be the blind means of its fulfilment, leave it always an open question. My zeal need not on that account be slacker than the most fanatical, but at the same time I remain towards it frostily cold, un-believing, and its most irreconcilable enemy; I remain its *judge*, because I am its owner.

Unselfishness grows rank as far as possessedness reaches, as much on possessions of the devil as on those of a good spirit: there vice, folly, and the like; here humility, devotion, and so forth.

Where could one look without meeting victims of self-renunciation? There sits a girl opposite me, who perhaps has been making bloody sacrifices to her soul for ten years already. Over the buxom form droops a deathly-tired head, and pale cheeks betray the slow bleeding away of her youth. Poor child, how often the passions may have beaten at your heart, and the rich powers of youth have demanded their right! When your head rolled in the soft pillow, how awakening nature quivered through your limbs, the blood swelled your veins, and fiery fancies poured the gleam of voluptuousness into your eyes! Then appeared the ghost of the soul and its external bliss. You were terrified, your hands folded themselves, your tormented eyes turned their look upward, you—prayed. The storms of nature were hushed, a calm glided over the ocean of your appetites. Slowly the weary eyelids sank over the life extinguished under them, the tension crept out unperceived from the rounded limbs, the boisterous waves dried up in the heart, the folded hands themselves rested a powerless weight on the unresisting bosom, one last faint 'Oh dear!' moaned itself away, and—*the soul was at rest*. You fell asleep, to awake in the morning to a new combat and a new—prayer. Now the habit of renunciation cools the heat of your desire, and the roses of your youth are growing pale in the—chlorosis of your heavenliness. The soul is saved, the body may perish! O Laïs, O Ninon,[1] how well you did to scorn this pale virtue. One free *grisette* against a thousand virgins grown grey in virtue!

The fixed idea may also be perceived as 'maxim',

---

[1] A reference to the beautiful Greek courtesan made famous by Demosthenes, and to Ninon de Lenclos (1620–1705), the worldly French *belle*, known among other things for her many amatory liaisons.

'principle', 'standpoint', and the like. Archimedes, to move the earth, asked for a standpoint *outside* it. Men sought continually for this standpoint, and every one seized upon it as well as he was able. This foreign standpoint is the *world of mind*, of ideas, thoughts, concepts, essences; it is *heaven*. Heaven is the 'standpoint' from which the earth is moved, earthly doings surveyed and — despised. To assure to themselves heaven, to occupy the heavenly standpoint firmly and for ever — how painfully and tirelessly humanity struggled for this!

Christianity has aimed to deliver us from a life determined by nature, from the appetites as actuating us, and so has meant that man should not let himself be determined by his appetites. This does not involve the idea that *he* was not to have appetites, but that the appetites were not to have him, that they were not to become *fixed*, uncontrollable, indissoluble. Now could not what Christianity (religion) contrived against the appetites be applied by us to its own precept that *mind* (thought, conceptions, ideas, faith) must determine us; could we not ask that neither should mind, or the conception, the idea, be allowed to determine us, to become fixed and inviolable or 'sacred'? Then it would end in the *dissolution of mind*, the dissolution of all thoughts, of all conceptions. As we there had to say, 'We are indeed to have appetites, but the appetites are not to have us,' so we should now say, 'We are indeed to have *mind*, but mind is not to have us.' If the latter seems lacking in sense, think of the fact that with so many a man a thought becomes a 'maxim', whereby he himself is made prisoner to it, so that it is not he that has the maxim, but rather it that has him. And with the maxim he has a 'permanent standpoint' again. The doctrines of the catechism become our *principles* before we find it out, and no longer brook rejection. Their thought, or — mind, has the sole power, and no protest of the 'flesh' is further listened to. Nevertheless it is only through the 'flesh' that I can break the tyranny of mind; for it is only when a man hears his flesh along with the rest of him that he hears himself wholly, and it is only when he wholly hears *himself* that he is a hearing or rational[1] being. The Christian does not hear the agony of his enthralled nature, but lives in 'humility'; therefore he does not grumble at the wrong which befalls his *person*; he thinks himself satisfied with the 'freedom of the spirit'. But, if the flesh once takes the floor, and its tone is 'passionate', 'indecorous', 'not well-disposed', 'spiteful' (as it cannot be otherwise), then he thinks he hears voices of devils, voices *against* the *spirit* (for decorum, passionlessness, kindly disposition, and the like, is—spirit), and is justly zealous against them. He could not be a Christian if he were willing to endure them. He listens only to morality, and slaps immorality in the mouth; he listens only to legality, and gags the lawless word. The *spirit* of morality and legality holds him a prisoner; a rigid, unbending *master*. They call that the 'mastery of the spirit'—it is at the same time the *standpoint* of the spirit.

And now whom do the ordinary liberal gentlemen mean to make free? Whose freedom is it that they cry out and thirst for? The *spirit's*! That of the spirit of morality, legality, piety, the fear of God. That is what the anti-liberal gentlemen also want, and the whole contention between the two turns on a matter of advantage—whether the latter are to be the only speakers, or the former are to receive a 'share in the enjoyment of the same advantage'. The *spirit* remains the absolute *lord* for both, and their only quarrel is over who shall occupy the hierarchical throne that pertains to the 'Vicegerent of the Lord'. The

[1] *vernünftig*, derived from *vernehmen*, to hear.

best of it is that one can calmly look upon the stir with the certainty that the wild beasts of history will tear each other to pieces just like those of nature; their putrefying corpses fertilize the ground for—our crops.

(Ego 78–82)

*   *   *

The difference is, then, whether feelings are imparted to me or only aroused. Those which are aroused are my own, egoistic, because they are not *as feelings* drilled into me, dictated to me, and pressed upon me; but those which are imparted to me I receive, with open arms—I cherish them in me as a heritage, cultivate them, and am *possessed* by them. Who is there that has never, more or less consciously, noticed that our whole education is calculated to produce *feelings* in us, impart them to us, instead of leaving their production to ourselves however they may turn out? If we hear the name of God, we are to feel veneration; if we hear that of the prince's majesty, it is to be received with reverence, deference, submission; if we hear that of morality, we are to think that we hear something inviolable; if we hear of the Evil One or evil ones, we are to shudder. The intention is directed to these *feelings*, and he who should hear with pleasure the deeds of the 'bad' would have to be 'taught what's what' with the rod of discipline. Thus stuffed with *imparted feelings*, we appear before the bar of majority and are 'pronounced of age'. Our equipment consists of 'elevating feelings, lofty thoughts, inspiring maxims, eternal principles'. The young are of age when they twitter like the old; they are driven through school to learn the old song, and, when they have this by heart, they are declared of age.

We *must not* feel at every thing and every name that

comes before us what we could and would like to feel thereat; at the name of God we must think of nothing laughable, feel nothing disrespectful, it being prescribed and imparted to us what and how we are to feel and think at mention of that name.

That is the meaning of the *care of souls* — that my soul or my mind be tuned as others think right, not as I myself would like it. How much trouble does it not cost one, finally to secure to oneself a feeling of one's *own* at the mention of at least this or that name, and to laugh in the face of many who expect from us a holy face and a composed expression at their speeches. What is imparted is *alien* to us, is not our own, and therefore is 'sacred', and it is hard work to lay aside the 'sacred dread of it'.

Today one again hears 'seriousness' praised, 'seriousness in the presence of highly important subjects and discussions', 'German seriousness', and so on. This sort of seriousness proclaims clearly how old and grave lunacy and possession have already become. For there is nothing more serious than a lunatic when he comes to the central point of his lunacy; then his great earnestness incapacitates him for taking a joke. (See madhouses.)

(Ego 83–5)

C.—THE HIERARCHY

Before the sacred, people lose all sense of power and all confidence; they occupy a *powerless* and *humble* attitude towards it. And yet no thing is sacred of itself, but by my *declaring it sacred*, by my declaration, my judgment, my bending the knee; in short, by my—conscience.

Sacred is everything which for the egoist is to be unapproachable, not to be touched, outside his *power*— above *him*; sacred, in a word, is every *matter of conscience,* for 'this is a matter of conscience to me' means simply 'I hold this sacred.'

For little children, just as for animals, nothing sacred exists, because, in order to make room for this conception, one must already have progressed so far in understanding that he can make distinctions like 'good and bad', 'warranted and unwarranted'; only at such a level of reflection or intelligence—the proper standpoint of religion—can unnatural (that is, brought into existence by thinking) *reverence*, 'sacred dread', step into the place of natural fear. To this sacred dread belongs holding something outside oneself for mightier, greater, better warranted, better; the attitude in which one acknowledges the might of something alien—not merely feels it, then, but expressly acknowledges it, admits it, yields, surrenders, lets himself be tied (devotion, humility, servility, submission). Here walks the whole ghostly troop of the 'Christian virtues'.

Everything towards which you cherish any respect or reverence deserves the name of sacred; you yourselves, too, say that you would feel a '*sacred dread*' of laying hands on it. And you give this tinge even to the unholy (gallows, crime, etc.). You have a horror of touching it. There lies in it something uncanny, that is, unfamiliar or *not your own*.

'If something or other did not rank as sacred in a man's mind, why, then all bars would be let down to self-will, to unlimited subjectivity!' Fear makes the beginning, and one can make himself fearful to the coarsest man; already, therefore, a barrier against his insolence. But in fear there always remains the attempt to liberate oneself from what is feared, by guile, deception, tricks, etc. In reverence,[1] on the contrary, it is quite otherwise. Here something is not only feared,[2] but also honoured[3]: what is feared has become an inward power which I can no longer get clear

[1] *Ehrfurcht.*   [2] *gefürchtet.*   [3] *geehrt.*

of; I honour it, am captivated by it and devoted to it, belong to it; by the honour which I pay it I am completely in its power, and do not even attempt liberation any longer. Now I am attached to it with all the strength of faith; I *believe*. I and what I fear are one; 'not I live, but the respected lives in me!' Because the spirit, the infinite, does not allow of coming to any end, therefore it is stationary; it fears *dying*, it cannot let go its dear Jesus, the greatness of finiteness is no longer recognized by its blinded eye; the object of fear, now raised to veneration, may no longer be handled; reverence is made eternal, the respected is deified. The man is now no longer employed in creating, but in *learning* (knowing, investigating), occupied with a fixed *object*, losing himself in its depths, without return to himself. The relation to this object is that of knowing, fathoming, basing, not that of *dissolution* (abrogation). 'Man is to be religious,' that is settled; therefore people busy themselves only with the question how this is to be attained, what is the right meaning of religiousness, etc. Quite otherwise when one makes the axiom itself doubtful and calls it in question, even though it should go to pieces. Morality too is such a sacred conception; one must be moral, and must look only for the right 'how', the right way to be so. One dares not go at morality itself with the question whether it is not itself an illusion; it remains exalted above all doubt, unchangeable. And so we go on with the sacred, grade after grade, from the 'holy' to the 'holy of holies'.

(Ego 92–4)

*　　*　　*

Hierarchy is dominion of thoughts, dominion of mind!
We are hierarchic to this day, kept down by those who are supported by thoughts. Thoughts are the sacred.

But the two are always clashing, now one and now the other giving the offence; and this clash occurs, not only in the collision of two men, but in one and the same man. For no cultured man is so cultured as not to find enjoyment in things too, and so be uncultured; and no uncultured man is totally without thoughts. In Hegel it comes to light at last what a longing for things even the most cultured man has, and what a horror of every 'hollow theory' he harbours. With him reality, the world of things, is altogether to correspond to the thought, and no concept is to be without reality. This caused Hegel's system to be known as the most objective, as if in it thought and thing celebrated their union. But this was simply the extremest case of violence on the part of thought, its highest pitch of despotism and sole dominion, the triumph of mind, and with it the triumph of *philosophy*. Philosophy cannot hereafter achieve anything higher, for its highest is the *omnipotence of mind*, the almightiness of mind.

Spiritual men have *taken into their head* something that is to be realized. They have *concepts* of love, goodness, and the like, which they would like to see *realized*; therefore they want to set up a kingdom of love on earth, in which no one any longer acts from selfishness, but each one 'from love'. Love is to *rule*. What they have taken into their head, what shall we call it but—*fixed idea*? Why, 'their head is *haunted*.' The most oppressive spook is *Man*. Think of the proverb, 'The road to hell is paved with good intentions.' The intention to realize humanity altogether in oneself, to become altogether man, is of such ruinous kind; here belong the intentions to become good, noble, loving, and so forth.

(*Ego* 95–6)

Who, then, is 'self-sacrificing'? In the full sense, surely, he who ventures everything else for *one thing*, one object, one will, one passion. Is not the lover self-sacrificing who forsakes father and mother, endures all dangers and privations, to reach his goal? Or the ambitious man, who offers up all his desires, wishes, and satisfactions to the single passion, or the avaricious man who denies himself everything to gather treasures, or the pleasure-seeker? He is ruled by a passion to which he brings the rest as sacrifices.

And are these self-sacrificing people perchance not selfish, not egoists? As they have only one ruling passion, so they provide for only one satisfaction, but for this the more strenuously; they are wholly absorbed in it. Their entire activity is egoistic, but it is a one-sided, unopened, narrow egoism; it is possessedness.

'Why, those are petty passions, by which, on the contrary, man must not let himself be enthralled. Man must make sacrifices for a great idea, a great cause!' A 'great idea', a 'good cause', is, it may be, the honour of God, for which innumerable people have met death; Christianity, which has found its willing martyrs; the Holy Catholic Church, which has greedily demanded sacrifices of heretics; liberty and equality, which were waited on by bloody guillotines.

He who lives for a great idea, a good cause, a doctrine, a system, a lofty calling, may not let any worldly lusts, any self-seeking interest, spring up in him. Here we have the concept of *clericalism*,[1] or, as it may also be called in its pedagogic activity, schoolmasterliness; for the idealists play the schoolmaster over us. The clergyman is especially

[1] As far as I can discover, apart from the isolated, and at that time unknown, exception of William Blake, Stirner is the first to use 'cleric' (*der Pfaff*) as the paradigm for the resentful, inhibited, devitalized victim-become-perpetrator of morality, the substitute for genuine inner authority. Apart from Nietzsche and his *asketische Priester* the most noteworthy reappearance of the 'cleric' comes in Julien Benda's influential book, *La Trahison des clercs* (1927).

called to live to the idea and to work for the idea, the truly
good cause. Therefore the people feel how little it befits
him to show worldly haughtiness, to desire good living, to
join in such pleasures as dancing and gaming—in short,
to have any other than a 'sacred interest'. Hence too,
doubtless, is derived the scanty salary of teachers, who are
to feel themselves repaid by the sacredness of their calling
alone, and to 'renounce' other enjoyments.

Even a directory of the sacred ideas, one or more of
which man is to look upon as his calling, is not lacking.
Family, fatherland, science, etc., may find in me a servant
faithful to his calling.

Here we come upon the old, old craze of the world,
which has not yet learned to do without clericalism—that
to live and work *for an idea* is man's calling, and according
to the faithfulness of its fulfilment his *human* worth is
measured.

This is the dominion of the idea; in other words, it is
clericalism. Thus Robespierre and St Just were priests
through and through, inspired by the idea, enthusiasts,
consistent instruments of this idea, idealistic men. So St
Just exclaims in a speech, 'There is something terrible in
the sacred love of country; it is so exclusive that it sacrifices
everything to the public interest without mercy, without
fear, without human consideration. It hurls Manlius down
the precipice; it sacrifices its private inclinations; it leads
Regulus to Carthage, throws a Roman into the chasm,
and sets Marat, as a victim of his devotion, in the
Pantheon.'

Now, over against these representatives of ideal or
sacred interests stands a world of innumerable 'personal'
profane interests. No idea, no system, no sacred cause is
so great as never to be outrivalled and modified by these
personal interests. Even if they are silent momentarily, and

in times of rage and fanaticism, yet they soon come upper-most again through 'the sound sense of the people'. Those ideas do not completely conquer till they are no longer hostile to personal interests, till they satisfy egoism.

The man who is just now crying herrings in front of my window has a personal interest in good sales, and, if his wife or anybody else wishes him the like, this remains a personal interest all the same. If, on the other hand, a thief deprived him of his basket, then there would at once arise an interest of many, of the whole city, of the whole country, or, in a word, of all who abhor theft; an interest in which the herring-seller's person would become in-different, and in its place the category of the 'robbed man' would come into the foreground. But even here all might yet resolve itself into a personal interest, each of the partakers reflecting that he must concur in the punish-ment of the thief because unpunished stealing might otherwise become general and cause him too to lose his own. Such a calculation, however, can hardly be assumed on the part of many, and we shall rather hear the cry that the thief is a 'criminal'. Here we have before us a judg-ment, the thief's action receiving its expression in the concept 'crime'. Now the matter stands thus: even if a crime did not cause the slightest damage either to me or to any of those in whom I take an interest, I should never-theless denounce it. Why? Because I am enthusiastic for *morality*, filled with the *idea* of morality; what is hostile to it I everywhere assail. Because in his mind theft ranks as abominable without any question, Proudhon, for instance, thinks that with the sentence 'Property is theft' he has at once put a brand on property. In the sense of the priestly, theft is always a *crime*, or at least a misdeed.

Here the personal interest is at an end. This particular person who has stolen the basket is perfectly indifferent to my person; it is only the thief, this concept of which that person presents a specimen, that I take an interest in. The thief and man are in my mind irreconcilable opposites; for one is not truly man when one is a thief; one degrades *Man* or 'humanity' in himself when one steals. Dropping out of personal concern, one gets into *philanthropism*, friendliness to man, which is usually misunderstood as if it was a love to men, to each individual, while it is nothing but a love of *Man*, the unreal concept, the spook. It is not *tous anthropous*, men, but *ton anthropon*, Man, that the philanthropist carries in his heart. To be sure, he cares for each individual, but only because he wants to see his beloved ideal realized everywhere.

So there is nothing said here of care for me, you, us; that would be personal interest, and belongs under the head of 'worldly love'. Philanthropism is a heavenly, spiritual, a—priestly love. *Man* must be restored in us, even if thereby we poor devils should come to grief. It is the same priestly principle as that famous *fiat justitia, pereat mundus*; man and justice are ideas, ghosts, for love of which everything is sacrified; therefore, the priestly spirits are the 'self-sacrificing' ones.

He who is infatuated with *Man* leaves persons out of account so far as that infatuation extends, and floats in an ideal, sacred interest. *Man*, you see, is not a person, but an ideal, a spook.

(*Ego* 97–101)

To the activity of priestly minds belongs especially what one often hears called '*moral influence*'.

Moral influence takes its start where *humiliation* begins; yes, it is nothing else than this humiliation itself, the breaking and bending of the mettle[1] down to humility.[2] If I call

---

[1] *Mut.*   [2] *Demut.*

to some one to run away when a rock is to be blasted, I exert no moral influence by this demand; if I say to a child, 'You will go hungry if you will not eat what is put on the table', this is not moral influence. But, if I say to it, 'You will pray, honour your parents, respect the crucifix, speak the truth, for this belongs to man and is man's calling', or even 'this is God's will', then moral influence is complete; then a man is to bend before the *calling* of man, be tractable, become humble, give up his will for an alien one which is set up as rule and law; he is to *abase* himself before something *higher*: self-abasement. 'He that abaseth himself shall be exalted.' Yes, yes, children must early be *made* to practise piety, godliness, and propriety; a person of good breeding is one into whom 'good maxims' have been *instilled* and *impressed*, poured in through a funnel, thrashed in and preached in.

If one shrugs his shoulders at this, at once the good wring their hands despairingly, and cry, 'But, for heaven's sake, if one is to give children no good instruction, why, then they will run straight into the jaws of sin, and become good-for-nothing hoodlums!' Gently, you prophets of evil. Good-for-nothing in your sense they certainly will become; but your sense happens to be a very good-for-nothing sense. The impudent lads will no longer let anything be whined and chattered into them by you, and will have no sympathy for all the follies for which you have been raving and drivelling since the memory of man began; they will abolish the law of inheritance; they will not be willing to *inherit* your stupidities as you inherited them from your fathers; they destroy *original sin*. If you command them, 'Bend before the Most High', they will answer, 'If he wants to bend us, let him come himself and do it; we, at least, will not bend of our own accord.' And, if you threaten them with his wrath and his punishment, they will take it like being threatened with the bogeyman. If you are no more successful in making them afraid of ghosts, then the dominion of ghosts is at an end, and fairy-tales find no—*faith*.

And is it not precisely the liberals again that press for good education and improvement of the educational system? For how could their liberalism, their 'liberty within the bounds of law', come about without discipline? Even if they do not exactly educate to the fear of God, yet they demand the *fear of Man* all the more strictly, and awaken 'enthusiasm for the truly human calling' by discipline.

(*Ego* 105–6)

*　　*　　*

Many a man renounces morals, but with great difficulty the conception, 'morality'. Morality is the 'idea' of morals, their intellectual power, their power over the conscience; on the other hand, morals are too material to rule the mind, and do not fetter an 'intellectual' man, a so-called independent, a 'freethinker'.

The Protestant may put it as he will, the 'holy Scripture', the 'Word of God', still remains sacred for him. He for whom this is no longer 'holy' has ceased to—be a Protestant. But herewith what is 'ordained' in it, the public authorities appointed by God, etc., also remain sacred for him. For him these things remain indissoluble, unapproachable, 'raised above all doubt'; and, as *doubt*, which in practice becomes a *buffeting*, is what is most man's own, these things remain 'raised' above himself. He who cannot *get away* from them will—*believe*; for to believe in them is to be *bound* to them. Through the fact that in Protestantism the *faith* becomes a more inward faith, the *servitude* has also become a more inward servitude; one has taken those sanctities up into himself, entwined them with all his thoughts and endeavours, made them a *'matter of conscience'*, constructed out of them a *'sacred duty'* for himself. Therefore what the Protestant's conscience cannot get away from is sacred to him, and *conscientiousness* most clearly designates his character.

Protestantism has actually put a man in the position of a country governed by secret police. The spy and eaves-dropper, 'conscience', watches over every motion of the mind, and all thought and action is for it a 'matter of conscience', that is, police business. This tearing apart of man into 'natural impulse' and 'conscience' (inner popu-lace and inner police) is what constitutes the Protestant. The reason of the Bible (in place of the Catholic 'reason of the Church') ranks as sacred, and this feeling and con-sciousness that the word of the Bible is sacred is called — conscience. With this, then, sacredness is 'laid upon one's conscience'. If one does not free himself from conscience, the consciousness of the sacred, he may act uncon-scientiously indeed, but never consciencelessly.

The Catholic finds himself satisfied when he fulfils the *command*; the Protestant acts according to his 'best judg-ment and conscience'. For the Catholic is only a *layman*; the Protestant is himself a *clergyman*.

(*Ego* 114–16)

A Jesuit may, as a good Catholic, hallow everything. He needs only, for example, to say to himself, 'I as a priest am necessary to the Church, but serve it more zealously when I appease my desires properly; consequently I will seduce this girl, have my enemy there poisoned, etc.; my end is holy because it is a priest's, consequently it hallows the means.' For in the end it is still done for the benefit of the

Church. Why should the Catholic priest shrink from handing Emperor Henry VII[1] the poisoned wafer for the — Church's welfare?

The genuinely Churchly Protestants inveighed against every 'innocent pleasure', because only the sacred, the spiritual, could be innocent. What they could not point out the holy spirit in, the Protestants had to reject — dancing, the theatre, ostentation in the church, and the like.

(*Ego* 119–20)

Great 'works of mind' were created almost solely by Protestants, as they alone were the true disciples and consummators of *mind*.

*   *   *

How little man is able to control! He must let the sun run its course, the sea roll its waves, the mountains rise to heaven. Thus he stands powerless before the *uncontrollable*. Can he keep off the impression that he is helpless against this gigantic world? It is a fixed *law* to which he must submit, it determines his *fate*. Now, what did pre-Christian humanity work towards? Towards getting rid of the irruptions of the destinies, not letting oneself be vexed by them. The Stoics attained this in apathy, declaring the attacks of nature *indifferent*, and not letting themselves be affected by them. Horace utters the famous *Nil admirari*, by which he likewise announces the indifference of the *other*, the

---

[1] Holy Roman Emperor of the House of Luxemburg (1308–13), who claimed to be independent of the spiritual power of the pope and encountered a coalition of power against him created in part by Pope Clement V. Stirner's historical reference, regardless of the objections which might be raised by the Jesuits, was incorrect, since the Society of Jesus was not founded until 1534.

world; it is not to influence us, not to rouse our astonishment. And that *impavidum ferient ruinae* expresses the very same *imperturbability* as Ps. xlvi 3: 'We do not fear, though the earth should perish.' In all this there is room made for the Christian proposition that the world is empty, for the Christian *contempt of the world*.

(*Ego* 120–1)

Cognition has its object in life. German thought seeks, more than that of others, to reach the beginnings and fountain-heads of life, and sees no life till it sees it in cognition itself. Descartes's *cogito, ergo sum* has the meaning 'One lives only when one thinks.' Thinking life is called 'intellectual life'! Only mind lives, its life is the true life. Then, just so in nature only the 'eternal laws', the mind or the reason of nature, are its true life. In man, as in nature, only the thought lives; everything else is dead! To this abstraction, to the life of generalities or of that which is *lifeless*, the history of mind had to come. God, who is spirit, alone lives. Nothing lives but the ghost.

(*Ego* 112)

Now nothing but *mind* rules in the world. An innumerable multitude of concepts buzz about in people's heads, and what are those doing who endeavour to get further? They are negating these concepts to put new ones in their place! They are saying, 'You form a false concept of right, of the State, of man, of liberty, of truth, of marriage; the concept of right, etc., is rather that one which we now set up.' Thus the confusion of concepts moves forward.

The history of the world has dealt cruelly with us, and the spirit has obtained an almighty power. You must have regard for my miserable shoes, which could protect your naked foot, my salt, by which your potatoes would become palatable, and my state carriage, whose possession would relieve you of all need at once; you must not reach out after them. Man is to recognize the *independence* of all these and innumerable other things: they are to rank in his mind as something that cannot be seized or approached, are to be kept away from him. He must have regard for it, respect it; woe to him if he stretches out his fingers desirously; we call that 'being light-fingered'!

How beggarly little is left us, yes, how really nothing! Everything has been removed, we must not venture on anything unless it is given us; we continue to live only by the *grace* of the giver. You must not pick up a pin, unless indeed you have got *leave* to do so. And got it from whom? From *respect*! Only when this lets you have it as property, only when you can *respect* it as property, only then may you take it. And again, you are not to conceive a thought, speak a syllable, commit an action, that should have their warrant in you alone, instead of receiving it from morality or reason or humanity. Happy *unconstraint* of the desirous man, how mercilessly people have tried to slay you on the alter of *constraint*!

But around the altar rise the arches of a church, and its walls keep moving farther and farther out. What they enclose is *sacred*. You can no longer get to it, no longer touch it. Shrieking with the hunger that devours you, you wander round about these walls in search of the little that is profane, and the circles of your course keep growing more and more extended. Soon that church will embrace the whole world, and you be driven out to the extreme edge; another step, and the *world of the sacred* has conquered: you sink into the abyss. Therefore take courage while it is yet time, wander about no longer in the profane where now it is dry feeding, dare the leap, and rush in through the gates into the sanctuary itself. If you *devour the sacred*, you have made it your *own*! Digest the sacramental wafer, and you are rid of it!

(*Ego* 125-7)

III. THE FREE[1]

A.—POLITICAL LIBERALISM

The human *religion* is only the last metamorphosis of the Christian religion. For liberalism is a religion because it separates my essence from me and sets it above me, because it exalts 'Man' to the same extent as any other religion does its God or idol, because it makes what is mine into something other-worldly, because in general it makes out of what is mine, out of my qualities and my property, something alien—to wit, an 'essence'; in short, because it sets me beneath Man, and thereby creates for me a 'vocation'.

(*Ego* 229)

*   *   *

The bourgeoisie[2] is nothing else than the thought that the State is all in all, the true man, and that the indi-

---

[1] Stirner is making an ironical reference to his contemporary philosophers, not only to the group called 'The Free Ones' of which he was a member. This chapter presents a critique of liberalist humanism and its exponents, who claimed to have emancipated themselves from Christian dogma. For Stirner liberalism has three faces: political liberalism or bourgeois ideology, social liberalism or communism, and humane liberalism as expounded by Bruno Bauer's school of 'criticism'. The third section on 'Humane Liberalism' is omitted here as it has little contemporary interest; Marx and Engels, earlier in 1844, had delivered in *The Holy Family* the first death-blow to Bauer's school—Stirner completed the job.

[2] Or 'citizenhood'. The word (*das Bürgertum*) means either the condition of being a citizen, or citizen-like principles, of the body of citizens or of the middle or business class, the bourgeoisie.

vidual's human value consists in being a citizen of the State. In being a good citizen he seeks his highest honour; beyond that he knows nothing higher than at most the antiquated—'being a good Christian'.

The bourgeoisie developed itself in the struggle against the privileged classes, by whom it was cavalierly treated as 'third estate' and confounded with the *canaille*. In other words, up to this time the State had recognized caste.[1] The son of a nobleman was selected for posts to which the most distinguished bourgeoisie aspired in vain. The civic feeling revolted against this. No more distinction, no giving preference to persons, no difference of classes! Let all be alike! No *separate interest* is to be pursued longer, but the *general interest of all*. The State is to be a fellowship of free and equal men, and every one is to devote himself to the 'welfare of the whole', to be dissolved in the *State*, to make the State his end and ideal. State! State! so ran the general cry, and thenceforth people sought for the 'right form of State', the best constitution, and so the State in its best conception. The thought of the State passed into all hearts and awakened enthusiasm; to serve it, this mundane god, became the new divine service and worship. The properly *political* epoch had dawned. To serve the State or the nation became the highest ideal, the State's interest the highest interest, State service (for which one does not by any means need to be an official) the highest honour.

So then the separate interests and personalities had been scared away, and sacrifice for the State had become the shibboleth. One must give up *himself*, and live only for the State. One must act 'disinterestedly', not want to benefit *himself*, but the State. Hereby the latter has become

[1] *Man hatte im Staate 'die ungleiche Person angesehen'*—there had been 'respect of unequal persons' in the State.

the true person, before whom the individual personality vanishes; not I live, but it lives in me. Therefore, in comparison with the former self-seeking, this was unselfishness and *impersonality* itself. Before this god—State —all egoism vanished, and before it all were equal; they were without any other distinction—men, nothing but men.

(*Ego* 129–30)

But, if the deserving count as the free (for what does the comfortable bourgeois, the faithful bureaucrat, lack of that freedom that his heart desires?), then the 'servants' are the—free. The obedient servant is the free man! What glaring nonsense! Yet this is the sense of the bourgeoisie, and its poet, Goethe, as well as its philosopher, Hegel,[1] succeeded in glorifying the dependence of the subject on the object, obedience to the objective world. He who only serves the cause, 'devotes himself entirely to it', has the true freedom. And among thinkers the cause was—*reason*, that which, like State and Church, gives—general laws, and puts the individual man in irons by the *thought of humanity*. It determines what is 'true', according to which one must then act. No more 'rational' people than the honest servants, who primarily are called good citizens as servants of the State.

Be rich as Croesus or poor as Job—the State of the bourgeoisie leaves that to your option; but only have a

[1] An irreverent charge, as Goethe and Hegel were still paid homage in Stirner's day as the twin giants standing astride the German literary and philosophical tradition which they had done so much to establish. Stirner was strongly influenced by both men; indeed, he draws heavily on Hegel's *Phenomenology*, that is, the Hegel who describes man as organically creating himself through the development of his consciousness. Stirner turns against him when he makes the jump to meet society with his concept of 'objective mind', or when in glorifying 'Reason' he is in danger of forgetting his own disdain for abstract thought, or again in his analysis of the State.

'good disposition'. This it demands of you, and counts it its most urgent task to establish this in all. Therefore it will keep you from 'evil promptings', holding the 'ill-disposed' in check and silencing their inflammatory discourses under censors' cancelling-marks or press-penalties and behind dungeon walls, and will, on the other hand, appoint people of 'good disposition' as censors, and in every way have a *moral influence* exerted on you by 'well-disposed and well-meaning' people. If it has made you deaf to evil promptings, then it opens your eare again all the more diligently to *good* promptings.

With the time of the bourgeoisie begins that of *liberalism*. People want to see what is 'rational', 'suited to the times', etc., established everywhere. The following definition of liberalism, which is supposed to be pro-nounced in its honour, characterizes it completely: 'Liberalism is nothing else than the knowledge of reason, applied to our existing relations.'* Its aim is a 'rational order', a 'moral behaviour', a 'limited freedom', not anarchy, lawlessness, selfhood. But, if reason rules, then the *person* succumbs. Art has for a long time not only acknowledged the ugly, but considered the ugly as neces-sary to its existence, and takes it up into itself; it needs the villain. In the religious domain, too, the extremest liberals go so far that they want to see the most religious man regarded as a citizen—that is, the religious villain; they want to see no more of trials for heresy. But against the 'rational law' no one is to rebel, otherwise he is threatened with the severest penalty. What is wanted is not free movement and realization of the person or of me, but of reason—a dominion of reason, a dominion. The liberals

* Georg Herwegh (ed.), *Ein und zwanzig Bogen aus der Schweiz* (Zürich and Winterthur, 1843) p. 12. This book, consisting of material by German radicals, was published in Switzerland to escape German press censorship laws.

are *zealots*, not exactly for the faith, for God, but certainly for *reason*, their master. They brook no lack of breeding, and therefore no self-development and self-determination; they *play the guardian* as effectively as the most absolute rulers.

(*Ego* 136–8)

The bourgeoisie professes a morality which is most closely connected with its essence. The first demand of this morality is to the effect that one should carry on a solid business, an honourable trade, lead a moral life. Immoral, to it, is the swindler, the courtesan, the thief, robber, and murderer, the gambler, the penniless man without a situation, the frivolous man. The doughty bourgeois designates the feeling against these 'immoral' people as his 'deepest indignation'.

All these lack settlement, the *solid* quality of business, a solid, seemly life, a fixed income, etc.; in short, they belong, because their existence does not rest on a *secure basis*, to the dangerous 'individuals or isolated persons', to the dangerous *proletariat*; they are 'individual bawlers' who offer no 'guarantee' and have 'nothing to lose', and so nothing to risk. The forming of family ties *binds* a man: he who is bound furnishes security, can be taken hold of; not so the street-walker. The gambler stakes everything on the game, ruins himself and others—no guarantee. All who appear to the bourgeois suspicious, hostile, and dangerous might be comprised under the name 'vagabonds'; every vagabondish way of living displeases him. For there are intellectual vagabonds too, to whom the hereditary dwelling-place of their fathers seems too cramped and oppressive for them to be willing to satisfy themselves with the limited space any more; instead of keeping within the limits of a temperate style of thinking, and taking as inviolable truth what furnishes comfort and tranquillity to thousands, they overlap all bounds of the traditional and run wild with their impudent criticism and untamed mania for doubt, these extravagating vagabonds. They form the class of the unstable, restless, changeable, of the proletariat, and, if they give voice to their unsettled nature, are called 'unruly fellows'.

Such a broad sense has the so-called proletariat, or pauperism. How much one would err if one believed the bourgeoisie to be desirous of doing away with poverty (pauperism) to the best of its ability! On the contrary, the good citizen helps himself with the incomparably comforting conviction that 'the fact is that the good things of fortune are unequally divided and will always remain so —according to God's wise decree.' The poverty which surrounds him in every alley does not disturb the true bourgeois further than that at most he clears his account with it by throwing an alms, or finds work and food for an 'honest and serviceable' fellow. But so much the more does he feel his quiet enjoyment clouded by *innovating* and *discontented* poverty, by those poor who no longer behave quietly and endure, but begin to *run wild* and become restless. Lock up the vagabond, thrust the breeder of unrest into the darkest dungeon! He wants to 'arouse dissatisfaction and incite people against existing institutions' in the State—stone him, stone him!

But from these identical discontented ones comes a reasoning somewhat as follows: It need not make any difference to the 'good citizens' who protects them and their principles, whether an absolute king or a constitutional one, a republic, if only they are protected. And what is their principle, whose protector they always 'love'? Not that of labour; not that of birth either. But that of *mediocrity*, of the golden mean; a little birth and a little labour, that is, an *interest-bearing possession*. Possession is here the fixed, the given, inherited (birth); interest-drawing is the exertion about it (labour); *labouring capital*, therefore. Only no immoderation, no ultra, no radicalism! Right of birth certainly, but only hereditary possessions; labour certainly, yet little or none at all of one's own, but labour of capital and of the—subject labourers.

If an age is imbued with an error, some always derive advantage from the error, while the rest have to suffer from it. In the Middle Ages the error was general among Christians that the church must have all power, or the supreme lordship on earth; the hierarchs believed in this 'truth' not less than the laymen, and both were spell-bound in the like error. But by it the hierarchs had the *advantage* of power, the laymen had to *suffer* subjection. However, as the saying goes, 'one learns wisdom by suffering'; and so the laymen at last learned wisdom and no longer believed in the medieval 'truth'.—A like relation exists between the bourgeoisie and the labouring class. Bourgeois and labourer believe in the 'truth' of *money*; they who do not possess it believe in it no less than those who possess it: the laymen, therefore, as well as the priests.

'Money governs the world' is the keynote of the civic epoch. A destitute aristocrat and a destitute labourer, as 'starvelings', amount to nothing so far as political consideration is concerned; birth and labour do not do it, but *money* brings *consideration*.[1] The possessors rule, but the State trains up from the destitute its 'servants', to whom, in proportion as they are to rule (govern) in its name, it gives money (a salary).[2]

---

[1] *das Geld gibt Geltung.*

[2] It is impossible to say where, in his economic ideas, if anywhere, Stirner anticipates Marx. In a number of places passages such as this one

I receive everything from the State. Have I anything without the *State's assent*? What I have without this it *takes* from me as soon as it discovers the lack of a 'legal title'. Do I not, therefore, have everything through its grace, its assent?

On this alone, on the *legal title*, the bourgeoisie rests. The bourgeois is what he is through the *protection of the State*, through the State's grace. He would necessarily be afraid of losing everything if the State's power were broken.

But how is it with him who has nothing to lose, how with the proletarian? As he has nothing to lose, he does not need the protection of the State for his 'nothing'. He may gain, on the contrary, if that protection of the State is withdrawn from the *protégé*.

Therefore the non-possessor will regard the State as a power protecting the possessor, which privileges the latter, but does nothing for him, the non-possessor, but to—suck his blood. The State is a—*State* of the bourgeois, is the estate of the bourgeoisie. It protects man not according to his labour, but according to his tractableness ('loyalty') —to wit, according to whether the rights entrusted to him by the State are enjoyed and managed in accordance with the will, that is, laws, of the State.

Under the *regime* of the bourgeoisie the labourers always fall into the hands of the possessors, of those who have at their disposal some bit of the State domains (and everything possessible in State domain belongs to the State, and is only a fief of the individual), especially

---

on the omnipotence of money in bourgeois society show a remarkable parallelism with sections of Marx's *1844 Manuscripts*, which were written at the same time—they were finished in Paris in August, a month or so before the first copies of Stirner's book were distributed. (See McLellan, *The Young Hegelians and Karl Marx*, pp. 132–6.)

money and land; of the capitalists, therefore. The labourer cannot *realize* his labour to the extent of the value that it has for the consumer. 'Labour is badly paid!' The capitalist has the greatest profit from it. — Well paid, and more than well paid, are only the labours of those who heighten the splendour and *dominion* of the State, the labours of high State *servants*. The State pays well that its 'good citizens', the possessors, may be able to pay badly without danger; it secures to itself by good payment its servants, out of whom it forms a protecting power, a 'police' (to the police belong soldiers, officials of all kinds, those of justice, education, etc. — in short, the whole 'machinery of the State') for the 'good citizens', and the 'good citizens' gladly pay high tax-rates to it in order to pay so much lower rates to their labourers.

But the class of labourers, because unprotected in what they essentially are (for they do not enjoy the protection of the State as labourers, but as its subjects they have a share in the enjoyment of the police, a so-called protection of the law), remains a power hostile to this State, this State of possessors, this 'citizen kingship'. Its principle, labour, is not recognized for its *value*; it is exploited, a spoil of the possessors, the enemy.

The labourers have the most enormous power in their hands, and, if they once became thoroughly conscious of it and used it, nothing would withstand them; they would only have to stop labour, regard the product of labour as theirs, and enjoy it. This is the sense of the labour disturbances which show themselves here and there.

The State rests on the — *slavery of labour*. If *labour* becomes *free*, the State is lost.

(*Ego* 147–52)

B.—SOCIAL LIBERALISM

The freedom of man is, in political liberalism, freedom from *persons*, from personal dominion, from the *master*; the securing of each individual person against other persons, personal freedom.

No one has any orders to give; the law alone gives orders.

But, even if the persons have become *equal*, yet their *possessions* have not. And yet the poor man *needs the rich*, the rich the poor, the former the rich man's money, the latter the poor man's labour. So no one needs another as a *person*, but needs him as a *giver*, and thus as one who has something to give, as holder or possessor. So what he *has* makes the *man*. And in *having*, or in 'possessions', people are unequal.

Consequently, social liberalism concludes, *no one must have*, as according to political liberalism *no one was to give orders*; as in that case the *State* alone obtained the command, so now *society* alone obtains the possessions.

For the State, protecting each one's person and property against the other, *separates* them from one another; each one *is* his special part and has his special part. He who is satisfied with what he is and has finds this state of things profitable; but he who would like to be and have more looks around for this 'more', and finds it in the power of other *persons*. Here he comes upon a contradiction: as a person no one is inferior to another, and yet one person *has* what another has not but would like to have. So, he concludes, the one person is more than the other, after all, for the former has what he needs, the latter has not; the former is a rich man, the latter a poor man.

He now asks himself further, are we to let what we rightly

buried come to life again? Are we to let this circuitously restored inequality of persons pass? No; on the contrary, we must bring quite to an end what was only half accomplished. Our freedom from another's person still lacks the freedom from what the other's person can command, from what he has in his personal power—in short, from 'personal property'. Let us then do away with *personal property*. Let no one have anything any longer, let every one be a—ragamuffin. Let property be *impersonal*, let it belong to—*society*.

Before the supreme *ruler*, the sole *commander*, we had all become equal, equal persons, that is, nullities.

Because in society the most oppressive evils make themselves felt, therefore the oppressed especially, and consequently the members of the lower regions of society, think they found the fault in society, and make it their task to discover the *right society*. This is only the old phenomenon —that one looks for the fault first in everything but *himself*, and consequently in the State, in the self-seeking of the rich, and so on, which yet have precisely our fault to thank for their existence.

The reflections and conclusions of communism[1] look very simple. As matters lie at this time—in the present situation with regard to the State, therefore—some, and they the majority, are at a disadvantage compared to others, the minority. In this *state* of things the former are in a *state of prosperity*, the latter in a *state of need*. Hence the present *state* of things, the State itself, must be done away with. And what in its place? Instead of the isolated state

[1] Stirner, like most of his contemporaries and even those who advocated collectivism, uses the terms 'socialism' and 'communism' interchangeably. And after all one can appropriately categorize Marxism from the middle of the century as the predominant element in the *socialist* movement. Stirner usually associates communism with the work of Wilhelm Christian Weitling (1809–71), the first German working-class socialist, and seems to have regarded Marx simply as one of Feuerbach's disciples.

of prosperity — a *general state of prosperity*, a *prosperity of all*.

Through the Revolution the bourgeoisie became omnipotent, and all inequality was abolished by every one's being raised or degraded to the dignity of a *citizen*: the common man — raised, the aristocrat — degraded; the *third* estate became sole estate, namely, the estate of — *citizens of the State*. Now communism responds: Our dignity and our essence consist not in our being all — the *equal children* of our mother, the State, all born with equal claim to her love and her protection, but in our all existing *for each other*. This is our equality, or herein we are *equal*, in that we, I as well as you and you and all of you, are active or 'labour' each one for the rest; in that each of us is a *labourer*, then. The point for us is not what we are *for the State* (citizens), not our *citizenship* therefore, but what we are *for each other*, that each of us exists only through the other, who, caring for my wants, at the same time sees his own satisfied by me. He labours for my clothing (tailor), I for his need of amusement (comedy-writer, rope-dancer), he for my food (farmer). I for his instruction (scientist). It is *labour* that constitutes our dignity and our — equality.

What advantage does citizenship bring us? Burdens! And how high is our labour appraised? As low as possible! But labour is our sole value all the same; that we are *labourers* is the best thing about us, this is our significance in the world, and therefore it must be our consideration too and must come to receive *consideration*. What can you meet us with? Surely nothing but — *labour* too. Only for labour or services do we owe you a recompense, not for your bare existence; not for what you are *for yourselves* either, but only for what you are *for us*. By what have you claims on us? Perhaps by your high birth? No, only by what you do for us that is desirable or useful. Be it thus then: we are willing to be worth to you only so much as we do for you; but you are to be held likewise by us. *Services* determine value, those services that are worth something to us, and consequently *labours for each other*, *labours for the common good*. Let each one be in the other's eyes a *labourer*. He who accomplishes something useful is inferior to none, or—all labourers (labourers, of course, in the sense of labourers 'for the common good', that is, communistic labourers) are equal. But, as the labourer is worth his wages,[1] let the wages too be equal.

As long as faith sufficed for man's honour and dignity, no labour, however harassing, could be objected to if it only did not hinder a man in his faith. Now, on the contrary, when every one is to cultivate himself into man, condemning a man to *machine-like labour* amounts to the same thing as slavery. If a factory worker must tire himself to death twelve hours and more, he is cut off from becoming man. Every labour is to have the intent that the man be satisfied. Therefore he must become a *master* in it too, be able to perform it as a totality. He who in a pin-factory only puts on the heads,[2] only draws the wire, works, as it were, mechanically, like a machine; he remains half-trained, does not become a master: his labour cannot *satisfy* him, it can only *fatigue* him. His labour is nothing by itself, has no object *in itself*, is nothing complete in itself; he labours only into another's hands, and is *used* (exploited) by this other. For this labourer in another's service there is no *enjoyment of a cultivated mind*, at most, crude amusements: *culture*, you see, is barred against him. To be a good Christian one

[1] In German an exact quotation of Luke x 7.
[2] A reference to Adam Smith's use of pin-manufacturing in *The Wealth of Nations* to explain the division of labour. This paragraph of Stirner's is very similar to the passages in Marx's *1844 Manuscripts* on the degradation which follows the division of labour.

needs only to *believe*, and that can be done under the most oppressive circumstances. Hence the Christian-minded take care only of the oppressed labourers' piety, their patience, submission, etc. Only so long as the down-trodden classes were *Christians* could they bear all their misery: for Christianity does not let their murmurings and exasperation rise. Now the *hushing* of desires is no longer enough, but their *sating* is demanded. The bourgeoisie has proclaimed the gospel of the *enjoyment of the world*, of material enjoyment, and now wonders that this doctrine finds adherents among us poor: it has shown that not faith and poverty, but culture and possessions, make a man blessed; we proletarians understand that too.

The bourgeoisie freed us from the orders and arbitrariness of individuals. But that arbitrariness was left which springs from the conjuncture of situations, and may be called the fortuity of circumstances; favouring *fortune*, and those 'favoured by fortune', still remain.

When, for example, a branch of industry is ruined and thousands of labourers become breadless, people think reasonably enough to acknowledge that it is not the individual who must bear the blame, but that 'the evil lies in the situation.' Let us change the situation then, but let us change it thoroughly, and so that its fortuity becomes powerless, and a *law*![1] Let us no longer be slaves of chance! Let us create a new order that makes an end of *fluctuations*. Let this order then be sacred!

Formerly one had to suit the *lords* to come to anything; after the Revolution the word was 'Grasp *fortune*!' Luck-hunting or hazard-playing, civil life was absorbed in this. Then, alongside this, the demand that he who has obtained something shall not frivolously stake it again.

[1] It was soon after Marx read Stirner's book that he wrote his famous Eleventh Feuerbach Thesis on changing the world.

Strange and yet supremely natural contradiction. Competition, in which alone civil or political life unrolls itself, is a game of luck through and through, from the speculations of the exchange down to the solicitation of offices, the hunt for customers, looking for work, aspiring to promotion and decorations, the second-hand dealer's petty haggling, etc. If one succeeds in supplanting and outbidding his rivals, then the 'lucky throw' is made; for it must be taken as a piece of luck to begin with that the victor sees himself equipped with an ability (even though it has been developed by the most careful industry) against which the others do not know how to rise, consequently that—no abler ones are found. And now those who ply their daily lives in the midst of these changes of fortune without seeing any harm in it are seized with the most virtuous indignation when their own principle appears in naked form and 'breeds misfortune' as—*hazard-playing*. Hazard-playing, you see, is too clear, too barefaced a competition, and, like every decided nakedness, offends honourable modesty.[1]

The socialists want to put a stop to this activity of chance, and to form a society in which men are no longer dependent on *fortune*, but free.

In the most natural way in the world this endeavour first utters itself as hatred of the 'unfortunate' against the 'fortunate', of those for whom fortune has done little or nothing, against those for whom it has done everything. But properly the ill-feeling is not directed against the fortunate, but against *fortune*, this rotten spot of the bourgeoisie.

As the communists first declare free activity to be man's

[1] Cf. Keynes's gently mocking description of the Stock Exchange as a gambling casino (*The General Theory of Employment, Interest, and Money* [Macmillan, London, 1936], chap. 12).

essence, they, like all workday dispositions, need a
Sunday; like all material endeavours, they need a God,
an uplifting and edification alongside their witless
'labour'.

That the communist sees in you the man, the brother, is
only the Sunday side of communism. According to the
workday side he does not by any means take you as man
simply, but as human labourer or labouring man. The
first view has in it the liberal principle; in the second,
illiberality is concealed. If you were a 'lazybones', he
would not indeed fail to recognize the man in you, but
would endeavour to cleanse him as a 'lazy man' from
laziness and to convert you to the *faith* that labour is
man's 'destiny and calling'.

(*Ego* 153–60)

By the principle of labour that of fortune or competition is
certainly outdone. But at the same time the labourer, in
his consciousness that the essential thing in him is 'the
labourer', holds himself aloof from egoism and subjects
himself to the supremacy of a society of labourers, as the
bourgeois clung with self-abandonment to the com-
petition-State. The beautiful dream of a 'social duty' still
continues to be dreamed. People think again that society
gives what we need, and we are *under obligations* to it on
that account, owe it everything. They are still at the
point of wanting to *serve* a 'supreme giver of all good'.
That society is no ego at all, which could give, bestow,
or grant, but an instrument or means, from which we may
derive benefit; that we have no social duties, but solely
interests for the pursuance of which society must serve
us; that we owe society no sacrifice, but, if we sacrifice
anything, sacrifice it to ourselves — of this the socialists
do not think, because they — as liberals — are imprisoned

in the religious principle, and zealously aspire after — a sacred society, such as the State was hitherto.

Society, from which we have everything, is a new master, a new spook, a new 'supreme being', which 'takes us into its service and allegiance'!

(Ego 161–2)

*   *   *

It is not man that makes up your greatness, but you create it, because you are more than man, and mightier than other — men.

It is believed that one cannot be more than man. Rather, one cannot be less!

(Ego 176)

*   *   *

I say: Liberate yourself as far as you can, and you have done your part; for it is not given to every one to break through all limits, or, more expressively: not to every one is that a limit which is a limit for the rest. Consequently, do not tire yourself with toiling at the limits of others; enough if you tear down yours. Who has ever succeeded in tearing down even one limit *for all men*? Are not countless persons today, as at all times, running about with all the 'limitations of humanity'? He who overturns one of *his* limits may have shown others the way and the means; the overturning of *their* limits remains their affair.

(Ego 187)

Political liberalism abolished the inequality of masters and servants; it made people masterless, anarchic. The master was now removed from the individual, the

'egoist', to become a ghost—the law or the State. Social
liberalism abolishes the inequality of possession, of the
poor and rich, and makes people *possessionless* or property-
less. Property is withdrawn from the individual and
surrendered to ghostly society. Humane liberalism makes
people *godless*, atheistic. Therefore the individual's God,
'My God', must be put an end to. Now masterlessness is
indeed at the same time freedom from service, possession-
lessness at the same time freedom from care, and godlessness at the same time freedom from prejudice: for with
the master the servant falls away; with possession, the
care about it; with the firmly-rooted God, prejudice.
But, since the master rises again as State, the servant
appears again as subject; since possession becomes the
property of society, care is begotten anew as labour; and,
since God as Man becomes a prejudice, there arises a new
faith, faith in humanity or liberty. For the individual's
God the God of all, to wit, 'Man', is now exalted; 'for it
is the highest thing in us all to be man.' But, as nobody
can become entirely what the idea 'man' imports, Man
remains to the individual a lofty other world, an unattained supreme being, a God. But at the same time this
is the 'true God', because he is fully adequate to us—to
wit, our own '*self*'; we ourselves, but separated from us
and lifted above us.

(*Ego* 189–90)

PART TWO · I

At the entrance of the modern time stands the 'God-Man'. At its exit will only the God in the God-man evaporate? And can the God-man really die if only the God in him dies? They did not think of this question, and thought they were through when in our days they brought to a victorious end the work of the Enlightenment the vanquishing of God: they did not notice that Man has killed God in order to become now —'*sole* God on high'. The *other world outside us* is indeed brushed away, and the great undertaking of the Enlighteners completed; but the *other world in us* has become a new heaven and calls us forth to renewed heaven-storming: God has had to give place, yet not to us, but to —Man. How can you believe that the God-man is dead before the Man in him, besides the God, is dead?[1]

IV. OWNNESS[2]

'Does not the spirit thirst for freedom?'—Alas, not my

[1] Nietzsche (*Die fröhliche Wissenschaft*, sec. 125 (1882)) was not the first to utter the cry which has been repeated so often even in our own day: 'God is dead!'

[2] This is a literal translation of the German word *Eigenheit*, which, with its root *eigen*, 'own', is used in this chapter in a way that the German dictionaries do not quite recognize. The author's conception being new, he had to make an innovation in the German language to express it. The translator is under the like necessity. In most passages 'self-ownership', or else 'personality', would translate the word, but there are some where the thought is so *eigen*, that is, so peculiar or so thoroughly the author's *own*, that no English word would express it.

spirit alone, my body too thirsts for it hourly! When before the odorous castle-kitchen my nose tells my palate of the savoury dishes that are being prepared therein, it feels a fearful pining at its dry bread; when my eyes tell the hardened back about soft down on which one may lie more delightfully than on its compressed straw, a suppressed rage seizes it; when—but let us not follow the pains farther.—And you call that a longing for freedom? What do you want to become free from, then? From your hard tack and your straw bed? Then throw them away!— But that seems not to serve you: you want rather to have the freedom to enjoy delicious foods and downy beds. Are men to give you this 'freedom'—are they to permit it to you? You do not hope that from their philanthropy, because you know they all think like—you: each is the nearest to himself! How, therefore, do you mean to come to the enjoyment of those foods and beds? Evidently not otherwise than in making them your property!

If you think it over rightly, you do not want the freedom to have all these fine things, for with this freedom you still do not have them; you want really to have them, to call them *yours* and possess them as *your property*. Of what use is a freedom to you, indeed, if it brings in nothing? And, if you became free from everything, you would no longer have anything; for freedom is empty of substance. Whoso knows not how to make use of it, for him it has no value, this useless permission; but how I make use of it depends on my peculiarity.[1]

I have no objection to freedom, but I wish more than freedom for you: you should not merely *be rid* of what you do not want; you should not only be a 'freeman', you should be an 'owner' too.

Free—from what? Oh! what is there that cannot be

[1] *Eigenheit.*

shaken off? The yoke of serfdom, of sovereignty, of aristocracy and princes, the dominion of the desires and passions; yes, even the dominion of one's own will, of self-will, for the completest self-denial is nothing but freedom—freedom, to wit, from self-determination, from one's own self. And the craving for freedom as for something absolute, worthy of every praise, deprived us of ownness; it created self-denial. However, the freer I become, the more compulsion piles up before my eyes; and the more impotent I feel myself. The unfree son of the wilderness does not yet feel anything of all the limits that crowd a civilized man: he seems to himself freer than this latter. In the measure that I conquer freedom for myself I create for myself new bounds and new tasks: If I have invented railroads, I feel myself weak again because I cannot yet sail through the skies like the bird; and, if I have solved a problem whose obscurity disturbed my mind, at once there await me innumerable others, whose perplexities impede my progress, dim my free gaze, make the limits of my *freedom* painfully sensible to me. 'Now that you have become free from sin, you have become servants of righteousness.'* Republicans in their broad freedom, do they not become servants of the law? How true Christian hearts at all times longed to 'become free', how they pined to see themselves delivered from the 'bonds of this earth-life'! They looked out towards the land of freedom. ('The Jerusalem that is above is the freewoman; she is the mother of us all.' Gal. iv 26.)

Being free from anything—means only being clear or rid. 'He is free from headache' is equal to 'he is rid of it.' 'He is free from this prejudice' is equal to 'he has never conceived it' or 'he has got rid of it.' In 'less' we complete

* Rom. vi 18.

the freedom recommended by Christianity, in sinless, godless, moralityless, etc.

Freedom is the doctrine of Christianity. 'Ye, dear brethren, are called to freedom.'* 'So speak and so do, as those who are to be judged by the law of freedom.'†

Must we then, because freedom betrays itself as a Christian ideal, give it up? No, nothing is to be lost, freedom no more than the rest; but it is to become our own, and in the form of freedom it cannot.

What a difference between freedom and ownness! One can get *rid* of a great many things, one yet does not get rid of all; one becomes free from much, not from everything. Inwardly one may be free in spite of the condition of slavery, although, too, it is again only from all sorts of things, not from everything; but from the whip, the domineering temper, of the master, one does not as slave become *free*. 'Freedom lives only in the realm of dreams!' Ownness, on the contrary, is my whole being and existence, it is I myself. I am free from what I am *rid* of, owner of what I have in my *power* or what I *control*. *My own* I am at all times and under all circumstances, if I know how to have myself and do not throw myself away on others. To be free is something that I cannot truly *will*, because I cannot make it, cannot create it: I can only wish it and — aspire towards it, for it remains an ideal, a spook. The fetters of reality cut the sharpest welts in my flesh every moment. But *my own* I remain. Given up as serf to a master, I think only of myself and my advantage; his blows strike me indeed, I am not *free* from them; but I endure them only for *my benefit*, perhaps in order to deceive him and make him secure by the semblance of patience, or, again, not to draw worse upon myself by insubordination. But, as I keep my eye on myself and my

* 1 Pet. ii 16.   † James ii 12.

selfishness, I take by the forelock the first good opportunity to trample the slave holder into the dust. That I then become *free* from him and his whip is only the consequence of my antecedent egoism. Here one perhaps says I was 'free' even in the condition of slavery — to wit, 'in itself' or 'inwardly'. But 'free in itself' is not 'really free', and 'inwardly' is not 'outwardly'. I was own, on the other hand, *my own*, altogether, inwardly and outwardly. Under the dominion of a cruel master my body is not 'free' from torments and lashes; but it is *my* bones that moan under the torture, *my* fibres that quiver under the blows, and *I* moan because *my* body moans. That *I* sigh and shiver proves that I have not yet lost *myself*, that I am still my own. My leg is not 'free' from the master's stick, but it is *my* leg and is inseparable. Let him tear it off me and look and see if he still has my leg! He retains in his hand nothing but the — corpse of my leg, which is as little my leg as a dead dog is still a dog: a dog has a pulsating heart, a so-called dead dog has none and is therefore no longer a dog.

If one opines that a slave may yet be inwardly free, he says in fact only the most indisputable and trivial thing. For who is going to assert that any man is *wholly* without freedom? If I am an eye-servant, can I therefore not be free from innumerable things, from faith in Zeus, from the desire for fame, and the like? Why then should not a whipped slave also be able to be inwardly free from un-Christian sentiments, from hatred of his enemy, etc.? He then has 'Christian freedom', is rid of the un-Christian; but has he absolute freedom, freedom from everything, as from the Christian delusion, or from bodily pain?

In the meantime, all this seems to be said more against names than against the thing. But is the name indifferent,

and has not a word, a shibboleth, always inspired and—
fooled men? Yet between freedom and ownness there lies
still a deeper chasm than the mere difference of the words.

All the world desires freedom, all long for its reign to
come. Oh, enchantingly beautiful dream of a blooming
'reign of freedom', a 'free human race'!—who has not
dreamed it? So men shall become free, entirely free, free
from all constraint! From all constraint, really from all?
Are they never to put constraint on themselves any more?
'Oh yes, that, of course; don't you see, that is no constraint at all?' Well, then at any rate they are to become
free from religious faith, from the strict duties of morality,
from the inexorability of the law, from—'What a fearful
misunderstanding!' Well, *what* are they to be free from
then, and what not?

The lovely dream is dissipated; awakened, one rubs his
half-opened eyes and stares at the prosaic questioner.
'What are men to be free from?'—From blind credulity,
cries one. What's that? exclaims another, all faith is
blind credulity; they must become free from all faith.
No, no, for God's sake—inveighs the first again—do not
cast all faith from you, or else the power of brutality
breaks in. We must have the republic—a third makes
himself heard—and become—free from all commanding
lords. There is no help in that, says a fourth: we only get a
new lord then, a 'dominant majority'; let us rather free
ourselves from this dreadful inequality.—O, hapless
equality, already I hear your plebeian roar again! How
I had dreamed so beautifully just now of a paradise of
freedom, and what—impudence and licentiousness now
raises its wild clamour! Thus the first laments, and gets on
his feet to grasp the sword against 'unmeasured freedom'.
Soon we no longer hear anything but the clashing of the
swords of the disagreeing dreamers of freedom.

What the craving for freedom has always come to has been the desire for a *particular* freedom, such as freedom of faith; the believing man wanted to be free and independent; of what? of faith perhaps? no! but of the inquisitors of faith. So now 'political or civil' freedom. The citizen wants to become free not from citizenhood, but from bureaucracy, the arbitrariness of princes, and the like. Prince Metternich[1] once said he had 'found a way that was adapted to guide men in the path of *genuine* freedom for all the future'. The Count of Provence[2] ran away from France precisely at the time when she was preparing the 'reign of freedom', and said, 'My imprisonment had become intolerable to me; I had only one passion, the desire for *freedom*; I thought only of it.'[3]

The craving for a *particular* freedom always includes the purpose of a new *dominion*, as it was with the Revolution, which indeed 'could give its defenders the uplifting feeling that they were fighting for freedom', but in truth only because they were after a particular freedom, therefore a new *dominion*, the 'dominion of the law'.

Freedom you all want, you want *freedom*. Why then do you higgle over a more or less? *Freedom* can only be the whole of freedom; a piece of freedom is not *freedom*. You despair of the possibility of obtaining the whole of freedom, freedom from everything—yes, you consider it insanity even to wish this?—Well, then leave off chasing

---

[1] Prince Metternich (1773–1859), the chief minister of Austria throughout the entire period from Napoleon's defeat to his own overthrow in 1848, was the very symbol of reaction to Stirner's liberal contemporaries.

[2] Brother of Louis XVI of France, who fled the country in the days after the uprising of the Paris mob which stormed the Bastille in July 1789.

[3] A corollary to Stirner's point about the hollowness of 'freedom from' is the key aphorism with which Nietzsche concludes his *Towards a Genealogy of Morals*: 'Man would rather have *the void* for his purpose than be *void* of purpose.'

after the phantom, and spend your pains on something better than the — *unattainable*.

(*Ego* 202–10)

But one needs only admonish you of yourselves to bring you to despair at once. 'What am I?' each of you asks himself. An abyss of lawless and unregulated impulses, desires, wishes, passions, a chaos without light or guiding star! How am I to obtain a correct answer, if, without regard to God's commandments or to the duties which morality prescribes, without regard to the voice of reason, which in the course of history, after bitter experiences, has exalted the best and most reasonable thing into law, I simply appeal to myself? My passion would advise me to do the most senseless thing possible. — Thus each deems himself the — devil; for if, so far as he is unconcerned about religion, he only deemed himself a beast, he would easily find that the beast, which does follow only *its* impulse (as it were, its advice), does not advise and impel itself to do the 'most senseless' things, but takes very correct steps. But the habit of the religious way of thinking has biased our mind so grievously that we are — terrified at *ourselves* in our nakedness and naturalness; it has degraded us so that we deem ourselves depraved by nature, born devils. Of course it comes into your head at once that your calling requires you to do the 'good', the moral, the right. Now, if you ask *yourselves* what is to be done, how can the right voice sound forth from you, the voice which points the way of the good, the right, the true? What concord have God and Belial?

But what would you think if one answered you by saying: 'That one is to listen to God, conscience, duties, laws, and so forth, is flim-flam with which people have stuffed your head and heart and made you crazy'? And if he asked you how it is that you know so surely that the voice of nature is a seducer? And if he even demanded of you to turn the thing about and actually to deem the voice of God and conscience to be the devil's work? There are such grace-less men; how will you settle them? You cannot appeal to your parsons, parents, and good men, for precisely these are designated by them as your *seducers*, as the true seducers and corrupters of youth, who busily sow broad-cast the tares of self-contempt and reverence to God, who fill young hearts with mud and young heads with stupidity.

(Ego 211–13)

If your efforts are ever to make 'freedom' the issue, then exhaust freedom's demands. Who is it that is to become free? You, I, we. Free from what? From everything that is not you, not I, not we. I, therefore, am the kernel that is to be delivered from all wrappings and—freed from all cramping shells. What is left when I have been freed from everything that is not I? Only I; nothing but I. But freedom has nothing to offer to this I himself. As to what is now to happen further after I have become free, free-dom is silent—as our governments, when the prisoner's time is up, merely let him go, thrusting him out into abandonment.

Now why, if freedom is striven after for love of the ego[1] after all—why not choose the ego itself as beginning, middle, and end? Am I not worth more than freedom? Is it not I that make myself free, am not I the first? Even unfree, even laid in a thousand fetters, I yet am; and I am

[1] *Das Ich*, the term Freud was to use as his concept of identity. Stirner capitalizes the first personal pronoun *ich* throughout this section. In the earlier paragraph there are further intimations of Freud where Stirner refers to the voice of conscience as the work of the devil.

not, like freedom, extant only in the future and in hopes, but even as the most abject of slaves I am—present.[1]

Think that over well, and decide whether you will place on your banner the dream of 'freedom' or the resolution of 'egoism', of 'ownness'. 'Freedom' awakens your *rage* against everything that is not you; 'egoism' calls you to *joy* over yourselves, to self-enjoyment; 'freedom' is and remains a *longing*, a romantic plaint, a Christian hope for unearthliness and futurity; 'ownness' is a reality, which *of itself* removes just so much unfreedom as by barring your own way hinders you. What does not disturb you, you will not want to renounce; and, if it begins to disturb you, why, you know that 'you must obey *yourselves* rather than men!'

Freedom teaches only: Get yourselves rid, relieve yourselves, of everything burdensome; it does not teach you who you yourselves are. Rid, rid! so call, get rid even of yourselves, 'deny yourselves'. But ownness calls you back to yourselves, it says 'Come to yourself!' Under the aegis of freedom you get rid of many kinds of things, but something new pinches you again: 'you are rid of the Evil One; evil is left.'[2] As *own* you are *really rid of everything*, and what clings to you *you have accepted*; it is your choice and your pleasure. The *own* man is the *free-born*, the man free to begin with; the free man, on the contrary, is only the *eleutheromaniac*, the dreamer and enthusiast.

The former is *originally free*, because he recognizes nothing but himself; he does not need to free himself first, because at the start he rejects everything outside himself, because he prizes nothing more than himself, rates

[1] Stirner's ontological statement, the existentialist 'I am—present', should be contrasted with Descartes's 'I think, therefore I am' and the romantic 'I feel, therefore I am.'

[2] A minor variation of Mephistopheles' words to Faust in the Witches' Kitchen: 'They [men] are rid of the Evil One; evils remain.' (*Faust*, 1, 2509)

nothing higher, because, in short, he starts from himself and 'comes to himself'. Constrained by childish respect, he is nevertheless already working at 'freeing' himself from this constraint. Ownness works in the little egoist, and procures him the desired—freedom.

Thousands of years of civilization have obscured to you what you are, have made you believe you are not egoists but are *called* to be idealists ('good men'). Shake that off! Do not seek for freedom, which does precisely deprive you of yourselves, in 'self-denial'; but seek for *yourselves*, become egoists, become each of you an *almighty ego*. Or, more clearly: Just recognize yourselves again, just recognize what you really are, and let go your hypocritical endeavours, your foolish mania to be something else than you are. Hypocritical I call them because you have yet remained egoists all these thousands of years, but sleeping, self-deceiving, crazy egoists, you Heautontimorumenoses, you self-tormentors. Never yet has a religion been able to dispense with 'promises', whether they referred us to the other world or to this ('long life', etc.); for man is *mercenary* and does nothing 'gratis'. But how about that 'doing the good for the good's sake' without prospect of reward? As if here too the pay was not contained in the satisfaction that it is to afford. Even religion, therefore, is founded on our egoism and—exploits it; calculated for our *desires*, it stifles many others for the sake of one. This then gives the phenomenon of *cheated* egoism, where I satisfy, not myself, but one of my desires, such as the impulse toward blessedness. Religion promises me the— 'supreme good'; to gain this I no longer regard any other of my desires, and do not slake them.—All your doings are *unconfessed*, secret, covert, and concealed egoism. But because they are egoism that you are unwilling to confess to yourselves, that you keep secret from yourselves, hence not manifest and public egoism, consequently unconscious egoism—therefore they are *not egoism*, but thraldom, service, self-renunciation; you are egoists, and you are not, since you renounce egoism. Where you seem most to be such, you have drawn upon the word 'egoist' —loathing and contempt.

I secure my freedom with regard to the world in the degree that I make the world my own, 'gain it and take possession of it' for myself, by whatever might, by that of persuasion, of petition, of categorical demand, yes, even by hypocrisy, cheating, etc.; for the means that I use for it are determined by what I am. If I am weak, I have only weak means, like the aforesaid, which yet are good enough for a considerable part of the world. Besides, cheating, hypocrisy, lying, look worse than they are. Who has not cheated the police, the law? Who has not quickly taken on an air of honourable loyalty before the constable who meets him, in order to conceal an illegality that may have been committed? He who has not done it has simply let violence be done to him; he was a *weakling* from— conscience. I know that my freedom is diminished even by my not being able to carry out my will on another object, be this other something without will, like a rock, or something with will, like a government, an individual; I deny my ownness when—in the presence of another—I give myself up, give way, desist, submit; therefore by *loyalty, submission*. For it is one thing when I give up my previous course because it does not lead to the goal, and therefore turn out of a wrong road; it is another when I yield myself a prisoner. I circumvent a rock that stands in my way, till I have powder enough to blast it; I circumvent the laws of a people, till I have gathered strength to overthrow them. Because I cannot grasp the moon, is it therefore to be 'sacred' to me, an Astarte? If I only could grasp you, I surely would, and, if I only find a means to get up to you, you shall not frighten me! You inapprehensible one, you shall remain inapprehensible to me only till I have acquired the might for apprehension and call you my *own*; I do not give myself up before you, but only bide my time. Even if for the present I put up with my inability to touch you, I yet remember it against you.

Vigorous men have always done so. When the 'loyal' had exalted an unsubdued power to be their master and had adored it, when they had demanded adoration from all, then there came some such son of nature who would not loyally submit, and drove the adored power from its inaccessible Olympus. He cried his 'Stand still' to the rolling sun, and made the earth go round; the loyal had to make the best of it; he laid his axe to the sacred oaks, and the 'loyal' were astonished that no heavenly fire consumed him; he threw the pope off Peter's chair, and the 'loyal' had no way to hinder it; he is tearing down the divine-right business, and the 'loyal' croak in vain, and at last are silent.

My freedom becomes complete only when it is my — *might*; but by this I cease to be a merely free man, and become an own man. Why is the freedom of the peoples a 'hollow word?' Because the peoples have no might! With a breath of the living ego I blow peoples over, be it the breath of a Nero, a Chinese emperor, or a poor writer. Why is it that the G——[1] legislatures pine in vain for freedom, and are lectured for it by the cabinet ministers? Because they are not of the 'mighty'! Might is a fine thing, and useful for many purposes; for 'one goes farther with a handful of might than with a bagful of right.'[2]

[1] Meaning 'German'. Written in this form because of the censorship.

[2] Stirner places himself firmly in the tradition in political philosophy which goes back to Plato's *Republic* and the Thrasymachus argument that 'might is right'. The most significant advocates of this 'realist' position were Machiavelli and Hobbes.

You long for freedom? You fools! If you took might, freedom would come of itself. See, he who has might 'stands above the law.' How does this prospect taste to you, you 'law-abiding' people? But you have no taste!

The cry for 'freedom' rings loudly all around. But is it felt and known what a donated or chartered freedom must mean? It is not recognized in the full amplitude of the word that all freedom is essentially — self-liberation — that I can have only so much freedom as I procure for myself by my ownness. Of what use is it to sheep that no one abridges their freedom of speech? They stick to bleating. Give one who is inwardly a Mohammedan, a Jew, or a Christian, permission to speak what he likes: he will yet utter only narrow-minded stuff. If, on the contrary, certain others rob you of the freedom of speaking and hearing, they know quite rightly wherein lies their temporary advantage, as you would perhaps be able to say and hear something whereby those 'certain' persons would lose their credit.

If they nevertheless give you freedom, they are simply knaves who give more than they have. For then they give you nothing of their own, but stolen wares: they give you your own freedom, the freedom that you must take for yourselves; and they *give* it to you only that you may not take it and call the thieves and cheats to account to boot. In their slyness they know well that given (chartered) freedom is no freedom, since only the freedom one *takes* for himself, therefore the egoist's freedom, rides with full sails. Donated freedom strikes its sails as soon as there comes a storm — or calm; it requires always a — gentle and moderate breeze.[1]

---

[1] Is this not Zarathustra speaking: the deft touch of language, the subtle twists of irony? The striking similarities between Nietzsche's style and Stirner's, instancing in both cases their best prose, exhibit a parallel

Here lies the difference between self-liberation and emancipation (manumission, setting free). Those who today 'stand in the opposition' are thirsting and screaming to be 'set free'. The princes are to 'declare their peoples of age', that is, emancipate them! Behave as if you were of age, and you are so without any declaration of majority; if you do not behave accordingly, you are not worthy of it, and would never be of age even by a declaration of majority. When the Greeks were of age, they drove out their tyrants, and, when the son is of age, he makes himself independent of his father. If the Greeks had waited till their tyrants graciously allowed them their majority, they might have waited long. A sensible father throws out a son who will not come of age, and keeps the house to himself; it serves the noodle right.

The man who is set free is nothing but a freed man, a *libertinus*, a dog dragging a piece of chain with him: he is an unfree man in the garment of freedom, like the ass in the lion's skin. Emancipated Jews are nothing bettered in themselves, but only relieved as Jews, although he who relieves their condition is certainly more than a churchly Christian, as the latter cannot do this without inconsistency. But, emancipated or not emancipated, Jew remains Jew; he who is not self-freed is merely an— emancipated man. The Protestant State can certainly set free (emancipate) the Catholics; but, because they do not make themselves free, they remain simply—Catholics.

Selfishness and unselfishness have already been spoken of. The friends of freedom are exasperated against selfishness because in their religious striving after freedom they

---

originality which strains the bounds of coincidence. While Stirner cannot sustain this plastically vital language as well as Nietzsche, neither does he lose himself in the wildly romantic imagery which decorates, and weakens, *Thus Spoke Zarathustra*.

cannot—free themselves from that sublime thing, 'self-renunciation'. The liberal's anger is directed against egoism, for the egoist, you know, never takes trouble about a thing for the sake of the thing, but for his sake: the thing must serve him. It is egoistic to ascribe to no thing a value of its own, an 'absolute' value, but to seek its value in me. One often hears that pot-boiling study which is so common counted among the most repulsive traits of egoistic behaviour, because it manifests the most shameful desecration of science; but what is science for but to be consumed? If one does not know how to use it for anything better than to keep the pot boiling, then his egoism is a petty one indeed, because this egoist's power is a limited power; but the egoistic element in it, and the desecration of science, only a possessed man can blame.

Incapable of letting the individual count as a unique one, Christianity thought of him only as a dependent, and was properly nothing but a *social theory*, a doctrine of living together, man with God as well as man with man. Therefore in it everything 'own' must fall into most woeful disrepute: selfishness, self-will, ownness, self-love, and the like. The Christian way of looking at things has on all sides gradually re-stamped honourable words into dishonourable; why should they not be brought into honour again? So *Schimpf* (insult, disgrace,) is in its old sense equivalent to jest, but for Christian seriousness pastime became a privation, for that seriousness cannot take a joke; *frech* (impudent) formerly meant only bold, brave; *Frevel* (wanton outrage) was only daring. It is well known how askance the word 'reason' was looked at for a long time.[1]

[1] Stirner here suggests the same process of the moralizing of ethically neutral words through history that Nietzsche was to propose as one of the important facets of the genealogy of morals.

Our language has settled itself pretty well to the Christian standpoint, and the general consciousness is still too Christian not to shrink in terror from everything un-Christian as from something incomplete or evil. Therefore 'selfishness' is in a bad way too.

Selfishness,[1] in the Christian sense, means something like this: I look only to see whether anything is of use to me as a sensual man. But is sensuality then the whole of my ownness? Am I in my own senses when I am given up to sensuality? Do I follow myself, my *own* determination, when I follow that? I am my *own* only when I am master of myself, instead of being mastered either by sensuality or by anything else (God, man, authority, law, State, Church); what is of use to me, this self-owned or self-appertaining one, my selfishness pursues.

(*Ego* 214–23)

Ownness includes in itself everything own, and brings to honour again what Christian language dishonoured. But ownness has not any alien standard either, as it is not in any sense an *idea* like freedom, morality, humanity, and the like: it is only a description of the—*owner*.

(*Ego* 224)

V. THE OWNER

A.—MY POWER

Whether I am in the right or not there is no judge but myself. Others can judge only whether they endorse my right, and whether it exists as right for them too.

In the meantime let us take the matter yet another way.

---

[1] *Eigennutz*, literally 'own-use'.

I am to reverence sultanic law in the sultanate, popular law in republics, canon law in Catholic communities. To these laws I am to subordinate myself; I am to regard them as sacred. A 'sense of right' and 'law-abiding mind' of such a sort is so firmly planted in people's heads that the most revolutionary persons of our day want to subject us to a new 'sacred law', the 'law of society', the law of mankind, the 'right of all', and the like. The right of 'all' is to go before *my* right. As a right of all it would indeed be my right among the rest, since I, with the rest, am included in all; but that it is at the same time a right of others, or even of all others, does not move me to its upholding. Not as a *right of all* will I defend it, but as *my* right; and then every other may see to it how he shall likewise maintain it for himself. The right of all (for example, to eat) is a right of every individual. Let each keep this right unabridged for *himself*, then all exercise it spontaneously; let him not take care for all, though— let him not grow zealous for it as for a right of all.

But the social reformers preach to us a *'law of society'*. There the individual becomes society's slave, and is in the right only when society *makes him out* in the right, when he lives according to society's *statutes* and so is— *loyal*. Whether I am loyal under a despotism or in a 'society' *à la* Weitling,[1] it is the same absence of right in so far as in both cases I have not *my* right but *foreign* right.

In consideration of right the question is always asked, 'What or who gives me the right to it?' Answer: God, love, reason, nature, humanity, etc. No, only *your might*, *your* power gives you the right (your reason, therefore, may give it to you).

(*Ego* 244–5)

---

[1] As has been noted, Stirner associates 'communism' with the name of Weitling.

The only thing I am not entitled to is what I do not do with a free cheer, that is, what I do not entitle myself to.

I decide whether it is the *right thing* in me; there is no right *outside* me. If it is right for me, it is right. Possibly this may not suffice to make it right for the rest; that is their care, not mine: let them defend themselves. And if for the whole world something were not right, but it were right for me, that is, I wanted it, then I would ask nothing about the whole world. So every one does who knows how to value *himself*, every one in the degree that he is an egoist; for might goes before right, and that— with perfect right.

Because I am 'by nature' a man I have an equal right to the enjoyment of all goods, says Babeuf.[1] Must he not also say: because I am 'by nature' a first-born prince I have a right to the throne? The rights of man and the 'well-earned rights' come to the same thing in the end, to wit, to *nature*, which *gives* me a right, that is, to *birth* (and, further, inheritance). 'I am born as a man' is equal to 'I am born as a king's son.' The natural man has only a natural right (because he has only a natural power) and natural claims: he has right of birth and claims of birth. But *nature* cannot entitle me, give me capacity or might, to that to which only my act entitles me. That the king's child sets himself above other children, even this is his act, which secures to him the precedence; and that the other children approve and recognize this act is their act, which makes them worthy to be—subjects.

Whether nature gives me a right, or whether God, the people's choice, etc., does so, all of that is the same *foreign* right, a right that I do not give or take to myself.

[1] François-Noël (Gracchus) Babeuf (1760–97) can be regarded as the first theorist of egalitarian communism, which with his followers he vigorously tried to put into practice in Paris in 1796; he was not only a precursor of Marx but of Bakunin and also of the French anarchist tradition.

Thus, the communists say, equal labour entitles man to equal enjoyment. Formerly the question was raised whether the 'virtuous' man must not be 'happy' on earth. The Jews actually drew this inference: 'That it may go well with thee on earth.' No, equal labour does not entitle you to it, but equal enjoyment alone entitles you to equal enjoyment. Enjoy, then you are entitled to enjoyment. But, if you have laboured and let the enjoyment be taken from you, then — 'it serves you right.'

If you *take* the enjoyment, it is your right; if, on the contrary, you only pine for it without laying hands on it, it remains as before, a 'well-earned right' of those who are privileged for enjoyment. It is *their* right, as by laying hands on it would become *your* right.

The conflict over the 'right of property' wavers in vehement commotion. The communists affirm* that 'the earth belongs rightfully to him who tills it, and its products to those who bring them out.' I think it belongs to him who knows how to take it, or who does not let it be taken from him, does not let himself be deprived of it. If he appropriates it, then not only the earth, but the right to it too, belongs to him. This is *egoistic right*: it is right for me, therefore it is right.

Aside from this, right does have 'a wax nose'. The tiger that assails me is in the right, and I who strike him down am also in the right. I defend against him not my *right*, but *myself*.

As human right is always something given, it always in reality reduces to the right which men give, 'concede', to each other. If the right to existence is conceded to new-born children, then they have the right: if it is not conceded to them, as was the case among the Spartans and ancient Romans, then they do not have it. For only

* A. Becker, *Die Volksphilosophie unserer Tage* (Neumünster, 1843), pp. 22f.

society can give or concede it to them; they themselves cannot take it, or give it to themselves. It will be objected, the children had nevertheless 'by nature' the right to exist; only the Spartans refused *recognition* to this right. But then they simply had no right to this recognition— any more than they had to recognition of their life by the wild beasts to which they were thrown.

People talk so much about *birthright*, and complain:

> There is—alas!—no mention of the rights
> That were born with us.[1]

What sort of right, then, is there that was born with me? The right to receive an entailed estate, to inherit a throne, to enjoy a princely or noble education; or, again, because poor parents begot me, to—get free schooling, be clothed out of contributions of alms, and at last earn my bread and my herring in the coal-mines or at the loom? Are these not birthrights, rights that have come down to me from my parents through *birth*? You think—no; you think these are only rights improperly so called, it is just these rights that you aim to abolish through the *real birthright*. To give a basis for this you go back to the simplest thing and affirm that every one is by birth *equal* to another—to wit, a *man*. I will grant you that every one is born as man, hence the new-born are therein *equal* to each other. Why are they? Only because they do not yet show and exert themselves as anything but bare— *children of men*, naked little human beings. But thereby they are at once different from those who have already made something out of themselves, who thus are no longer bare 'children of man', but—children of their own

---

[1] *Vom Rechte, das mit uns geboren ist,*
Von dem ist leider! nie die Frage.
(Mephistopheles in *Faust*, 1, 1978–9).

creation. The latter possesses more than bare birthrights: they have *earned* rights. What an antithesis, what a field of combat! The old combat of the birthrights of man and well-earned rights. Go right on appealing to your birthrights; people will not fail to oppose to you the well-earned. Both stand on the 'ground of right'; for each of the two has a 'right' against the other, the one the birthright of natural right, the other the earned or 'well-earned' right.

(*Ego* 247–51)

It is said that punishment is the criminal's right. But impunity is just as much his right. If his understanding succeeds, it serves him right, and, if it does not succeed, it likewise serves him right. You make your bed and lie in it. If some one goes foolhardily into dangers and perishes in them, we are apt to say, 'It serves him right; he would have it so.' But, if he conquered the dangers, if his *might* was victorious, then he would be in the *right* too. If a child plays with the knife and gets cut, it is served right; but, if it doesn't get cut, it is served right too. Hence right befalls the criminal, doubtless, when he suffers what he risked; why, what did he risk it for, since he knew the possible consequences? But the punishment that we decree against him is only our right, not his. Our right reacts against his, and he is — 'in the wrong at last' because — we get the upper hand.

*   *   *

But what is right, what is matter of right in a society, is voiced too — in the *law*.[1]

Whatever the law may be, it must be respected by the —

[1] *Gesetz*, statute; no longer the same German word as 'right'.

loyal citizen. Thus the law-abiding mind of Old England is eulogized. To this that Euripidean sentiment (*Orestes,* 418) entirely corresponds: 'We serve the gods, whatever the gods are.' *Law as such, God as such,* thus far we are today.

People are at pains to distinguish *law* from arbitrary *orders,* from an ordinance: the former comes from a duly entitled authority. But a law over human action (ethical law, State law, etc.) is always a *declaration of will,* and so an order. Yes, even if I myself gave myself the law, it would yet be only my order, to which in the next moment I can refuse obedience. One may well enough declare what he will put up with, and so deprecate the opposite of the law, making known that in the contrary case he will treat the transgressor as his enemy; but no one has any business to command *my* actions, to say what course I shall pursue and set up a code to govern it. I must put up with it that he treats me as his *enemy,* but never that he makes free with me as his *creature,* and that he makes *his* reason, or even unreason, my plumb-line.

States last only so long as there is a *ruling will* and this ruling will is looked upon as tantamount to the own will. The lord's will is—law. What do your laws amount to if no one obeys them? What your orders, if nobody lets himself be ordered? The State cannot forbear the claim to determine the individual's will, to speculate and count on this. For the State it is indispensable that nobody have an *own will*; if one had, the State would have to exclude (lock up, banish, etc.) this one; if all had, they would do away with the State. The State is not thinkable without lordship and servitude (subjection); for the State must will to be the lord of all that it embraces, and this will is called the 'will of the State'.

He who, to hold his own, must count on the absence of

will in others is a thing made by these others, as the master is a thing made by the servant. If submissiveness ceased, it would be all over with lordship.[1]

The *own will* of Me is the State's destroyer; it is therefore branded by the State as 'self-will'. Own will and the State are powers in deadly hostility, between which no 'eternal peace' is possible. As long as the State asserts itself, it represents own will, its ever-hostile opponent, as unreasonable, evil; and the latter lets itself be talked into believing this—nay, it really is such, for no more reason than this, that it still lets itself be talked into such belief: it has not yet come to itself and to the consciousness of its dignity; hence it is still incomplete, still amenable to fine words.

Every State is a *despotism*, be the despot one or many, or (as one is likely to imagine about a republic) if all be lords, that is, despotize one over another. For this is the case when the law given at any time, the expressed volition of (it may be) a popular assembly, is thenceforth to be *law* for the individual, to which *obedience is due* from him or toward which he has the *duty* of obedience. If one were even to conceive the case that every individual in the people had expressed the same will, and hereby a complete 'collective will' had come into being, the matter would still remain the same. Would I not be bound today and henceforth to my will of yesterday? My will would in this case be *frozen*. Wretched *stability*! My creature—to wit, a particular expression of will—would have become my commander. But I in my will, I the creator, should be hindered in my flow and my dissolution. Because I was a fool yesterday I must remain such my life long. So in the State-life I am at best—I might just as well say, at worst—a bondman of myself. Because I was a willer

---

[1] An allusion to Hegel's master–slave dialectic.

yesterday, I am today without will: yesterday voluntary, today involuntary.

How change it? Only by recognizing no *duty*, not *binding* myself nor letting myself be bound. If I have no duty, then I know no law either.

'But they will bind me!' My will nobody can bind, and my disinclination remains free.

'Why, everything must go topsy-turvy if every one could do what he would!' Well, who says that every one can do everything? What are you there for, pray, you who do not need to put up with everything? Defend yourself, and no one will do anything to you! He who would break your will has to do with you, and is your *enemy*. Deal with him as such. If there stand behind you for your protection some millions more, then you are an imposing power and will have an easy victory. But, even if as a power you overawe your opponent, still you are not on that account a hallowed authority to him, unless he be a simpleton. He does not owe you respect and regard, even though he will have to consider your might.

We are accustomed to classify States according to the different ways in which 'the supreme might' is distributed. If an individual has it—monarchy; if all have it—democracy; and so on. Supreme might, then! Might against whom? Against the individual and his 'self-will'. The State practices 'violence', the individual must not do so. The State's behaviour is violence, and it calls its violence 'law'; that of the individual, 'crime'. Crime,[1] then —so the individual's violence is called; and only by crime does he overcome[2] the State's violence when he thinks that the State is not above him, but he is above the State.[3]

[1] *Verbrechen.*

[2] *brechen.*

[3] Here is the root and crux of the notion of 'repressive tolerance', introduced a century and a quarter ago. Herbert Marcuse is responsible for its

Now, if I wanted to act ridiculously, I might, as a well-meaning person, admonish you not to make laws which impair my self-development, self-activity, self-creation. I do not give this advice. For, if you should follow it, you would be unwise, and I should have been cheated of my entire profit. I request nothing at all from you; for, whatever I might demand, you would still be dictatorial lawgivers, and must be so, because a raven cannot sing, nor a robber live without robbery. Rather do I ask those who would be egoists what they think the more egoistic — to let laws be given them by you, and to respect those that are given, or to practice *refractoriness*, yes, complete disobedience. Good-hearted people think the laws ought to prescribe only what is accepted in the people's feeling as right and proper. But what concern is it of mine what is accepted in the nation and by the nation? The nation will perhaps be against the blasphemer; therefore a law against blasphemy. Am I not to blaspheme on that account? Is this law to be more than an 'order' to me? I put the question.

Solely from the principle that all *right* and all *authority* belong to the *collectivity of the people* do all forms of government arise. For none of them lacks this appeal to the collectivity, and the despot, as well as the president or any aristocracy, acts and commands 'in the name of the State'. They are in possession of the 'authority of the State', and it is perfectly indifferent whether, were this possible, the people as a *collectivity* (all individuals) exercise this State-*authority*, or whether it is only the representatives of this collectivity, be there many of them as in aristocracies or one as in monarchies. Always the

current popularity: see *A Critique of Pure Tolerance* (including essays by Robert Paul Wolff, Barrington Moore Jr. and Herbert Marcuse) (Cape, London, 1969).

collectivity is above the individual, and has a power which is called *legitimate*, which is law.

Over against the sacredness of the State, the individual is only a vessel of dishonour, in which 'exuberance, malevolence, mania for ridicule and slander, frivolity', are left as soon as he does not deem that object of veneration, the State, to be worthy of recognition. The spiritual *haughtiness* of the servants and subjects of the State has fine penalties against unspiritual 'exuberance'.

(*Ego* 254–9)

*   *   *

What is the ordinary criminal but one who has committed the fatal mistake of endeavouring after what is the people's instead of seeking for what is his? He has sought despicable *alien* goods, has done what believers do who seek after what is God's. What does the priest who admonishes the criminal do? He sets before him the great wrong of having desecrated by his act what was hallowed by the State, its property (in which, of course, must be included even the life of those who belong to the State); instead of this, he might rather hold up to him the fact that he has befouled *himself* in not despising the alien thing, but thinking it worth stealing; he could, if he were not a parson. Talk with the so-called criminal as with an egoist, and he will be ashamed, not that he transgressed against your laws and goods, but that he considered your laws worth evading, your goods worth desiring; he will be ashamed that he did not — despise you and yours together, that he was too little an egoist. But you cannot talk egoistically with him, for you are not so great as a criminal, you — commit no crime! You do not know that an ego who is his own cannot desist from being a criminal, that crime is his life. And yet you should know it, since you believe that 'we are all miserable sinners'; but you think surreptitiously to get beyond sin, you do not comprehend—for you are devil-fearing—that guilt is the value of a man. Oh, if you were guilty! But now you are 'righteous'. Well—just put everything nicely to rights for your master!

When the Christian consciousness, or the Christian man, draws up a criminal code, what can the concept of *crime* be there but simply—*heartlessness*? Each severing and wounding of a *heart relation*, each *heartless behaviour* towards a sacred being, is crime. The more heartfelt the relation is supposed to be, the more scandalous is the deriding of it, and the more worthy of punishment the crime. Everyone who is subject to the lord should love him; to deny this love is a high treason worthy of death. Adultery is a heartlessness worthy of punishment; one has no heart, no enthusiasm, no pathetic feeling for the sacredness of marriage. So long as the heart or soul dictates laws, only the heartful or soulful man enjoys the protection of the laws. That the man of soul makes laws means properly that the *moral* man makes them: what contradicts these men's 'moral feeling', this they penalize. How should disloyalty, secession, breach of oaths—in short, all *radical breaking off*, all tearing asunder of venerable *ties*—not be flagitious and criminal in their eyes?

(*Ego* 264–6)

One sees here how it is 'Man' again who sets on foot even the concept of crime, of sin, and therewith that of right. A man in whom I do not recognize 'man' is 'sinner, a guilty one'.

Only against a sacred thing are there criminals; you against me can never be a criminal, but only an opponent.

But not to hate him who injures a sacred thing is in itself a crime, as St Just cries out against Danton: 'Are you not a criminal and responsible for not having hated the enemies of the fatherland?' —

If, as in the Revolution, what 'Man' is is apprehended as 'good citizen', then from this concept of 'Man' we have the well-known 'political offences and crimes'.

(*Ego* 267)

According to the liberal way of thinking, right is to be obligatory for me because it is thus established by *human reason*, against which *my reason* is 'unreason'. Formerly people inveighed in the name of divine reason against weak human reason; now, in the name of strong human reason, against egoistic reason, which is rejected as 'unreason'. And yet none is real but this very 'unreason'. Neither divine nor human reason, but only your and my reason existing at any given time, is real, as and because you and I are real.

The thought of right is originally my thought; or, it has its origin in me. But, when it has sprung from me, when the 'Word' is out, then it has 'become flesh', it is a *fixed idea*. Now I no longer get rid of the thought; however I turn, it stands before me. Thus men have not become masters again of the thought 'right', which they themselves created; their creature is running away with them. This is absolute right, that which is absolved or unfastened from me. We, revering it as absolute, cannot devour it again, and it takes from us the creative power: the creature is more than the creator, it is 'in and for itself'.

(*Ego* 269)

*   *   *

The 'equality of right' is a phantom just because right is nothing more and nothing less than admission, *a matter of grace*, which, be it said, one may also acquire by his desert; for desert and grace are not contradictory, since even grace wishes to be 'deserved' and our gracious smile falls only to him who knows how to force it from us.

So people dream of 'all citizens of the State having to stand side by side, with equal rights'. As citizens of the State they are certainly all equal for the State. But it will divide them, and advance them or put them in the rear, according to its special ends, if on no other account; and still more must it distinguish them from one another as good and bad citizens.

(*Ego* 270–1)

The last and most decided opposition, that of unique against unique, is at bottom beyond what is called opposition, but without having sunk back into 'unity' and unison. As unique you have nothing in common with the other any longer, and therefore nothing divisive or hostile either; you are not seeking to be in the right against him before a *third* party, and are standing with him neither 'on the ground of right' nor on any other common ground. The opposition vanishes in complete — *severance* or singleness. This might indeed be regarded as the new point in common or a new parity, but here the parity consists precisely in the disparity, and is itself nothing but disparity, a par of disparity, and that only for him who institutes a 'comparison'.

The polemic against privilege forms a characteristic feature of liberalism, which fumes against 'privilege' because it itself appeals to 'right'. Further than to fuming it cannot carry this; for privileges do not fall before right falls, as they are only forms of right. But right falls apart into its nothingness when it is swallowed up by might, when one understands what is meant by 'Might goes before right'. All right explains itself then as privilege, and privilege itself as power, as — *superior power*.

But must not the mighty combat against superior power show quite another face than the modest combat against privilege, which is to be fought out before a first judge, 'right', according to the judge's mind?

(Ego 273-4)

* * *

I do not demand any right, therefore I need not recognize any either. What I can get by force I get by force, and what I do not get by force I have no right to, nor do I give myself airs, or consolation, with my imprescriptible right.

With absolute right, right itself passes away; the dominion of the 'concept of right' is cancelled at the same time. For it is not to be forgotten that hitherto concepts, ideas, or principles ruled us, and that among these rulers the concept of right, or of justice, played one of the most important parts.

Entitled or unentitled — that does not concern me, if I am only *powerful*, I am of myself *empowered*, and need no other empowering or entitling.

Right — is a bat in the belfry, put there by a spook; power — that am I myself, I am the powerful one and owner of power. Right is above me, is absolute, and exists in one higher, as whose grace it flows to me: right is a gift of grace from the judge; power and might exist only in me the powerful and mighty.

(Ego 275)

B.—MY INTERCOURSE

The Christian people has produced two societies whose duration will keep equal measure with the permanence of that people: these are the societies *State* and *Church*. Can they be called a union of egoists?[1] Do we in them pursue an egoistic, personal, own interest, or do we pursue a popular, an interest of the Christian *people*, to wit, a State, and Church interest? Can I and may I be myself in them? May I think and act as I will, may I reveal myself, live myself out, busy myself? Must I not leave untouched the majesty of the State, the sanctity of the Church?

Well, I may not do so as I will. But shall I find in any society such an unmeasured freedom of may-ing? Certainly not! Accordingly we might be content? Not a bit! It is a different thing whether I rebound from an ego or from a people, a generalization. There I am my opponent's opponent, born his equal; here I am a despised opponent, bound and under a guardian: there I stand man to man; here I am a schoolboy who can accomplish nothing against his comrade because the latter has called father and mother to aid and has crept under the apron, while I am well scolded as an ill-bred brat, and I must not 'argue': there I fight against a bodily enemy; here against mankind, against a generalization, against a 'majesty', against a spook. But to me no majesty, nothing sacred, is a limit; nothing that I know how to overpower. Only that which I cannot overpower still limits my might; and I of limited might am temporarily a limited I, not

[1] Stirner calls his own 'ideal type' of society the Union of Egoists, a voluntary coalition of individuals who associate together in order to mutually enhance their individual powers. There are striking links with modern 'self-realization' movements and the rhetoric of 'doing your own thing'.

limited by the might *outside* me, but limited by my *own* still deficient might, by my *own impotence*. However, 'the Guard dies, but does not surrender!' Above all, only a bodily opponent!

(*Ego* 278–9)

But of what concern to me is the common weal? The common weal as such is not *my weal*, but only the furthest extremity of *self-renunciation*. The common weal may cheer aloud while I must 'come to heel', the State may shine while I starve. In what lies the folly of the political liberals but in their opposing the people to the government and talking of people's rights? So there is the people going to be of age, etc. As if one who has no mouth could be *mündig*![1] Only the individual is able to be *mündig*.

(*Ego* 279–80)

In general, all States, constitutions, churches, have sunk by the *secession* of individuals; for the individual is the irreconcilable enemy of every *generality*, every *tie*, every fetter. Yet people fancy to this day that man needs 'sacred ties': he, the deadly enemy of every 'tie'. The history of the world shows that no tie has yet remained unrent, shows that man tirelessly defends himself against ties of every sort; and yet, blinded, people think up new ties again and again, and think that they have arrived at the right one if one puts upon them the tie of a so-called free constitution, a beautiful, constitutional tie; decoration ribbons, the ties of confidence between '——', do seem gradually to have become somewhat infirm, but people have made no further progress than from apronstrings to garters and collars.

[1] This is the word for 'of age'; but it is derived from *Mund*, 'mouth', and refers properly to the right of speaking through one's own *mouth*.

Everything sacred is a tie, a fetter.

Everything sacred is and must be perverted by perverters of the law; therefore our present time has
multitudes of such perverters in all spheres. They are
preparing the way for the break-up of law, for lawlessness.

Poor Athenians who are accused of pettifoggery and
sophistry! poor Alcibiades, of intrigue! Why, that was just
your best point, your first step in freedom. Your Aeschy-
lus, Herodotus, etc., only wanted to have a free Greek
people; you were the first to surmise something of *your*
freedom.

A people represses those who tower above *its majesty*, by
ostracism against too-powerful citizens, by the Inquisition
against the heretics of the Church, by the—Inquisition
against traitors in the State.

For the people is concerned only with its self-assertion;
it demands 'patriotic self-sacrifice' from everybody. To
it, accordingly, every one *in himself* is indifferent, a nothing,
and it cannot do, not even suffer, what the individual and
he alone must do—to wit, *turn him to account*. Every people,
every State, is unjust toward the *egoist*.

As long as there still exists even one institution which
the individual may not dissolve, the ownness and self-
appurtenance of Me is still very remote. How can I be
free when I must bind myself by oath to a constitution,
a charter, a law, 'vow body and soul' to my people? How
can I be my own when my faculties may develop only so
far as they 'do not disturb the harmony of society'
(Weitling)?

The fall of peoples and mankind will invite *me* to my
rise.

Listen, even as I am writing this, the bells begin to
sound, that they may jingle in for tomorrow the festival

of the thousand years' existence of our dear Germany.[1] Sound, sound its knell! You do sound solemn enough, as if your tongue was moved by the presentiment that it is giving convoy to a corpse. The German people and German peoples have behind them a history of a thousand years: what a long life! Oh, go to rest, never to rise again—that all may become free whom you so long have held in fetters.—The *people* is dead.—Up with *me*!

O thou my much-tormented German people—what was thy torment? It was the torment of a thought that cannot create itself a body, the torment of a walking spirit that dissolves into nothing at every cock-crow and yet pines for deliverance and fulfilment. In me too thou hast lived long, thou dear—thought, thou dear—spook. Already I almost fancied I had found the word of thy deliverance, discovered flesh and bones for the wandering spirit; then I hear them sound, the bells that usher thee into eternal rest; then the last hope fades out, then the notes of the last love die away, then I depart from the desolate house of those who now are dead and enter at the door of the—living one: For only he who is alive is in the right.

Farewell, thou dream of so many millions; farewell, thou who hast tyrannized over thy children for a thousand years!

Tomorrow they carry thee to the grave; soon thy sisters, the peoples, will follow thee. But, when they have all followed, then — —mankind is buried, and I am my own, I am the laughing heir!

* * *

[1] Written in 1843, the thousandth anniversary of the Treaty of Verdun, when the empire of Charlemagne was divided into three parts, the part from the Rhine to the easterly marches of the empire becoming what was essentially Germany upon unification in 1871, though it was a confederation of several separate political units in Stirner's time.

THE STATE[1]

The word *Gesellschaft* (society) has its origin in the word *Sal* (hall). If one hall encloses many persons, then the hall causes these persons to be in society. They *are* in society, and at most constitute a *salon*-society by talking in the traditional forms of *salon* idiom. When it comes to real *intercourse*, this is to be regarded as independent of society: it may occur or be lacking, without altering the nature of what is named society. Those who are in the hall are a society even as mute persons, or when they put each other off solely with empty phrases of courtesy. Intercourse is mutuality, it is the action, the *commercium*, of individuals; society is only community of the hall, and even the statues of a museum-hall are in society, they are 'grouped'. People are accustomed to say 'they *haben inne*[2] this hall in common,' but the case is rather that the hall has us *inne* or in it. So far the natural signification of the word society. In this it comes out that society is not generated by me and you, but by a third factor which makes associates out of us two, and that it is just this third factor that is the creative one, that which creates society.

Just so a prison society or prison companionship (those who enjoy[3] the same prison). Here we already hit upon a third factor fuller of significance than was that merely local one, the hall. Prison no longer means a space only, but a space with express reference to its inhabitants: for it is a prison only through being destined for prisoners,

[1] I have added sub-headings in a number of places in this long section, 'My Intercourse', of Chapter V.

[2] 'Occupy'; literally, 'have within'.

[3] The word *Genosse*, 'companion', signifies originally a companion in *enjoyment*.

without whom it would be a mere building. What gives a common stamp to those who are gathered in it? Evidently the prison, since it is only by means of the prison that they are prisoners. What, then, determines the *manner of life* of the prison society? The prison! What determines their intercourse? The prison too, perhaps? Certainly they can enter upon intercourse only as prisoners, only so far as the prison laws allow it; but that *they themselves* hold intercourse, I with you, this the prison cannot bring to pass; on the contrary, it must have an eye to guarding against such egoistic, purely personal intercourse (and only as such is it really intercourse between me and you). That we *jointly* execute a job, run a machine, effectuate anything in general—for this a prison will indeed provide; but that I forget that I am a prisoner, and engage in intercourse with you who likewise disregard it, brings danger to the prison, and not only cannot be caused by it, but must not even be permitted. For this reason the saintly and moral-minded French chamber decides to introduce solitary confinement, and other saints will do the like in order to cut off 'demoralizing intercourse'. Imprisonment is the established and—sacred condition, to injure which no attempt must be made. The slightest push of that kind is punishable, as is every uprising against a sacred thing by which man is to be charmed and chained.

Like the hall, the prison does form a society, a companionship, a communion (as in a communion of labour), but no *intercourse*, no reciprocity, no *union*. On the contrary, every union in the prison bears within it the dangerous seed of a 'plot', which under favourable circumstances might spring up and bear fruit.

(Ego 283–7)

Which of the two lies nearer my heart, the good of the

family or my good?[1] In innumerable cases both go peace-
fully together; the advantage of the family is at the same
time mine, and *vice versa*. Then it is hard to decide whether
I am thinking *selfishly* or *for the common benefit*, and perhaps
I complacently flatter myself with my unselfishness. But
there comes the day when a necessity of choice makes me
tremble, when I have it in mind to dishonour my family
tree, to affront parents, brothers, and kindred. What then?
Now it will appear how I am disposed at the bottom of
my heart; now it will be revealed whether piety ever stood
above egoism for me, now the selfish one can no longer
skulk behind the semblance of unselfishness. A wish rises
in my soul, and, growing from hour to hour, becomes a
passion. To whom does it occur at first blush that the
slightest thought which may result adversely to the
spirit of the family (piety) bears within it a transgression
against this? Nay, who at once, in the first moment,
becomes completely conscious of the matter? It happens
so with Juliet in *Romeo and Juliet*. The unruly passion can
at last no longer be tamed, and undermines the building
of piety.

(*Ego* 289–90)

But now sometimes a wish glimmers in a less passionate
and wilful heart than Juliet's. The pliable girl brings
herself as a *sacrifice* to the peace of the family. One might
say that here too selfishness prevailed, for the decision
came from the feeling that the pliable girl felt herself
more satisfied by the unity of the family than by the fulfilment of her wish. That might be; but what if there
remained a sure sign that egoism had been sacrificed to

---

[1] Stirner has been discussing the family as a ritual community, like the
prison, with sacred laws and the cohesive bond of piety, against which the
individual son must become a criminal in order to free himself.

piety? What if, even after the wish that had been directed against the peace of the family was sacrificed, it remained at least as a recollection of a 'sacrifice' brought to a sacred tie? What if the pliable girl were conscious of having left her self-will unsatisfied and humbly subjected herself to a higher power? Subjected and sacrificed, because the superstition of piety exercised its dominion over her!

There egoism won, here piety wins and the egoistic heart bleeds; there egoism was strong, here it was — weak. But the weak, as we have long known, are the — unselfish. For them, for these its weak members, the family cares, because they *belong* to the family, do not belong to themselves and care for themselves. This weakness Hegel praises when he wants to have match-making left to the choice of the parents.

$$(Ego\ 290\text{--}1)$$

Well, the egoist has broken the ties of the family and found in the State a lord to shelter him against the grievously affronted spirit of the family. But where has he run now? Straight into a new *society*, in which his egoism is awaited by the same snares and nets that it has just escaped. For the State is likewise a society, not a union; it is the broadened *family* ('Father of the Country — Mother of the Country — children of the country').

* * *

What is called a State is a tissue and plexus of dependence and adherence; it is a *belonging together*, a holding together, in which those who are placed together fit themselves to each other, or, in short, mutually depend on each other: it is the *order* of this *dependence*. Suppose the king, whose authority lends authority to all down to the beadle, should vanish: still all in whom the will for order was awake would keep order erect against the disorders of bestiality. If disorder were victorious, the State would be at an end.

But is this thought of love, to fit ourselves to each other, to adhere to each other and depend on each other, really capable of winning us? According to this the State should be *love* realized, the being for each other and living for each other of all. Is not self-will being lost while we attend to the will for order? Will people not be satisfied when order is cared for by authority, when authority sees to it that no one 'gets in the way of' another; when, then, the *herd* is judiciously distributed or ordered? Why, then everything is in 'the best order', and it is this best order that is called—State!

Our societies and States *are* without our *making* them, are united without our uniting, are predestined and established, or have an independent standing[1] of their own, are the indissolubly established against us egoists. The fight of the world today is, as it is said, directed against the 'established'. Yet people are wont to misunderstand this as if it were only to be an exchange of what is now established for another, a better, established system. But war might rather be declared against establishment itself, the *State*, not a particular State, not any such thing as the mere condition of the State at the time; it is not another State (such as a 'people's State') that men aim at, but their *union*, uniting, this ever-fluid uniting of everything standing.—A State exists even without my co-operation: I am born in it, brought up in it, under obligations to it, and must 'do it homage'.[2] It takes me up into its 'favour,'[3]

[1] It should be remembered that in German the words 'establish' and 'State' are both derived from the root *stand*.

[2] *huldigen.*

[3] *Huld.*

and I live by its 'grace'. Thus the independent establishment of the State founds my lack of independence; its
condition as a 'natural growth', its organism, demands
that my nature do not grow freely, but be cut to fit it.
That *it* may be able to unfold in natural growth, it applies
to me the shears of 'civilization'; it gives me an education
and culture adapted to it, not to me, and teaches me to
respect the laws, to refrain from injury to State property
(that is, private property), to reverence divine and earthly
highness, etc.; in short, it teaches me to be—*unpunishable*,
'sacrificing' my ownness to 'sacredness' (everything possible is sacred; property, others' life, etc.). In this consists
the sort of civilization and culture that the State is able
to give me: it brings me up to be a 'serviceable instrument', a 'serviceable member of society'.

(*Ego* 292–4)

People talk of the tolerance, the leaving opposite tendencies
free, and the like, by which civilized States are distinguished. Certainly some are strong enough to look with
complacency on even the most unrestrained meetings,
while others charge their catchpole to go hunting for
tobacco-pipes. Yet for one State as for another the play
of individuals among themselves, their buzzing to and
fro, their daily life, is an *incident* which it must be content
to leave to themselves because it can do nothing with this.
Many, indeed, still strain at gnats and swallow camels,
while others are shrewder. Individuals are 'freer' in the
latter, because less pestered. But *I* am free in *no* State.
The lauded tolerance of States is simply a tolerating of
the 'harmless', the 'not dangerous'; it is only elevation
above petty-mindedness, only a more estimable, grander,
prouder—despotism. A certain State seemed for a while

to mean to be pretty well elevated above *literary* combats, which might be carried on with all heat; England is elevated above *popular turmoil* and — tobacco-smoking. But woe to the literature that deals blows at the State itself, woe to the mobs that 'endanger' the State. In that certain State they dream of a 'free science', in England of a 'free popular life'.

The State does let individuals *play* as freely as possible, only they must not be in *earnest*, must not forget *it*. Man must not carry on intercourse with man *unconcernedly*, not without 'superior oversight and mediation'. I must not execute all that I am able to, but only so much as the State allows; I must not turn to account *my* thoughts, nor *my* work, nor, in general, anything of mine.

The State always has the sole purpose to limit, tame, subordinate, the individual — to make him subject to some *generality* or other; it lasts only so long as the individual is not all in all, and it is only the clearly marked *restriction of me*, my limitation, my slavery. Never does a State aim to bring in the free activity of individuals, but always that which is bound to the *purpose of the State*. Through the State nothing *in common* comes to pass either, as little as one can call a piece of cloth the common work of all the individual parts of a machine; it is rather the work of the whole machine as a unit, *machine work*. In the same style everything is done by the *State machine* too; for it moves the clockwork of the individual minds, none of which follow their own impulse. The State seeks to hinder every free activity by its censorship, its supervision, its police, and holds this hindering to be its duty, because it is in truth a duty of self-preservation. The State wants to make something out of man, therefore there live in it only *made* men; everyone who wants to be his own self is its opponent and is nothing. 'He is nothing' means as much as, the State does not make use of him, grants him no position, no office, no trade, and the like.

(*Ego* 297–9)

The best State will clearly be that which has the most loyal citizens, and the more the devoted mind for *legality* is lost, so much the more will the State, this system of morality, this moral life itself, be diminished in force and quality. With the 'good citizens' the good State too perishes and dissolves into anarchy and lawlessness. 'Respect for the law!' By this cement the total of the State is held together. 'The law is *sacred*, and he who affronts it a *criminal*.' Without crime no State: the moral world— and this the State is—is crammed full of scamps, cheats, liars, thieves. Since the State is the 'lordship of law', its hierarchy, it follows that the egoist, in all cases where *his* advantage runs against the State's, can satisfy himself only by crime.

(*Ego* 313–14)

What a folly, to ask of the State's authority that it should enter into an honourable fight with the individual, and, as they express themselves in the matter of freedom of the press, share sun and wind equally! If the State, this thought, is to be a *de facto* power, it simply must be a superior power against the individual. The State is 'sacred' and must not expose itself to the 'impudent attacks' of individuals. If the State is *sacred*, there must be censorship. The political liberals admit the former and dispute the inference. But in any case they concede repressive measures to it, for—they stick to this, that State is *more* than the individual and exercises a justified revenge, called punishment.

Punishment has a meaning only when it is to afford

expiation for the injuring of a *sacred* thing. If something is sacred to anyone, he certainly deserves punishment when he acts as its enemy. A man who lets a man's life continue in existence *because* to him it is sacred and he has a *dread* of touching it is simply a—*religious* man.

Weitling lays crime at the door of 'social disorder', and lives in the expectation that under communistic arrangements crimes will become impossible, because the temptations to them, such as money, fall away. As, however, his organized society is also exalted into a sacred and inviolable one, he miscalculates in that good-hearted opinion. Such as with their mouth professed allegiance to the communistic society, but worked underhand for its ruin, would not be lacking. Besides, Weitling has to keep on with 'curative means against the natural remainder of human diseases and weaknesses', and 'curative means' always announce to begin with that individuals will be looked upon as 'called' to a particular 'salvation' and hence treated according to the requirements of this 'human calling'. *Curative means* or *healing* is only the reverse side of *punishment*, the *theory of cure* runs parallel with the *theory of punishment*; if the latter sees in an action a sin against right, the former takes it for a sin of the man *against himself*, as a decadence from his health. But the correct thing is that I regard it either as an action that *suits me* or as one that *does not suit me*, as hostile or friendly to *me*, that I treat it as my *property*, which I cherish or demolish. 'Crime' or 'disease' is not either of them an *egoistic* view of the matter, a judgment *starting from me*, but starting from *another*—to wit, whether it injures *right*, general right, or the *health* partly of the individual (the sick one), partly of the generality (*society*). 'Crime' is treated inexorably, 'disease' with 'loving gentleness, compassion' and the like.

Punishment follows crime. If crime falls because the sacred vanishes, punishment must not less be drawn into its fall; for it too has significance only over against something sacred. Ecclesiastical punishments have been abolished. Why? Because how one behaves towards the 'holy God' is his own affair. But, as this one punishment, *ecclesiastical punishment*, has fallen, so all *punishments* must fall. As sin against the so-called God is a man's own affair, so is that against every kind of the so-called sacred. According to our theories of penal law, with whose 'improvement in conformity to the times' people are tormenting themselves in vain, they want to *punish* men for this or that 'inhumanity'; and therein they make the silliness of these theories especially plain by their consistency, hanging the little thieves and letting the big ones run. For injury to property they have the house of correction, and for 'violence to thought', suppression of 'natural rights of man', only—representations and petitions.

The criminal code has continued existence only through the sacred, and perishes of itself if punishment is given up. Now they want to create everywhere a new penal law, without indulging in a misgiving about punishment itself. But it is exactly punishment that must make room for satisfaction, which, again, cannot aim at satisfying right or justice, but at procuring *us* a satisfactory outcome. If one does to us what we *will not put up with*, we break his power and bring our own to bear: we satisfy *ourselves* on him, and do not fall into the folly of wanting to satisfy right (the spook). It is not the *sacred* that is to defend itself against man, but man against man; as *God* too, you know, no longer defends himself against man, God to whom formerly (and in part, indeed, even now) all the 'servants of God' offered their hands to punish the blasphemer, as they still at this very day lend their hands to the sacred. This devotion to the sacred brings it to pass also that, without lively participation of one's own, one only delivers misdoers into the hands of the police and courts; a non-participating making over to the authorities, 'who, of course, will best administer sacred matters'. The people is quite crazy for hounding the police on against everything that seems to it to be immoral, often only unseemly, and this popular rage for the moral protects the police institution more than the government could in any way protect it.

In crime the egoist has hitherto asserted himself and mocked at the sacred; the break with the sacred, or rather of the sacred, may become general. A revolution never returns, but a mighty, reckless, shameless, conscienceless, proud — *crime*, does it not rumble in distant thunders, and do you not see how the sky grows presciently silent and gloomy?

(Ego 315–19)

*   *   *

At this point the 'Nationals' may be brought to mind. To demand of the thirty-eight states of Germany that they shall act as *one nation* can only be put alongside the senseless desire that thirty-eight swarms of bees, led by thirty-eight queen bees, shall unite themselves into one swarm. *Bees* they all remain; but it is not the bees as bees that belong together and can join themselves together, it is only that the *subject* bees are connected with the *ruling* queens. Bees and peoples are destitute of will, and the *instinct* of their queens leads them.

If one were to point the bees to their beehood, in which at any rate they are all equal to each other, one would be doing the same thing that they are now doing so stormily in pointing the Germans to their Germanhood. Why, Germanhood is just like beehood in this very thing, that it bears in itself the necessity of cleavages and separations, yet without pushing on to the last separation, where, with the complete carrying through of the process of separating, its end appears: I mean, to the separation of man from man. Germanhood does indeed divide itself into different peoples and tribes, beehives; but the individual who has the quality of being a German is still as powerless as the isolated bee. And yet only individuals can enter into union with each other, and all alliances and leagues of peoples are and remain mechanical compoundings, because those who come together, at least so far as the 'peoples' are regarded as the ones that have come together, are *destitute of will*. Only with the last separation does separation itself end and change to unification.

(*Ego* 303–4)

How ridiculously sentimental when one German grasps another's hand and presses it with sacred awe because 'he too is a German'! With that he is something great! But this will certainly still be thought touching as long as people are enthusiastic for 'brotherliness', as long as they have a *'family disposition'*. From the superstition of 'piety', from 'brotherliness' or 'childlikeness' or however else the soft-hearted piety-phrases run—from the *family spirit*—the Nationals, who want to have a great *family of Germans*, cannot liberate themselves.

(*Ego* 304–5)

As with the Greeks, there is now a wish to make man a *zoon politicon*, a citizen of the State or political man. So he ranked for a long time as a 'citizen of heaven'. But the Greek fell into ignominy along with his *State*, the citizen of heaven likewise falls with heaven; we, on the other hand, are not willing to go down along with the *people*, the nation and nationality, not willing to be merely *political* men or politicians. Since the Revolution they have striven to 'make the people happy', and in making the people happy, great, and the like, they make us unhappy: the people's good hap is—my mishap.

(*Ego* 307)

The egoist is to himself the warder of the human, and has nothing to say to the State except 'Get out of my sunshine.' Only when the State comes in contact with his ownness does the egoist take an active interest in it. If the condition of the State does not bear hard on the closet-philosopher, is he to occupy himself with it because it is his 'most sacred duty'? So long as the State does according to his wish, what need has he to look up from his studies? Let those who from an interest of their own want to have conditions otherwise busy themselves with them. Not now, nor evermore, will 'sacred duty' bring people to reflect about the State—as little as they become disciples of science, artists, etc., from 'sacred duty'. Egoism alone can impel them to it, and will as soon as things have become much worse. If you showed people that their egoism demanded that they busy themselves with State affairs, you would not have to call on them long; if, on the other hand, you appeal to their love of fatherland and the like, you will long preach to deaf hearts in behalf of this 'service of love'. Certainly, in your sense the egoists will not participate in State affairs at all.

(*Ego* 307–8)

He in whose head or heart or both the *State* is seated, he
who is possessed by the State, or the *believer in the State*, is
a politician, and remains such to all eternity.

'The State is the most necessary means for the complete development of mankind.' It assuredly has been so as
long as we wanted to develop mankind; but, if we want
to develop ourselves, it can be to us only a means of
hindrance.

Can State and people still be reformed and bettered
now? As little as the nobility, the clergy, the church, etc.:
they can be abrogated, annihilated, done away with,
not reformed. Can I change a piece of nonsense into
sense by reforming it, or must I drop it outright?

Henceforth what is to be done is no longer about the
State (the form of the State, etc.), but about me. With
this all questions about the prince's power, the constitution, and so on, sink into their true abyss and their true
nothingness. I, this nothing, shall put forth my *creations*
from myself.

*   *   *

THE PARTY

To the chapter of society belongs also 'the party', whose
praise has of late been sung.

In the State the *party* is current. 'Party, party, who
should not join one!' But the individual is *unique*, not a
member of the party. He unites freely, and separates
freely again. The party is nothing but a State in the
State, and in this smaller bee-State 'peace' is also to rule
just as in the greater. The very people who cry loudest
that there must be an *opposition* in the State inveigh against
every discord in the party. A proof that they too want

only a — State. All parties are shattered not against the State, but against the unique one.[1]

One hears nothing more often now than the admonition to remain true to his party; party men despise nothing so much as a mugwump. One must run with his party through thick and thin, and unconditionally approve and represent its chief principles. It does not indeed go quite so badly here as with closed societies, because these bind their members to fixed laws or statutes (such as the religious orders, the Society of Jesus, etc.). But yet the party ceases to be a union at the same moment at which it makes certain principles *binding* and wants to have them assured against attacks; but this moment is the very birth-act of the party. As party it is already a *born society*, a dead union, an idea that has become fixed. As party of absolutism it cannot will that its members should doubt the irrefragable truth of this principle; they could cherish this doubt only if they were egoistic enough to want still to be something outside their party, non-partisans. Non-partisans they cannot be as party-men, but only as egoists. If you are a Protestant and belong to that party, you must only justify Protestantism, at most 'purge' it, not reject it; if you are a Christian and belong among men to the Christian party, you cannot be beyond this as a member of this party, but only when your egoism, non-partisanship, impels you to it. What exertions the Christians, down to Hegel and the communists, have put forth to make their party strong! They stuck to it that Christianity must contain the eternal truth, and that one needs only to get at it, make sure of it, and justify it.

[1] Stirner again anticipates and perhaps generates one of the key perspectives of the radical critics today of advanced industrial society, one particularly prominent in the work of Herbert Marcuse: we live in an age of 'consensus politics', where the opposition party is as much a tool of the prevailing society ideology as the governing one.

In short, the party cannot bear non-partisanship, and it is in this that egoism appears. What matters the party to me? I shall find enough anyhow who *unite* with me without swearing allegiance to my flag.

He who passes over from one party to another is at once abused as a 'turncoat'. Certainly *morality* demands that one stand by his party, and to become apostate from it is to spot oneself with the stain of 'faithlessness'; but ownness knows no commandment of 'faithfulness', 'attachment', and the like, ownness permits everything, even apostasy, defection. Unconsciously even the moral themselves let themselves be led by this principle when they have to judge one who passes over to *their* party — indeed they are making proselytes; they should only at the same time acquire a consciousness of the fact that one must commit *immoral* actions in order to commit his own — here, that one must break faith, yes, even his oath, in order to determine himself instead of being determined by moral considerations. In the eyes of people of strict moral judgment an apostate always shimmers in equivocal colours, and will not easily obtain their confidence; for there sticks to him the taint of 'faithlessness', of an immorality. In the lower man[1] this view is found almost generally; advanced thinkers fall here too, as always, into an uncertainty and bewilderment, and the contradiction necessarily founded in the principle of morality does not, on account of the confusion of their concepts, come clearly to their consciousness. They do not venture to call the apostate downright immoral, because they themselves entice to apostasy, to defection from one religion to another; still, they cannot give up the standpoint of

---

[1] Cf. Nietzsche's 'slave morality' and his 'lower' or 'herd' type — Stirner also uses the image of the herd.

morality either. And yet here the occasion was to be seized to step outside of morality.

Are the Own or Unique perchance a party? How could they be *own* if they were such as *belonged* to a party!

Or is one to hold with no party? In the very act of joining them and entering their circle one forms a *union* with them that lasts as long as party and I pursue one and the same goal. But today I still share the party's tendency, as by tomorrow I can do so no longer and I become 'untrue' to it. The party has nothing *binding* (obligatory) for me, and I do not have respect for it; if it no longer pleases me, I become its foe.

(Ego 309–12)

*   *   *

PROPERTY[1]

I want to raise the value of myself, the value of ownness, and should I cheapen property? No, as I was not respected hitherto because people, mankind, and a thousand other generalities were put higher, so property too has to this day not yet been recognized in its full value.

---

[1] The revaluation of property (*Eigenthum*), the rediscovery of man's proper-ties, is at the core of Stirner's endeavour to instate the individual at the centre of the cosmos, as the measure of all things. Property is not to be valued in itself, for value is only something that is realized in consumption. When Stirner exhorts 'Get the value out of yourself!' 'Consume yourself!' he implies that self and property are fundamentally inseparable, that the individual builds his own identity through expressing himself in consumption. The value placed on an article and the possessor's self-valuation are interdependent, and any view which somehow treats man as independent from commodities (and for Stirner people are to be consumed 'creatively' in a similar way to impersonal objects) segregates him from his means to fulfilment. It is understandable, in this light, that Stirner should seek to devalue economic activity which is not germane to the enjoyment of life; this entails a critique of *Homo-economicus*, the cleric in material garb.

Property too was only the property of a ghost, the people's property; my whole existence 'belonged to the fatherland'; *I* belonged to the fatherland, the people, the State, and therefore also everything that I called *my own*. It is demanded of States that they do away with pauperism. It seems to me this is asking that the State should cut off its own head and lay it at its feet; for so long as the State is the ego the individual ego must remain a poor devil, a non-ego. The State has an interest only in being itself rich; whether Michael is rich and Peter poor is alike to it; Peter might also be rich and Michael poor. It looks on indifferently as one grows poor and the other rich, unruffled by this alternation. As *individuals* they are really equal before its face; in this it is just: before it both of them are—nothing, as we 'are altogether sinners before God'; on the other hand, it has a very great interest in this, that those individuals who make it their ego should have a part in *its* wealth; it makes them partakers in *its property*. Through property, with which it rewards the individuals, it tames them; but this remains *its* property, and every one has the usufruct of it only so long as he bears in himself the ego of the State, or is a 'loyal member of society'; in the opposite case the property is confiscated, or made to melt away by vexatious lawsuits. The property, then, is and remains *State property*, not property of the ego. That the State does not arbitrarily deprive the individual of what he has from the State means simply that the State does not rob itself. He who is State-ego, a good citizen or subject, holds his fief undisturbed as *such an ego*, not as being an ego of his own. According to the code, property is what I call mine 'by virtue of God and law'. But it is mine by virtue of God and law only so long as—the State has nothing against it.

In expropriations, disarmaments, and the like (as, when the exchequer confiscates inheritances if the heirs do not put in an appearance early enough) how plainly the otherwise veiled principle that only the *people*, 'the State', is proprietor, while the individual is feoffee, strikes the eye!

The State, I mean to say, cannot intend that anybody should *for his own sake* have property or actually be rich, or even well-to-do; it can acknowledge nothing, yield nothing, grant nothing to me as me. The State cannot check pauperism, because the poverty of possession is a poverty of me. He who *is* nothing but what chance or another—to wit, the State—makes out of him also *has* quite rightly nothing but what another gives him. And this other will *give* him only what he *deserves*, what he is worth by *service*. It is not he that realizes a value from himself; the State realizes a value from him.

National economy busies itself much with this subject. It lies far out beyond the 'national', however, and goes beyond the concepts and horizon of the State, which knows only State property and can distribute nothing else. For this reason it binds the possessions of property to *conditions*—as it binds everything to them, as in marriage, allowing validity only to the marriage sanctioned by it, and wresting this out of my power. But property is *my* property only when I hold it *unconditionally*: only I, an *unconditional* ego, have property, enter a relation of love, carry on free trade.[1]

---

[1] Stirner was familiar with the work of the major economists and his use of the term 'free trade' is intended to slight its economic usage as a technical description of the relationship between tariff laws and the import of commodities. He seeks to draw back such an *alienating* abstraction into the orbit of the individual; free trade, for him, refers to consumers creating their own code of intercourse, and finding the mode of consumption which suits their particular needs. At the meal table it is our thoughts, our affections, our spontaneous expressions much more than the fruit of our barter with the greengrocer which we seek to trade freely.

The State has no anxiety about me and mine, but about itself and its: I count for something to it only as *its child*, as 'a son of the country'; as *ego* I am nothing at all for it. For the State's understanding, what befalls me as ego is something accidental, my wealth as well as my impoverishment. But, if I with all that is mine am an accident in the State's eyes, this proves that it cannot comprehend *me*: *I* go beyond its concepts, or, its understanding is too limited to comprehend me. Therefore it cannot do anything for me either.

Pauperism is the *valuelessness of me*, the phenomenon that I cannot realize value from myself. For this reason State and pauperism are one and the same. The State does not let me come to my value, and continues in existence only through my valuelessness: it is for ever intent on *getting benefit* from me, exploiting me, turning me to account, using me up, even if the use it gets from me consists only in my supplying a *proles* (*proletariat*); it wants me to be 'its creature'.

Pauperism can be removed only when I as ego *realize value* from myself, when I give my own self value, and make my price myself. I must rise in revolt to rise in the world.

What I produce, flour, linen, or iron and coal, which I toilsomely win from the earth, is my work that I want to realize value from. But then I may long complain that I am not paid for my work according to its value: the payer will not listen to me, and the State likewise will maintain an apathetic attitude so long as it does not think it must 'appease' me that *I* may not break out with my dreaded might. But this 'appeasing' will be all, and, if it comes into my head to ask for more, the State turns against me with all the force of its lion-paws and eagle-claws: for it is the king of beasts, it is lion and eagle. If

I refuse to be content with the price that it fixes for my ware and labour, if I rather aspire to determine the price of my ware myself, that is, 'to pay myself', in the first place I come into a conflict with the buyers of the ware. If this were stilled by a mutual understanding, the State would not readily make objections; for how individuals get along with each other troubles it little, so long as therein they do not get in its way. Its damage and its danger begin only when they do not agree, but, in the absence of a settlement, take each other by the hair. The State cannot endure that man stand in a direct relation to man; it must step between as — *mediator*, must — *intervene*. What Christ was, what the saints, the Church were, the State has become — to wit, 'mediator'. It tears man from man to put itself between them as 'spirit'. The labourers who ask for higher pay are treated as criminals as soon as they want to *compel* it. What are they to do? Without compulsion they do not get it, and in compulsion the State sees a self-help, a determination of price by the ego, a genuine, free realization of value from his property, which it cannot admit of. What then are the labourers to do? Look to themselves and ask nothing about the State? — —

But, as is the situation with regard to my material work, so it is with my intellectual too. The State allows me to realize value from all my thoughts and to find customers for them (I do realize value from them, in the very fact that they bring me honour from the listeners, and the like); but only so long as *my* thoughts are — *its* thoughts. If, on the other hand, I harbour thoughts that it cannot approve (make its own), then it does not allow me at all to realize value from them, to bring them into *exchange*, into *commerce*. *My* thoughts are free only if they are granted to me by the State's *grace*, if they are the State's thoughts. It lets me philosophize freely only so far as I approve myself a 'philosopher of State'; *against* the State I must not philosophize, gladly as it tolerates my helping it out of its 'deficiencies', 'furthering' it. — Therefore, as I may behave only as an ego most graciously permitted by the State, provided with its testimonial of legitimacy and police pass, so too it is not granted me to realize value from what is mine, unless this proves to be its, which I hold as fief from it. My ways must be its ways, or else it distrains me; my thoughts its thoughts, or else it stops my mouth.

The State has nothing to be more afraid of than the value of me, and nothing must it more carefully guard against than every occasion that offers itself to me for *realizing value* from myself. *I* am the deadly enemy of the State, which always hovers between the alternatives, it or I. Therefore it strictly insists not only on not letting *me* have a standing, but also on keeping down what is *mine*. In the State there is no property, no property of the individual, but only State property. Only through the State have I what I have, as I am only through it what I am. My private property is only that which the State leaves to me of *its own, cutting off* others from it (depriving them, making it private): it is State property.

But, in opposition to the State, I feel more and more clearly that there is still left me a great might, the might over myself, over everything that pertains only to me and that *exists* only in being my own.

What do I do if my ways are no longer its ways, my thoughts no longer its thoughts? I look to myself, and ask nothing about it! In *my* thoughts, which I get sanctioned by no assent, grant, or grace, I have my real property, a property with which I can trade. For as mine they are my *creatures*, and I am in a position to give them away in return for *other* thoughts: I give them up and take in exchange for them others, which then are my new purchased property.

What then is *my* property? Nothing but what is in my *power*! To what property am I entitled? To every property to which I—*empower* myself. I give myself the right of property in taking property to myself, or giving myself the proprietor's *power*, full power, empowerment.[1]

Everything over which I have might that cannot be torn from me remains my property; well, then let might decide about property, and I will expect everything from my might! Alien might, might that I leave to another, makes me an owned slave: then let my own might make me an owner. Let me then withdraw the might that I have conceded to others out of ignorance regarding the strength of my *own* might! Let me say to myself, what my might reaches to is my property; and let me claim as property everything that I feel myself strong enough to attain, and let me extend my actual property by as much as *I* entitle, that is, empower, myself to take.

Here egoism, selfishness, must decide; not the principle of *love*, not love-motives like mercy, gentleness, good nature, or even justice and equity (for *justitia* too is a phenomenon of—love, a product of love): love knows only *sacrifices* and demands 'self-sacrifice'.

Egoism does not think of sacrificing anything, giving away anything that it wants; it simply decides, what I want I must have and will procure.

---

[1] Stirner takes up the basic Hobbesian insight that social and political life is conducted in terms of power and coercion, and turns it into a principle for individual action. Instead of drawing the inference that a strong State is necessary to avert the 'war of all against all' he finds the roots of liberation—and, in essence, sets the way for Nietzsche's 'will to power'.

All attempts to enact rational laws about property have put out from the bay of *love* into a desolate sea of regulations. Even socialism and communism cannot be excepted from this. Every one is to be provided with adequate means, for which it is little to the point whether one socialistically finds them still in a personal property, or communistically draws them from the community of goods. The individual's mind in this remains the same; it remains a mind of dependence. The distributing *board of equity* lets me have only what the sense of equity, its *loving* care for all, prescribes. For me, the individual, there lies no less of a check in *collective wealth* than in that of *individual others*; neither that is mine, nor this: whether the wealth belongs to the collectivity, which confers part of it on me, or to individual possessors, is for me the same constraint, as I cannot decide about either of the two. On the contrary, communism, by the abolition of all personal property, only presses me back still more into dependence on another, to wit, on the generality or collectivity; and, loudly as it always attacks the 'State', what it intends is itself again a State, a *status*, a condition hindering my free movement, a sovereign power over me. Communism rightly revolts against the pressure that I experience from individual proprietors; but still more horrible is the might that it puts in the hands of the collectivity.

Egoism takes another way to root out the non-possessing rabble. It does not say: Wait for what the board of equity will—bestow on you in the name of the collectivity (for such bestowal took place in 'States' from the most ancient times, each receiving 'according to his desert', and therefore according to the measure in which each was able to *deserve* it, to acquire it by *service*) but: Take hold, and take what you require! With this the war of all against all is declared. I alone decide what I will have.[1]

'Now, that is truly no new wisdom, for self-seekers have acted so at all times!' Not at all necessary either that the thing be new, if only *consciousness* of it is present. But this latter will not be able to claim great age, unless perhaps one counts in the Egyptian and Spartan law; for how little current it is appears even from the stricture above, which speaks with contempt of 'self-seekers'. One is to know just this, that the procedure of taking hold is not contemptible, but manifests the pure deed of the egoist at one with himself.

Only when I expect neither from individuals nor from a collectivity what I can give to myself, only then do I slip out of the snares of—love; the rabble ceases to be rabble only when it *takes hold*. Only the dread of taking hold, and the corresponding punishment thereof, makes it a rabble. Only that taking hold is *sin*, crime—only this dogma creates a rabble. For the fact that the rabble remains what it is, it (because it allows validity to that dogma) is to blame as well as, more especially, those who 'self-seekingly' (to give them back their favourite word) demand that the dogma be respected. In short, the lack of *consciousness* of that 'new wisdom', the old consciousness of sin, alone bears the blame.

If men reach the point of losing respect for property, every one will have property, as all slaves become free men as soon as they no longer respect the master as master. *Unions* will then, in this matter too, multiply the individual's means and secure his assailed property.

According to the communists' opinion the commune should be proprietor. On the contrary, *I* am proprietor,

[1] In this section the elitist and fascist elements of Stirner's anarchism become explicit.

and I only come to an understanding with others about my property. If the commune does not do what suits me, I rise against it and defend my property. I am proprietor, but property is *not sacred*. I should be merely possessor? No, hitherto one was only possessor, secured in the possession of a parcel by leaving others also in possession of a parcel; but now *everything* belongs to me, I am proprietor of *everything that I require* and can get possession of. If it is said socialistically, society gives me what I require—then the egoist says, I take what I require. If the communists conduct themselves as ragamuffins, the egoist behaves as proprietor.

(Ego 333–42)

Property, therefore, should not and cannot be abolished; it must rather be torn from ghostly hands and become *my* property; then the erroneous consciousness, that I cannot entitle myself to as much as I require, will vanish. —

'But what cannot man require!' Well, whoever requires much, and understands how to get it, has at all times helped himself to it, as Napoleon did with the Continent and France with Algiers. Hence the exact point is that the respectful 'rabble' should learn at last to help itself to what it requires. If it reaches out too far for you, why, then, defend yourselves. You have no need at all to good-heartedly—bestow anything on it; and, when it learns to know itself, it—or rather: whoever of the rabble learns to know himself, he—casts off the rabble-quality in refusing your alms with thanks. But it remains ridiculous that you declare the rabble 'sinful and criminal' if it is not pleased to live from your favours because it can do something in its own favour. Your bestowals cheat it and put it off. Defend your property, then you will be strong; if, on the other hand, you want to retain your ability to bestow, and perhaps actually have the more political rights the more alms (poor-rates) you can give, this will work just as long as the recipients let you work it.

In short, the property question cannot be solved so amicably as the socialists, yes, even the communists, dream. It is solved only by the war of all against all. The poor become free and proprietors only when they—*rise*. Bestow ever so much on them, they will still always want more; for they want nothing less than that at last—nothing more be bestowed.[1]

It will be asked, but how then will it be when the have-nots take heart? Of what sort is the settlement to be? One might as well ask that I cast a child's nativity. What a slave will do as soon as he has broken his fetters, one must—wait.

(*Ego* 342-4)

*   *   *

COMPETITION

Is 'free competition' then really 'free'? nay, is it really a 'competition'—to wit, one of *persons*—as it gives itself out to be because on this title it bases its right? It originated, you know, in persons becoming free of all personal rule. Is a competition 'free' which the State, this ruler in the civic principle, hems in by a thousand barriers? There is a rich manufacturer doing a brilliant business, and I should like to compete with him. 'Go ahead', says the State; 'I have no objection to make to your *person* as

---

[1] Again, as soon as individual 'up-rising' becomes mass 'up-rising' the danger of the slide from anarchism into fascism is present. The content of this paragraph is at the 'root of the Right'.

competitor.' Yes, I reply, but for that I need a space for
buildings, I need money! 'That's bad; but, if you have
no money, you cannot compete. You must not take
anything from anybody, for I protect property and grant
it privileges.' Free competition is not 'free', because I
lack the THINGS for competition. Against my *person* no
objection can be made, but because I have not the things
my person too must step to the rear. And who has the
necessary things? Perhaps that manufacturer? Why, from
him I could take them away! No, the State has them as
property, the manufacturer only as fief, as possession.

But, since it is no use trying it with the manufacturer, I
will compete with that professor of jurisprudence; the
man is a nincompoop, and I, who know a hundred times
more than he, shall make his class-room empty. 'Have you
studied and graduated, friend?' No, but what of that? I
understand abundantly what is necessary for instruction
in that department. 'Sorry, but competition is not "free"
here. Against your person there is nothing to be said, but
the *thing*, the doctor's degree is lacking. And this degree I,
the State, demand. Ask me for it respectfully first; then
we will see what is to be done."

This, therefore, is the 'freedom' of competition. The
State, *my lord*, first qualifies me to compete.

But do *persons* really compete? No, again *things* only!
Moneys in the first place, etc.

In the rivalry one will always be left behind another
(as, a poetaster behind a poet). But it makes a difference
whether the means that the unlucky competitor lacks are
personal or material, and likewise whether the material
means can be won by *personal energy* or are to be obtained
only by *grace*, only as a present; as when the poorer man
must leave, that is, present, to the rich man his riches.
But, if I must all along wait for the State's *approval* to

obtain or to use (as in the case of graduation) the means, I have the means by the *grace of the State*.*

Free competition, therefore, has only the following meaning: To the State all rank as its equal children, and every one can scud and run to earn the *State's goods and largesse*. Therefore all do chase after havings, holdings, possessions (be it of money or offices, titles of honour, etc.), after the *things*.

In the mind of the bourgeoisie every one is possessor or 'owner'. Now, whence comes it that the great majority have in fact next to nothing? From this, that the great majority are already joyful over being possessors at all, even though it be of some rags, as children are joyful in their first trousers or even the first penny that is presented to them. More precisely, however, the matter is to be taken as follows. Liberalism came forward at once with the declaration that it belonged to man's essence not to be property, but proprietor. As the consideration here was about 'man', not about the individual, the how-much (which formed exactly the point of the individual's special interest) was left to him. Hence the individual's egoism retained room for the freest play in this how-much, and carried on an indefatigable competition.

However, the lucky egoism had to become a snag in the way of the less fortunate, and the latter, still keeping its feet planted on the principle of humanity, put forward the question as to how-much of possession, and answered it to the effect that 'man must have as much as he requires.'

* In colleges and universities poor men compete with rich. But they are able to do so in most cases only through scholarships, which — a significant point — almost all come down to us from a time when free competition was still far from being a controlling principle. The principle of competition founds no scholarship, but says, Help yourself; provide yourself the means. What the State gives for such purposes it pays out from interested motives, to educate 'servants' for itself.

Will it be possible for *my* egoism to let itself be satisfied with that? What 'man' requires furnishes by no means a scale for measuring me and my needs; for I may have use for less or more. I must rather have so much as I am competent to appropriate.

Competition suffers from the unfavourable circumstance that the *means* for competing are not at every one's command, because they are not taken from personality, but from accident. Most are *without means*, and for this reason *without goods*.

(*Ego* 345–8)

But is my work then really, as the communists suppose, my sole competence? or does not this consist rather in everything that I am competent for? And does not the workers' society itself have to concede this, in supporting also the sick, children, old men—in short, those who are incapable of work? These are still competent for a good deal, for instance, to preserve their life instead of taking it. If they are competent to cause you to desire their continued existence, they have a power over you. To him who exercised utterly no power over you, you would vouchsafe nothing; he might perish.

Therefore, what you are *competent* for is your *competence*! If you are competent to furnish pleasure to thousands, then thousands will pay you an honorarium for it; for it would stand in your power to forbear doing it, hence they must purchase your deed. If you are not competent to *captivate* any one, you may simply starve.

Now am I, who am competent for much, perchance to have no advantage over the less competent?

We are all in the midst of abundance; now shall I not help myself as well as I can, but only wait and see how much is left me in an equal division?

Against competition there rises up the principle of ragamuffin society — *distribution*.

To be looked upon as a mere *part*, part of society, the individual cannot bear — because he is *more*; his uniqueness puts from it this limited conception.

Hence he does not await his competence from the sharing of others, and even in the workers' society there arises the misgiving that in an equal distribution the strong will be exploited by the weak; he awaits his competence rather from himself, and says now, what I am competent to have, that is my competence.

What competence does not the child possess in its smiling, its playing, its screaming! in short, in its mere existence! Are you capable of resisting its desire? Or do you not hold out to it, as mother, your breast; as father, as many of your possessions as it needs? It compels you, therefore it possesses what you call yours.

If your person is of consequence to me, you pay me with your very existence; if I am concerned only with one of your qualities, then your compliance, perhaps, or your aid, has a value (a money value) for me, and I *purchase* it.

If you do not know how to give yourself any other than a money value in my estimation, there may arise the case of which history tells us, that Germans, sons of the fatherland, were sold to America. Should those who let themselves to be traded in be worth more to the seller? He preferred the cash to this living ware that did not understand how to make itself precious to him. That he discovered nothing more valuable in it was assuredly a defect of his competence; but it takes a rogue to give more than he has. How should he show respect when he did not have it, no, hardly could have it for such a rabble![1]

[1] The preceding paragraphs advocating competition as the fundamental socio-economic principle suggest that Stirner follows in the track of *laissez-*

You behave egoistically when you respect each other neither as possessors nor as ragamuffins or workers, but as a part of your competence, as *'useful bodies'*. Then you will neither give anything to the possessor ('proprietor') for his possessions, nor to him who works, but only to him whom *you require*. The North Americans ask themselves, Do we require a king? and answer: not a farthing are he and his work worth to us.

If it is said that competition throws every thing open to all, the expression is not accurate, and it is better put thus: competition makes everything purchasable. In *abandoning*[1] it to them, competition leaves it to their appraisal[2] or their estimation, and demands a price[3] for it.

But the would-be buyers mostly lack the means to make themselves buyers: they have no money. For money, then, the purchasable things are indeed to be had ('For money everything is to be had!'), but it is exactly money that is lacking. Where is one to get money, this current or circulating property? Know then, you have as much money[4] as you have—might; for you count[5] for as much as you make yourself count for.

One pays not with money, of which there may come a lack, but with his competence, by which alone we are 'competent'; for one is proprietor only so far as the arm of our power reaches.

Weitling has thought out a new means of payment—

---

faire economics. He does affirm the essentials of economic individualism, but only in generalizing them to every sphere of social action. The purely economic trade of *laissez-faire* and the restless accumulation of capitalist individualism constitute the gross drudgeries of life for him. A valuable existence pays for itself.

[1] *preisgeben.*
[2] *Preis.*
[3] *Preis.*
[4] *Geld.*
[5] *gelten.*

work. But the true means of payment remains, as always, *competence*. With what you have 'within your competence' you pay. Therefore think on the enlargement of your competence.

This being admitted, they are nevertheless right on hand again with the motto, 'To each according to his competence!'[1] Who is to *give* to me according to my competence? Society? Then I should have to put up with its estimation. Rather, I shall *take* according to my competence.

'All belongs to all!' This proposition springs from the same unsubstantial theory. To each belongs only what he is competent for. If I say, The world belongs to me, properly that too is empty talk, which has a meaning only in so far as I respect no alien property. But to me belongs only as much as I am competent for, or have within my competence.

One is not worthy to have what one, through weakness, lets be taken from him; one is not worthy of it because one is not capable of it.

They raise a mighty uproar over the 'wrong of a thousand years' which is being committed by the rich against the poor. As if the rich were to blame for poverty, and the poor were not in like manner responsible for riches! Is there another difference between the two than that of competence and incompetence, of the competent and incompetent? Wherein, pray, does the crime of the rich consist? 'In their hardheartedness.' But who then have maintained the poor? Who have cared for their nourishment? Who have given alms, those alms that have even their name from mercy (*eleemosyne*)? Have not the

[1] Stirner's argument here, as far as it is intended as a critique of communism, becomes inconsistent; communism is normally associated with the motto, '*From* each according to his ability, *to* each according to his need.'

rich been 'merciful' at all times? Are they not to this day
'tender-hearted', as poor-taxes, hospitals, foundations of
all sorts, etc., prove?

But all this does not satisfy you! Doubtless, then, they
are to *share* with the poor? Now you are demanding that
they shall abolish poverty. Apart from the point that
there might be hardly one among you who would act so,
and that this one would be a fool for it, do ask yourselves:
why should the rich let go their fleeces and give up *themselves*, thereby pursuing the advantage of the poor rather
than their own? You, who have your thaler daily, are
rich above thousands who live on four groschen. Is it
for your interest to share with the thousands, or is it not
rather for theirs? — —

With competition is connected less the intention to do
the thing *best* than the intention to make it as *profitable*,
as productive, as possible. Hence people study to get into
the civil service (pot-boiling study), study cringing and
flattery, routine and 'acquaintance with business', work
'for appearance'. Hence, while it is apparently a matter
of doing 'good service', in truth only a 'good business' and
earning of money are looked out for. The job is done only
ostensibly for the job's sake, but in fact on account of the
gain that it yields. One would indeed prefer not to be
censor, but one wants to be—advanced; one would like
to judge, administer, etc., according to his best convictions, but one is afraid of transference or even dismissal;
one must, above all things—live.

Thus these goings-on are a fight for *dear life*, and, in
gradation upward, for more or less of a 'good living'.

And yet, withal, their whole round of toil and care
brings in for most only 'bitter life' and 'bitter poverty'.
All the bitter painstaking for this!

Restless acquisition does not let us take breath, take a

calm *enjoyment*: we do not get the comfort of our possessions.

But the organization of labour touches only such labours as others can do for us, slaughtering, tillage, and the like; the rest remain egoistic, because no one can in your stead elaborate your musical compositions, carry out your projects of painting, etc.; nobody can replace Raphael's labours. The latter are labours of a unique person, which only he is competent to achieve, while the former deserved to be called 'human', since what is anybody's *own* in them is of slight account, and almost 'any man' can be trained to it.

Now, as society can regard only labours for the common benefit, *human* labours, he who does anything *unique* remains without its care; indeed, he may find himself disturbed by its intervention. The unique person will work himself forth out of society all right, but society brings forth no unique person.

Hence it is at any rate helpful that we come to an agreement about *human* labours, that they may not, as under competition, claim all our time and toil. So far communism will bear its fruits. For before the dominion of the bourgeoisie even that for which all men are qualified, or can be qualified, was tied up to a few and withheld from the rest: it was a privilege. To the bourgeoisie it looked equitable to leave free all that seemed to exist for every 'man'. But, because left free, it was yet given to no one, but rather left to each to be got hold of by his *human* power. By this the mind was turned to the acquisition of the human, which henceforth beckoned to every one; and there arose a movement which one hears so loudly bemoaned under the name of 'materialism'.

Communism seeks to check its course, spreading the belief that the human is not worth so much discomfort, and, with sensible arrangements, could be gained without the great expense of time and powers which has hitherto seemed requisite.

But for whom is time to be gained? For what does man require more time than is necessary to refresh his wearied powers of labour? Here communism is silent.

For what? To take comfort in himself as the unique, after he has done his part as man!

In the first joy over being allowed to stretch out their hands towards everything human, people forgot to want anything else; and they competed away vigorously, as if the possession of the human were the goal of all our wishes.

But they have run themselves tired, and are gradually noticing that 'possession does not give happiness'. Therefore they are thinking of obtaining the necessary by an easier bargain, and spending on it only so much time and toil as its indispensableness exacts. Riches fall in price, and contented poverty, the carefree ragamuffin, becomes the seductive ideal.

Should such human activities, that everyone is confident of his capacity for, be highly salaried, and sought for with toil and expenditure of all life-forces? Even in the every-day form of speech, 'If I were minister, or even (the —,) then it should go quite otherwise', that confidence expresses itself—that one holds himself capable of playing the part of such a dignitary; one does get a perception that to things of this sort there belongs not uniqueness, but only a culture which is attainable, even if not exactly by all, at any rate by many; that for such a thing one need only be an ordinary man.

If we assume that, as *order* belongs to the essence of the State, so *subordination* too is founded in its nature, then we see that the subordinates, or those who have received preferment, disproportionately *overcharge* and *overreach* those who are put in the lower ranks. But the latter take heart (first from the socialist standpoint, but certainly with egoistic consciousness later, of which we will therefore at once give their speech some colouring) for the question, by what then is your property secure, you creatures of preferment? — and give themselves the answer, by our refraining from interference! And so by *our* protection! And what do you give us for it? Kicks and disdain you give to the 'common people'; police supervision, and a catechism with the chief sentence 'Respect what is *not yours*, what belongs to *others*! respect others, and especially your superiors!' But we reply, 'If you want our respect, *buy* it for a price agreeable to us. We will leave you your property, if you give a due equivalent for this leaving.' Really, what equivalent does the general in time of peace give for the many thousands of his yearly income? — another for the sheer hundred-thousands and millions yearly? What equivalent do you give for our chewing potatoes and looking calmly on while you swallow oysters? Only buy our oysters as dear as we have to buy your potatoes, then you may go on eating them. Or do you suppose the oysters do not belong to us as much as to you? You will make an outcry over *violence* if we reach out our hands and help consume them, and you are right. Without violence we do not get them, as you no less have them by doing violence to us.

But take the oysters and have done with it, and let us consider our nearer property, labour; for the other is only possession. We distress ourselves twelve hours in the sweat of our face, and you offer us a few groschen for it. Then take the like for your labour too. Are you not willing? You fancy that our labour is richly repaid with that wage, while yours on the other hand is worth a wage of many thousands. But, if you did not rate yours so high, and gave us a better chance to realize value from ours, then we might well, if the case demanded it, bring to pass still more important things than you do for the many thousand thalers; and, if you got only such wages as we, you would soon grow more industrious in order to receive more. But, if you render any service that seems to us worth ten and a hundred times more than our own labour, why, then you shall get a hundred times more for it too; we, on the other hand, think also to produce for you things for which you will requite us more highly than with the ordinary day's wages. We shall be willing to get along with each other all right, if only we have first agreed on this—that neither any longer needs to—*present* anything to the other. Then we may perhaps actually go so far as to pay even the cripples and sick and old an appropriate price for not parting from us by hunger and want; for, if we want them to live, it is fitting also that we—purchase the fulfilment of our will. I say 'purchase', and therefore do not mean a wretched 'alms'. For their life is the property even of those who cannot work; if we (no matter for what reason) want them not to withdraw this life from us, we can mean to bring this to pass only by purchase; indeed, we shall perhaps (maybe because we like to have friendly faces about us) even want a life of comfort for them. In short, we want nothing presented by you, but neither will we present you with anything. For centuries we have handed alms to you from good-hearted—stupidity, have doled out the mite of the poor and given to the masters the things that are—not the masters'; now just open your wallet, for henceforth our wares rise in price quite enormously. We do not want to take from you anything, anything at all, only you are to pay better for what you want to have. What then have you? 'I have an estate of a thousand acres.' And I am your ploughman, and will henceforth attend to your fields only for one thaler a day wages. 'Then I'll take another'. You won't find any, for we ploughmen are no longer doing otherwise, and, if one puts in an appearance who takes less, then let him beware of us. There is the housemaid, she too is now demanding as much, and you will no longer find one below this price. 'Why, then it is all over with me.' Not so fast! You will doubtless take in as much as we; and, if it should not be so, we will leave you enough to live like us. 'But I am accustomed to live better.' We have nothing against that, but it is not our look-out; if you can clear more, go ahead. Are we to hire out under rates, that you may have a good living? The rich man always puts off the poor with the words, 'What does your want concern me? See to it how you make your way through the world; that is *your affair*, not mine.' Well, let us let it be our affair, then, and let us not let the means that we have to realize value from ourselves be pilfered from us by the rich. 'But you uncultured people really do not need so much.' Well, we are taking somewhat more in order that for it we may procure the culture that we perhaps need. 'But, if you thus bring down the rich, who is then to support the arts and sciences hereafter?' Oh, well, we must make it up by numbers; we club together, that gives a nice little sum—besides, you rich men now buy only the most tasteless books and the most lamentable Madonnas or a pair of lively dancer's legs. 'O ill-starred equality!' No, my good old sir, nothing of equality. We only want to count for what we are worth, and, if you are worth more, you shall count for more right along. We only want to be *worth our price*, and think to show ourselves worth the price that you will pay.

Is the State likely to be able to awaken so secure a

temper and so forceful a self-consciousness in the menial? Can it make man feel himself? Indeed, may it even do so much as set this goal for itself? Can it want the individual to recognize his value and realize this value from himself? Let us keep the parts of the double question separate, and see first whether the State can bring about such a thing. As the unanimity of the ploughmen is required, only this unanimity can bring it to pass, and a State law would be evaded in a thousand ways by competition and in secret. But can the State bear with it? The State cannot possibly bear with people's suffering coercion from another than it; it could not, therefore, admit the self-help of the unanimous ploughmen against those who want to engage for lower wages. Suppose, however, that the State made the law, and all the ploughmen were in accord with it: could the State bear with it then?

In the isolated case—yes; but the isolated case is more than that, it is a case of *principle*. The question therein is of the whole range of *the ego's self-realization of value from himself*, and therefore also of his self-consciousness *against* the State. So far the communists keep company; but, as self-realization of value from self necessarily directs itself against the State, so it does against *society* too, and therewith reaches out beyond the commune and the communistic—out of egoism.

(Ego 349–61)

But, even if these offices may vest in every one, yet it is only the individual's unique force, peculiar to him alone, that gives them, so to speak, life and significance. That he does not manage his office like an 'ordinary man', but puts in the competence of his uniqueness, this he is not yet paid for when he is paid only in general as an official or a minister. If he has done it so as to earn your thanks, and you wish to retain this thankworthy force of the unique one, you must not pay him like a mere man who performed only what was human, but as one who accomplishes what is unique. Do the like with your labour, do!

There cannot be a general schedule-price fixed for my uniqueness as there can for what I do as man. Only for the latter can a schedule-price be set.

Go right on, then, setting up a general appraisal for human labours, but do not deprive your uniqueness of its desert.

Human or *general* needs can be satisfied through society; for satisfaction of *unique* needs you must do some seeking. A friend and a friendly service, or even an individual's service, society cannot procure you. And yet you will every moment be in need of such a service, and on the slightest occasions require somebody who is helpful to you. Therefore do not rely on society, but see to it that you have the wherewithal to—purchase the fulfilment of your wishes.

Whether money is to be retained among egoists? To the old stamp an inherited possession adheres. If you no longer let yourselves be paid with it, it is ruined: if you do nothing for this money, it loses all power. Cancel the *inheritance*, and you have broken off the executor's court-seal. For now everything is an inheritance, whether it be already inherited or await its heir. If it is yours, wherefore do you let it be sealed up from you? Why do you respect the seal?

But why should you not create a new money? Do you then annihilate the ware in taking from it the hereditary stamp? Now, money is a ware, and an essential *means* or competence. For it protects against the ossification of resources, keeps them in flux and brings to pass their exchange. If you know a better medium of exchange, go ahead; yet it will be a 'money' again. It is not the money that does you damage, but your incompetence to take it. Let your competence take effect, collect yourselves, and there will be no lack of money—of your money, the money of *your* stamp. But working I do not call 'letting your competence take effect'. Those who are only 'looking for work' and 'willing to work hard' are preparing for their own selves the infallible upshot—to be out of work.

Good and bad luck depend on money. It is a power in the bourgeois period for this reason, that it is only wooed on all hands like a girl, indissolubly wedded by nobody. All the romance and chivalry of *wooing* for a dear object come to life again in competition. Money, an object of longing, is carried off by the bold 'captains of industry'.

He who has luck takes home the bride. The ragamuffin has luck; he takes her into his household, 'society', and destroys the virgin. In his house she is no longer bride, but wife; and with her virginity her family name is also lost. As housewife the maiden Money is called 'Labour', for 'Labour' is her husband's name. She is a possession of her husband's.

To bring this figure to an end, the child of Labour and Money is again a girl, an unwedded one and therefore Money but with the certain descent from Labour, her father. The form of the face, the 'effigy', bears another stamp.

Finally, as regards competition once more, it has a continued existence by this very means, that all do not attend to *their affair* and come to an *understanding* with each other about it. Bread is a need of all the inhabitants of a city; therefore they might easily agree on setting up a public bakery. Instead of this, they leave the furnishing of the needful to the competing bakers. Just so meat to the butchers, wine to wine merchants, etc.

Abolishing competition is not equivalent to favouring the guild. The difference is this: In the *guild*, baking, etc., is the affair of the guild-brothers; in *competition*, the affair of chance competitors; in the *union*, of those who require baked goods, and therefore my affair, yours, the affair of neither the guild nor the concessionary baker, but the affair of the *united*.[1]

If *I* do not trouble myself about *my* affair, I must be *content* with what it pleases others to vouchsafe me. To have bread is my affair, my wish and desire, and yet people leave that to the bakers and hope at most to obtain through their wrangling, their getting ahead of each other, their rivalry—in short, their competition—an advantage which one could not count on in the case of the guild-brothers who were lodged *entirely* and *alone* in the proprietorship of the baking franchise.—What everyone requires, everyone should also take a hand in procuring and producing; it is *his* affair, his property, not the property of the guild or concessionary master.

Let us look back once more. The world belongs to the children of this world, the children of men; it is no longer God's world, but man's. As much as every man can procure of it, let him call his; only the true man, the State, human society or mankind, will look to it that each shall make nothing else his own than what he appropriates as man, in human fashion. Inhuman appropriation is that which is not consented to by man, that is, it is a 'criminal' appropriation, as the human, *vice versa*, is a 'rightful' one, one acquired in the 'way of law'.

[1] Marx and Engels, in *The German Ideology*, are particularly critical of this utopian aspect of Stirner's socio-economic theory, which pays no heed to the exigencies of production and competition in capitalist society; they dub it 'mediaeval philistinism'.

So they talk since the Revolution.

But my property is not a thing, since this has an existence independent of me; only my might is my own. Not this tree, but my might or control over it, is what is mine.

Now, how is this might perversely expressed? They say I have a *right* to this tree, or it is my *rightful* property. So I have *earned* it by might. That the might must last in order that the tree may also be *held*—or better, that the might is not a thing existing of itself, but has existence solely in the *mighty ego*, in me the mighty—is forgotten. Might, like other of my *qualities* (humanity, majesty, etc.), is exalted to something existing of itself, so that it still exists long after it has ceased to be *my* might. Thus transformed into a ghost, might is—*right*. This *eternalized* might is not extinguished even with my death, but is transferred or 'bequeathed'.

Things now really belong not to me, but to right.

On the other side, this is nothing but a hallucination. For the individual's might becomes permanent and a right only by others joining their might with his. The delusion consists in their believing that they cannot withdraw their might. The same phenomenon over again; might is separated from me. I cannot take back the might that I gave to the possessor. One has 'granted power of attorney', has given away his power, has renounced coming to a better mind.

The proprietor can give up his might and his right to a thing by giving the thing away, squandering it, and the like. And *we* should not be able likewise to let go the might that we lend to him?

The rightful man, the *just*, desires to call nothing his own that he does not have 'rightly' or have the right to, and therefore only *legitimate property*.

Now, who is to be judge, and adjudge his right to him? At last, surely, Man, who imparts to him the rights of man: then he can say, in an infinitely broader sense than Terence, *humani nihil a me alienum puto*, that is, *the human is my property*. However he may go about it, so long as he occupies this standpoint he cannot get clear of a judge; and in our time the multifarious judges that had been selected have set themselves against each other in two persons at deadly enmity — to wit, in God and Man. The one party appeal to divine right, the other to human right or the rights of man.

So much is clear, that in neither case does the individual do the entitling himself.

Just pick me out an action today that would not be a violation of right! Every moment the rights of man are trampled under foot by one side, while their opponents cannot open their mouth without uttering a blasphemy against divine right. Give an alms, you mock at a right of man, because the relation of beggar and benefactor is an inhuman relation; utter a doubt, you sin against a divine right. Eat dry bread with contentment, you violate the right of man by your equanimity; eat it with discontent, you revile divine right by your repining. There is not one among you who does not commit a crime at every moment; your speeches are crimes, and every hindrance to your freedom of speech is no less a crime. Ye are criminals altogether!

Yet you are so only in that you all stand on the *ground of right*, in that you do not even know, and understand how to value, the fact that you are criminals.

Inviolable or *sacred* property has grown on this very ground; it is a *juridical concept*.

A dog sees the bone in another's power, and stands off only if it feels itself too weak. But man respects the other's *right* to his bone. The latter action, therefore, ranks as *human*, the former as *brutal* or 'egoistic'.

And as here, so in general, it is called '*human*' when one sees in everything something *spiritual* (here right), makes everything a ghost and takes his attitude towards it as towards a ghost, which one can indeed scare away at its appearance, but cannot kill. It is human to look at what is individual not as individual, but as a generality.

In nature as such I no longer respect anything, but know myself to be entitled to everything against it; in the tree in that garden, on the other hand, I must respect *alienness* (they say, in a one-sided fashion, 'property'), I must keep my hand off it. This comes to an end only when I can indeed leave that tree to another as I leave my stick, etc., to another, but do not in advance regard it as alien to me, sacred. Rather, I commit no *crime* by felling it, if I will, and it remains my property, however long I resign it to others: it is and remains *mine*. In the banker's fortune I as little see anything alien as Napoleon did in the territories of kings: we have no *fear* of '*conquering*' it, and we look about us for the means thereto. We strip off from it, therefore, the *spirit* of *alienness*, of which we had been afraid.

Therefore it is necessary that I do not lay claim to anything more *as man*, but to everything as I, this I; and accordingly to nothing human, but to mine; that is, nothing that pertains to me as man, but—what I will and because I will it.

Rightful, or legitimate, property of another will be only that which *you* are content to recognize as such. If your content ceases, then this property has lost legitimacy for you, and you will laugh at absolute right to it.

(*Ego* 362–9)

* * *

FREEDOM OF THE PRESS—A PARADIGM OF 'FREEDOM FROM'

What a sighing for liberty of the press! What then is the press to be liberated from? Surely from a dependence, a belonging, and a liability to service! But to liberate himself from that is everyone's affair, and it may with safety be assumed that, when you have delivered yourself from liability to service, that which you compose and write will also belong to you as your *own* instead of having been thought and indicted *in the service* of some power. What can a believer in Christ say and have printed, that should be freer from that belief in Christ than he himself is? If I cannot or may not write something, perhaps the primary fault lies with *me*. Little as this seems to hit the point, so near is the application nevertheless to be found. By a press-law I draw a boundary for my publications, or let one be drawn, beyond which wrong and its *punishment* follows. I myself *limit* myself.

If the press was to be free, nothing would be so important as precisely its liberation from every coercion that could be put on it in the *name of a law*. And, that it might come to that, I my own self should have to have absolved myself from obedience to the law.

Certainly, the absolute liberty of the press is, like every absolute liberty, a nonentity. The press can become free from full many a thing, but always only from what I too am free from. If we make ourselves free from the sacred, if we have become *graceless* and *lawless*, our words too will become so.

As little as *we* can be declared clear of every coercion in the world, so little can our writing be withdrawn from it. But as free as we are, so free we can make it too.

It must therefore become our *own*, instead of, as hitherto, serving a spook.

People do not yet know what they mean by their cry for liberty of the press. What they ostensibly ask is that the State shall set the press free; but what they are really after, without knowing it themselves, is that the press become free from the State, or clear of the State. The former is a *petition to* the State, the latter an *insurrection against* the State. As a 'petition for right', even as a serious demanding of the right of liberty of the press, it presupposes the State as the giver, and can hope only for a *present*, a permission, a chartering. Possible, no doubt, that a State acts so senselessly as to grant the demanded present; but you may bet everything that those who receive the present will not know how to use it so long as they regard the State as a truth: they will not trespass against this 'sacred thing', and will call for a penal press-law against everyone who would be willing to dare this.

In a word, the press does not become free from what I am not free from.

Do I perhaps hereby show myself an opponent of the liberty of the press? Or the contrary, I only assert that one will never get it if one wants only it, the liberty of the press, if one sets out only for an unrestricted permission. Only beg from the start for this permission: you may wait for ever for it, for there is no one in the world who could give it to you. As long as you want to have yourselves 'entitled' to the use of the press by a permission, you live in vain hope and complaint.

'Nonsense! Why, you yourself, who harbour such thoughts as stand in your book, can unfortunately bring them to publicity only through a lucky chance or by stealth; nevertheless you will inveigh against one's pressing and importuning his own State till it gives the refused permission to print?' But an author thus addressed would perhaps—for the impudence of such people goes far—give the following reply: 'Consider well what you say! What then do I do to procure myself liberty of the press for my book? Do I ask for permission, or do I not rather, without any question of legality, seek a favourable occasion and grasp it in complete recklessness of the State and its wishes? I—the terrifying word must be uttered—I cheat the State. You unconsciously do the same. From your tribunes you talk it into the idea that it must give up its sanctity and inviolability, it must lay itself bare to the attacks of writers, without needing on that account to fear danger. But you are imposing on it; for its existence is done for as soon as it loses its unapproachability. To *you* indeed it might well accord liberty of writing, as England has done; you are *believers in the State* and incapable of writing against the State, however much you would like to reform it and 'remedy its defects'. But what if opponents of the State availed themselves of free utterance, and stormed out against Church, State, morals, and everything 'sacred' with inexorable reasons? You would then be the first, in terrible agonies, to call into life the *September laws*.[1] Too late would you then rue the stupidity that earlier made you so ready to fool and palaver into compliance the State, or the government of the State.—But I prove by my act only two things. This for one, that the liberty of the press is always bound to 'favourable opportunities', and accordingly will never be an absolute liberty; but secondly this, that he who would enjoy it must seek out and, if possible, create the favourable opportunity, availing himself of his *own advantage* against the State; and counting

---

[1] A series of very repressive measures enacted in France in September 1835 in the reign of Louis Philippe; one of them was a severe press restriction, aimed at curtailing the expression of radical views and opinions.

himself and his will more than the State and every
'superior' power. Not in the State, but only against it, can
the liberty of the press be carried through; if it is to be
established, it is to be obtained not as the consequence of a
petition but as the work of an *insurrection*. Every petition and
every motion for liberty of the press is already an insurrection, be it conscious or unconscious: a thing which
Philistine halfness alone will not and cannot confess to
itself until, with a shrinking shudder, it shall see it clearly
and irrefutably by the outcome. For the requested liberty
of the press has indeed a friendly and well-meaning face at
the beginning, as it is not in the least minded ever to let
the 'insolence of the press' come into vogue; but little by
little its heart grows more hardened, and the inference
flatters its way in that really a liberty is not a liberty if it
stands in the *service* of the State, or morals, or of the law.
A liberty indeed from the coercion of censorship, it is yet
not a liberty from the coercion of law. The press, once
seized by the lust for liberty, always wants to grow freer,
till at last the writer says to himself, really I am not wholly
free till I ask about nothing; and writing is free only when
it is my *own*, dictated to me by no power or authority, by
no faith, no dread; the press must not be free — that is too
little — it must be *mine*: — *ownness of the press* or *property in
the press*, that is what I will take.'[1]

(*Ego* 371-6)

'Let my people, if they will, go without liberty of free
press, I will manage to print by force or ruse; I get my
permission to print only from — *myself* and my strength.

'If the press is *my own*, I as little need a permission of the
State for employing it as I seek that permission in order to

---

[1] An anticipation of modern underground rhetoric as much as fascist
attitudes to the press.

blow my nose. The press is my *property* from the moment when nothing is more to me than myself; for from this moment State, Church, people, society, and the like, cease, because they have to thank for their existence only the disrespect that I have for myself, and with the vanishing of this undervaluation they themselves are extinguished: they exist only when they exist *above me*, exist only as *powers* and *power-holders*. Or can you imagine a State whose citizens one and all think nothing of it? It would be as certainly a dream, an existence in seeming, as "united Germany".

'The press is my own as soon as I myself am my own, a self-owned man: to the egoist belongs the world, because he belongs to no power of the world.

'With this my press might still be very *unfree*, as at this moment. But the world is large, and one helps himself as well as he can. If I were willing to abate from the *property* of my press, I could easily attain the point where I might everywhere have as much printed as my fingers produced. But, as I want to assert my property, I must necessarily swindle my enemies. "Would you not accept their permission if it were given you?" Certainly, with joy; for their permission would be to me a proof that I had fooled them and started them on the road to ruin. I am not concerned for their permission, but so much the more for their folly and their overthrow. I do not sue for their permission as if I flattered myself (like the political liberals) that we both, they and I, could make out peaceably alongside and with each other, yes, probably raise and prop each other; but I sue for it in order to make them bleed to death by it, that the permitters themselves may cease at last. I act as a conscious enemy, overreaching them and *utilizing* their heedlessness.

'The press is *mine* when I recognize outside myself no

judge whatever over its utilization, when my writing is no longer determined by morality or religion or respect for the State laws or the like, but by me and my egoism!'

(*Ego* 376–8)

The liberty of the press is also demanded under the name of a 'general human right'. Against this the objection was well-founded that not every man knew how to use it rightly, for not every individual was truly man. Never did a government refuse it to *Man* as such; but *Man* writes nothing, for the reason that he is a ghost. It always refused it to *individuals* only, and gave it to others, its organs. If then one would have it for all, one must assert outright that it is due to the individual, me, not to man or to the individual so far as he is man. Besides, another than a man (a beast) can make no use of it. The French government, for example, does not dispute the liberty of the press as a right of man, but demands from the individual a security for his really being man; for it assigns liberty of the press not to the individual, but to man.

Under the exact pretence that it was *not human*, what was mine was taken from me! What was human was left to me undiminished.

Liberty of the press can bring about only a *responsible* press; the *irresponsible* proceeds solely from property in the press.

(*Ego* 379–80)

*   *   *

LOVE

'God is love! All times and all races recognize in this word the central point of Christianity.' God, who is love, is an officious God: he cannot leave the world in peace, but wants to make it *blest*. 'God became man to make men divine.'[1] He has his hand in the game everywhere, and nothing happens without it; everywhere he has his 'best purposes', his 'incomprehensible plans and decrees'. Reason, which he himself is, is to be forwarded and realized in the whole world. His fatherly care deprives us of all independence. We can do nothing sensible without its being said, God did that, and can bring upon ourselves no misfortune without hearing, God ordained that; we have nothing that we have not from him, he 'gave' everything. But, as God does, so does Man. God wants perforce to make the world *blest*, and Man wants to make it *happy*, to make all men happy. Hence every 'man' wants to awaken in all men the reason which he supposes his own self to have: everything is to be rational throughout. God torments himself with the devil, and the philosopher does it with unreason and the accidental. God lets no being go *its own* gait, and Man likewise wants to make us walk only in human wise.

But whoso is full of sacred (religious, moral, humane) love loves only the spook, the 'true man', and persecutes with dull mercilessness the individual, the real man, under the phlegmatic legal title of measures against the 'un-man'. He finds it praiseworthy and indispensable to exercise pitilessness in the harshest measure; for love to the spook or generality commands him to hate him who is not ghostly, the egoist or individual; such is the meaning of the renowned love-phenomenon that is called 'justice'.[2]

[1] Athanasius.

[2] For Stirner the cleric's morality promotes more than a hypocritical partition of the world into good and evil, which in itself is quite harmless. It breeds that kind of resentment which Nietzsche was to analyse so profoundly (*Towards a Genealogy of Morals*, especially Book 1, sec. 10), the reactive emotion through which the inhibited and frustrated type vents its

The criminally arraigned man can expect no for-
bearance, and no one spreads a friendly veil over his
unhappy nakedness. Without emotion the stern judge
tears the last rags of excuse from the body of the poor
accused; without compassion the jailer drags him into his
damp abode; without placability, when the time of
punishment has expired, he thrusts the branded man again
among men, his good, Christian, loyal brethren, who contemptuously spit on him. Yes, without grace a criminal
'deserving of death' is led to the scaffold, and before the
eyes of a jubilant crowd the appeased moral law celebrates
its sublime — revenge. For only one can live, the moral law
or the criminal. Where criminals live unpunished, the
moral law has fallen; and, where this prevails, those must
go down. Their enmity is indestructible.

The Christian age is precisely that of *mercy, love,*
solicitude to have men receive what is due them, yes, to
bring them to fulfil their human (divine) calling. Therefore the principle has been put foremost for intercourse,
that this and that is man's essence and consequently his
calling, to which either God has called him or (according
to the concepts of today) his being man (the species) calls
him. Hence the zeal for conversion. That the communists
and the humane expect from man more than the Christians
do does not change the standpoint in the least. Man shall
get what is human! If it was enough for the pious that
what was divine became his part, the humane demand
that he be not curtailed of what is human. Both set themselves against what is egoistic. Of course; for what is
egoistic cannot be accorded to him or vested in him

---

envy and hate of anything that is self-affirming and joyous. The cleric
sets himself up as society's moral barometer and with strict conscientiousness—that 'great jail built about the mind of man by religion', as Stirner
calls it—mercilessly represses the 'immoral'.

(a fief); he must procure it for himself. Love imparts the former, the latter can be given to me by myself alone.

(*Ego* 382–4)

Am I perchance to have no lively interest in the person of another, are *his* joy and *his* weal not to lie at my heart, is the enjoyment that I furnish him not to be more to me than other enjoyments of my own? On the contrary, I can with joy sacrifice to him numberless enjoyments, I can deny myself numberless things for the enhancement of *his* pleasure, and I can hazard for him what without him was the dearest to me, my life, my welfare, my freedom. Why, it constitutes my pleasure and my happiness to refresh myself with his happiness and his pleasure. But *myself, my own self*, I do not sacrifice to him, but remain an egoist and —enjoy him. If I sacrifice to him everything that but for my love to him I should keep, that is very simple, and even more usual in life than it seems to be; but it proves nothing more than that this one passion is more powerful in me than all the rest. Christianity too teaches us to sacrifice all other passions to this. But, if to one passion I sacrifice others, I do not on that account go so far as to sacrifice *myself*, nor sacrifice anything of that whereby I truly am myself; I do not sacrifice my peculiar value, my *ownness*. Where this bad case occurs, love cuts no better figure than any other passion that I obey blindly. The ambitious man, who is carried away by ambition and remains deaf to every warning that a calm moment begets in him, has let this passion grow up into a despot against whom he abandons all power of dissolution; he has given up himself, because he cannot *dissolve* himself, and consequently cannot absolve himself from the passion; he is possessed.

I love men too—not merely individuals, but everyone. But I love them with the consciousness of egoism; I love them because love makes *me* happy, I love because loving is natural to me, because it pleases me. I know no 'commandment of love'.[1] I have a *fellow-feeling* with every feeling being, and their torment torments, their refreshment refreshes me too; I can kill them, not torture them. *Per contra*, the high-souled, virtuous Philistine prince Rudolph in *The Mysteries of Paris*,[2] because the wicked provoke his 'indignation', plans their torture. That fellow-feeling proves only that the feeling of those who feel is

[1] Stirner's central insight into the essentially egoistic nature of every human act becomes more than the truism it appears at first when it is introduced as the key to an understanding of the many different facets of behaviour. With its ancillary recognition that the repression of egoistic drives leads to a confusion of the individual's sense of self, and an emasculation of his *joie de vivre*, the case par excellence being 'love', Stirner has developed a powerful critical perspective, one which finds fuller extension in the work of Nietzsche and Freud. Freud's own views on love, as summarized by Philip Rieff, are strikingly parallel to Stirner's:

> Loving, the body is loved, and thus any object is absorbed into the subject; even adult loves retain their autistic and self-regarding character. That love must serve the self or the self will shrink from it, that the self may chase love round an object back to itself again — this is Freud's brilliant and true insight, reminiscent of La Rochefoucauld's keen detection of the ego behind the curtain. To care is the polite form of desire; the man who desires nothing cares for nothing. All loves are unmasked as self-satisfactions: from the love of the child for the parent-provider, to the love of spouses which reincarnates these parent-images, to the parent's 'narcissistic' love for his own children. (Philip Rieff, *Freud: The Mind of the Moralist* (Gollancz, London, 1959), p. 158.)

[2] To Stirner the high-priest of the contemporary world was Eugène Sue (1804–57), whose gospel was the best-selling novel, *Les Mystères de Paris*. Sue was widely celebrated as the originator of a new social conscience, Europe's Charles Dickens, exposing the misery and injustice suffered by the lower classes of Paris. Stirner, however, in 1843 saw the prophet of a new religion in this man, who 'knows no other happiness than in honest people, no other greatness than in morality, no other human values than virtue and godliness'. (Stirner, *Mysterien von Paris von Eugène Sue*, republished in *Kleinere Schriften*, pp. 278–95.) Sue's vision was a prudishly sentimental one: his hero, altruistically dedicated to leading simpler folk from wickedness towards the redemption found in good thoughts, good feelings, and good deeds, is one of those spotless embodiments of virtue and nobility that so captured the Victorian imagination. Stirner feared that the world would be enslaved by his precious virtue.

mine too, my property; in opposition to which the pitiless dealing of the 'righteous' man (as against notary Ferrand) is like the unfeelingness of that robber [Procrustes] who cut *off* or stretched his prisoners' legs to the measure of his bedstead: Rudolph's bedstead, which he cuts men to fit, is the concept of the 'good'. The feeling for right, virtue, etc., makes people hard-hearted and intolerant. Rudolph does not feel like the notary, but the reverse; he feels that 'it serves the rascal right'; that is no fellow-feeling.

You love man, therefore you torture the individual man, the egoist; your philanthropy (love of men) is the tormenting of men.

If I see the loved one suffer, I suffer with him, and I know no rest till I have tried everything to comfort and cheer him; if I see him glad, I too become glad over his joy. From this it does not follow that suffering or joy is caused in me by the same thing that brings out this effect in him, as is sufficiently proved by every bodily pain which I do not feel as he does; his tooth pains him, but his pain pains me.

But, because I cannot bear the troubled crease on the beloved forehead, for that reason, and therefore for my sake, I kiss it away. If I did not love this person, he might go right on making creases, they would not trouble me; I am only driving away *my* trouble.

How now, has anybody or anything, whom and which I do not love, a *right* to be loved by me? Is my love first, or is his right first? Parents, kinsfolk, fatherland, nation, native town, etc., finally fellow-men in general ('brothers, fraternity'), assert that they have a right to my love, and lay claim to it without further ceremony. They look upon it as *their property*, and upon me, if I do not respect this, as a robber who takes from them what pertains to them and is theirs. I *should* love. If love is a commandment and law, then I must be educated into it, cultivated up to it, and, if I trespass against it, punished. Hence people will exercise as strong a 'moral influence' as possible on me to bring me to love. And there is no doubt that one can work up and seduce men to love as one can to other passions — if you like, to hate. Hate runs through whole races merely because the ancestors of the one belonged to the Guelphs, those of the other to the Ghibellines.

However, love is not a commandment, but, like each of my feelings, *my property*. *Acquire*, purchase, my property, and then I will make it over to you. A church, a nation, a fatherland, a family, etc., that does not know how to acquire my love, I need not love; and I fix the purchase-price of my love quite at my pleasure.

Selfish love is far distant from unselfish, mystical, or romantic love. One can love everything possible, not merely men, but an 'object' in general (wine, one's fatherland, etc.). Love becomes blind and crazy by a *must* taking it out of my power (infatuation), romantic by a *should* entering into it, by the 'objects' becoming sacred for me, or my becoming bound to it by duty, conscience, oath. Now the object no longer exists for me, but I for it.

Love is a possessedness, not as my feeling — as such I rather keep it in my possession as property — but through the alienness of the object. For religious love consists in the commandment to love in the beloved a 'holy one', or to adhere to a holy one; for unselfish love there are objects *absolutely lovable* for which my heart is to beat, such as fellow-men, or my wedded mate, kinsfolk, etc. Holy Love loves the holy in the beloved, and therefore exerts itself also to make of the beloved more and more a holy one (a 'man').

The beloved is an object that *should* be loved by me. He

is not an object of my love on account of, because of, or by, my loving him, but is an object of love in and of himself. Not I make him an object of love, but he is such to begin with; for it is here irrelevant that he has become so by my choice, if so it be (as with a *fiancée*, a spouse, and the like), since even so he has in any case, as the person once chosen, obtained a 'right of his own to my love', and I, because I have loved him, am under obligation to love him for ever. He is therefore not an object of *my* love, but of love in general: an object that *should* be loved. Love appertains to him, is due to him, or is his *right*, while I am under *obligation* to love him. My love, the toll of love that I pay him, is in truth *his* love, which he only collects from me as toll.

Every love to which there clings but the smallest speck of obligation is an unselfish love, and, so far as this speck reaches, a possessedness. He who believes that he *owes* the object of his love anything loves romantically or religiously.

Family love, as it is usually understood as 'piety', is a religious love; love of fatherland, preached as 'patriotism', likewise. All our romantic loves move in the same pattern: everywhere the hypocrisy, or rather self-deception, of an 'unselfish love', an interest in the object for the object's sake, not for my sake and mine alone.

Religious or romantic love is distinguished from sensual love by the difference of the object indeed, but not by the dependence of the relation to it. In the latter regard both are possessedness; but in the former the one object is profane, the other sacred. The dominion of the object over me is the same in both cases, only that it is one time a sensuous one, the other time a spiritual (ghostly) one. My love is my own only when it consists altogether in a selfish and egoistic interest, and when consequently the object of my love is really *my* object or my property. I owe my property nothing, and have no duty to it, as little as I might have a duty to my eye; if nevertheless I guard it with the greatest care, I do so on my account.

Antiquity lacked love as little as do Christian times; the god of love is older than the God of Love. But the mystical possessedness belongs to the moderns.

The possessedness of love lies in the alienation of the object, or in my powerlessness as against its alienness and superior power. To the egoist nothing is high enough for him to humble himself before it, nothing so independent that he would live for love of it, nothing so sacred that he would sacrifice himself to it. The egoist's love rises in selfishness, flows in the bed of selfishness, and empties into selfishness again.

Whether this can still be called love? If you know another word for it, go ahead and choose it; then the sweet word love may wither with the departed world; for the present I at least find none in our *Christian* language, and hence stick to the old sound and 'love' *my* object, my — property.

(Ego 385–91)

Towards the world, especially towards men, I am to *assume a particular feeling*, and 'meet them with love', with the feeling of love, from the beginning. Certainly, in this there is revealed far more free-will and self-determination than when I let myself be stormed, by way of the world, by all possible feelings, and remain exposed to the most chequered, most accidental impressions. I go to the world rather with a preconceived feeling, as if it were a prejudice and a preconceived opinion; I have prescribed to myself in advance my behaviour towards it, and, despite all its temptations, feel and think about it only as I have once determined to. Against the dominion of the world I secure myself by the principle of love; for, whatever may come,

I—love. The ugly, for example, makes a repulsive impression on me; but, determined to love, I master this impression as I do every antipathy.

But the feeling to which I have determined and—condemned myself from the start is a *narrow* feeling, because it is a predestined one, of which I myself am not able to get clear or to declare myself clear. Because preconceived, it is a *prejudice*. *I* no longer show myself in face of the world, but my love shows itself. The *world* indeed does not rule me, but so much the more inevitably does the spirit of *love* rule this spirit.

If I first said, I love the world, I now add likewise: I do not love it, for I *annihilate* it as I annihilate myself; I *dissolve* it. I do not limit myself to one feeling for men, but give free play to all that I am capable of. Why should I not dare speak it out in all its glaringness? Yes, I *utilize* the world and men! With this I can keep myself open to every impression without being torn away from myself by one of them. I can love, love with a full heart, and let the most consuming glow of passion burn in my heart, without taking the beloved one for anything else than the *nourishment* of my passion, on which it ever refreshes itself anew. All my care for him applies only to the *object of my love*, only to him whom my love *requires*, only to him, the 'warmly loved'. How indifferent would he be to me without this—my love! I feed only my love with him, I *utilize* him for this only: I *enjoy* him.

Let us choose another convenient example. I see how men are fretted in dark superstition by a host of spectres. If to the extent of my powers I let a bit of daylight fall in on the nocturnal spookery, is it perchance because love for you inspires this in me? Do I write out of love for men? No, I write because I want to procure for *my* thoughts an existence in the world; and, even if I foresaw that these thoughts would deprive you of your rest and your peace, even if I saw the bloodiest wars and the fall of many generations springing up from this seed of thought—I should nevertheless scatter it. Do with it what you will and can, that is your affair and does not trouble me. You will perhaps have only trouble, combat, and death from it, very few will draw joy from it. If your weal lay at my heart, I should act as the Church did in withholding the Bible from the laity, or Christian governments, which make it a sacred duty for themselves to 'protect the common people from bad books'.[1]

But not only not for your sake, not even for truth's sake either do I speak out what I think. No—

> I sing as sings the bird
> That perches on the bough;
> The song that wells from me
> Is pay enough for now.

I sing because—I am a singer. But I *use*[2] you for it because I—need[3] ears.

Where the world comes in my way—and it comes in my way everywhere—I consume it to quiet the hunger of my egoism. For me you are nothing but—my food, even as I too am fed upon and turned to use by you. We have only one relation to each other, that of *usableness*, of utility, of use. We owe *each other* nothing, for what I seem to owe you I owe at most to myself. If I show you a cheery air in order to cheer you likewise, then your cheeriness is of consequence to *me*, and my air serves *my* wish; to a

[1] Probably the answer Nietzsche would have given to the critics, such as Lukács (*Die Zerstörung der Vernunft*), who, pointing to his influence on fascist ideology, argue that a writer is responsible for how other men use his thought.

[2] *gebrauche*.

[3] *brauche*.

thousand others, whom I do not aim to cheer, I do not show it.

(Ego 392–5)

*   *   *

THE SAVING LIE[1]

Those who educate us make it their concern early to break us of lying and to inculcate the principle that one must always tell the truth. If selfishness were made the basis for this rule, everyone would easily understand how by lying he fools away that confidence in him which he hopes to awaken in others, and how correct the maxim proves. Nobody believes a liar even when he tells the truth. Yet, at the same time, he would also feel that he had to meet with truth only him whom *he* authorized to hear the truth. If a spy walks in disguise through the enemy camp, and is asked who he is, the askers are assuredly entitled to inquire after his name, but the disguised man does not give them the right to learn the truth from him; he tells them what he likes, only not the fact. And yet morality demands, 'Thou shalt not lie!' By morality those persons are vested with the right to expect the truth; but by me they are not vested with that right, and I recognize only the right that *I* impart. In a gathering of revolutionaries the police force their way in and ask the orator for his name; everybody knows that the police have the right to do so, but they do not have it from the *revolutionary*, since he is their enemy; he tells them a false name and — cheats them with a lie. The police do not act so foolishly either as

[1] Ibsen introduced the notion of the 'saving lie' and 'life lie' in *The Wild Duck* (1884); his interpretation is slightly different from Stirner's.

to count on their enemies' love of truth; on the contrary, they do not believe without further ceremony, but have the questioned individual 'identified' if they can. Indeed, the State everywhere proceeds incredulously with individuals, because in their egoism it recognizes its natural enemy; it invariably demands a 'voucher', and he who cannot show vouchers falls a prey to its investigating inquisition. The State does not believe nor trust the individual, and so of itself places itself with him in the *convention of lying*; it trusts me only when it has *convinced* itself of the truth of my statement, for which there often remains to it no other means than the oath. How clearly, too, this (the oath) proves that the State does not count on our credibility and love of truth, but on our *interest*, our selfishness: it relies on our not wanting to fall foul of God by a perjury.

(*Ego* 395–6)

How would it be, now, if we changed the thing a little and wrote, A perjury and lie for—*my sake*? Would not that be pleading for every baseness? It seems so, assuredly, only in this it is altogether like the 'for God's sake'. For was not every baseness committed for God's sake, were not all the scaffolds filled for his sake and all the *autos-da-fé* held for his sake, was not all stupefaction introduced for his sake? And do they not today still for God's sake fetter the mind in tender children by religious education? Were not sacred vows broken for his sake, and do not missionaries and priests still go around every day to bring Jews, heathen, Protestants or Catholics, to treason against the faith of their fathers—for his sake? And that should be worse with the *for my sake*? What then does *on my account* mean? There people immediately think of '*filthy lucre*'. But he who acts from love of filthy lucre does it on his own account indeed, as there is nothing anyhow that one does not do for his own sake—among other things, everything that is done for God's glory; yet he, for whom he seeks the lucre, is a slave of lucre, not raised above lucre; he is one who belongs to lucre, the money-bag, not to himself; he is not his own. Must not a man whom the passion of avarice rules follow the commands of this *master*? And, if a weak good-naturedness once beguiles him, does this not appear as simply an exceptional case of precisely the same sort as when pious believers are sometimes forsaken by their Lord's guidance and ensnared by the arts of the 'devil'? So an avaricious man is not a self-owned man, but a servant; and he can do nothing for his own sake without at the same time doing it for his lord's sake—precisely like the godly man.

(Ego 398–9)

It is despicable to deceive a confidence that we voluntarily call forth; but it is no shame to egoism to let everyone who wants to get us into his power by an oath bleed to death by the unsuccessfulness of his untrustful craft. If you have wanted to bind me, then learn that I know how to burst your bonds.

The point is whether I give the confider the right to confidence. If the pursuer of my friend asks me where he has fled to, I shall surely put him on a false trail. Why does he ask precisely me, the pursued man's friend? In order not to be a false, traitorous friend, I prefer to be false to the enemy. I might certainly in courageous con-scientiousness, answer, 'I will not tell' (so Fichte decides the case); by that I should salve my love of truth and do for my friend as much as—nothing, for, if I do not mislead the enemy, he may accidentally take the right street, and my love of truth would have given up my friend as a prey, because it hindered me from the—courage for a lie. He

who has in the truth an idol, a sacred thing, must *humble
himself* before it, must not defy its demands, not resist
courageously; in short, he must renounce the *heroism of the
lie*. For to the lie belongs not less courage than to the truth:
a courage that young men are most apt to be defective
in, who would rather confess the truth and mount
the scaffold for it than confound the enemy's power by the
impudence of a lie. To them the truth is 'sacred', and the
sacred at all times demands blind reverence, submission,
and self-sacrifice. If you are not impudent, not mockers of
the sacred, you are tame and its servants. Let one but lay
a grain of truth in the trap for you, you peck at it to a
certainty, and the fool is caught. You will not lie? Well,
then, fall as sacrifices to the truth and become—martyrs!
Martyrs!—for what? For yourselves, for self-ownership?
No, for your goddess—the truth. You know only two
services, only two kinds of servants: servants of the truth
and servants of the lie. Then in God's name serve the
truth!

Others, again, serve the truth also; but they serve it 'in
moderation', and make a great distinction between a
simple lie and a lie sworn to. And yet the whole chapter
of the oath coincides with that of the lie, since an oath, as
everybody knows, is only a strongly assured statement.
You consider yourselves entitled to lie, if only you do not
swear to it besides? One who is particular about it must
judge and condemn a lie as sharply as a false oath. But
now there has been kept up in morality an ancient point of
controversy, which is customarily treated of under the
name of the 'lie of necessity'. No one who dares plead for
this can consistently put from him an 'oath of necessity'.
If I justify my lie as a lie of necessity, I should not be so
pusillanimous as to rob the justified lie of the strongest
corroboration. Whatever I do, why should I not do it

entirely and without reservations (*reservatio mentalis*)? If I once lie, why then not lie completely, with entire consciousness and all my might? As a spy I should have to swear to each of my false statements at the enemy's demand; determined to lie to him, should I suddenly become cowardly and undecided in face of an oath? Then I should have been ruined in advance for a liar and spy; for, you see, I should be voluntarily putting into the enemy's hands a means to catch me. — The State too fears the oath of necessity, and for this reason does not give the accused a chance to swear. But you do not justify the State's fear; you lie, but do not swear falsely. If you show someone a kindness, and he is not to know it, but he guesses it and tells you so to your face, you deny; if he insists, you say, 'Honestly, no!' If it came to swearing, then you would refuse; for, from fear of the sacred, you always stop half way. *Against* the sacred you have no *will of your own*. You lie in — moderation, as you are free 'in moderation', religious 'in moderation' (the clergy are not to 'encroach'; over this point the most rapid of controversies is now being carried on, on the part of the university against the Church), monarchically disposed 'in moderation' (you want a monarch limited by the constitution, by a fundamental law of the State), everything nicely *tempered*, lukewarm, half God's, half the devil's.

There was a university where the custom was that every word of honour that must be given to the university judge was looked upon by the students as null and void. For the students saw in the demanding of it nothing but a snare, which they could not escape otherwise than by taking away all its significance. He who at that same university broke his word of honour to one of his fellows was infamous; he who gave it to the university judge derided, in union with these very fellows, the dupe who fancied that a word had the same value among friends and among foes. It was less a correct theory than the constraint of practice that had there taught the students to act so, as, without that means of getting out, they would have been pitilessly driven to treachery against their comrades. But, as the means approved itself in practice, so it has its theoretical probation too. A word of honour, an oath, is one only for him whom I entitle to receive it; he who forces me to it obtains only a forced, a *hostile* word, the word of a foe, whom one has no right to trust; for the foe does not give us the right.[1]

(*Ego* 401–4)

THE UNION

Not isolation or being alone, but society, is man's original state. Our existence begins with the most intimate conjunction, as we are already living with our mother before we breathe; when we see the light of the world, we at once lie on a human being's breast again, her love cradles us in the lap, leads us in the harness, and chains us to her person with a thousand ties. Society is our *state of nature*. And this is why, the more we learn to feel ourselves, the connection that was formerly most intimate becomes ever looser and the dissolution of the original society more unmistakable. To have once again for herself the child that once lay under her heart, the mother must fetch it from the street and from the midst of its playmates. The child prefers the *intercourse* that it enters into with *its fellows* to

[1] Stirner believed in the romantic vision of friendship so popular in nineteenth-century Germany (even Zarathustra came to preach 'not the neighbour, but the friend'). Schiller gave birth in *Don Carlos* (1787) to the idea that deep and lasting fulfilment can only be found in friendship, and that, particularly when confronted by the impersonal State and its sterile political goals, the core of humanity lies in the trust and intimacy to be found with the elect friend.

the *society* that it has not entered into, but only been born in.

But the dissolution of *society* is *intercourse* or *union*. A society does assuredly arise by union too, but only as a fixed idea arises by a thought—to wit, by the vanishing of the energy of the thought (the thinking itself, this restless taking back all thoughts that make themselves fast) from the thought. If a union[1] has crystallized into a society, it has ceased to be a coalition;[2] for coalition is an incessant self-uniting; it has become a unitedness, come to a standstill, degenerated into a fixity; it is—*dead* as a union, it is the corpse of the union or the coalition, it is—society, community. A striking example of this kind is furnished by the *party*.

(*Ego* 406–7)

But in reference to *liberty*, State and union are subject to no essential difference. The latter can just as little come into existence, or continue in existence, without liberty's being limited in all sorts of ways, as the State is compatible with unmeasured liberty. Limitation of liberty is inevitable everywhere, for one cannot get *rid* of everything; one cannot fly like a bird merely because one would like to fly so, for one does not get free from his own weight; one cannot live under water as long as he likes, like a fish, because one cannot do without air and cannot get free from this indispensable necessity; and the like. As religion, and most decidedly Christianity, tormented man with the demand to realize the unnatural and self-contradictory, so it is to be looked upon only as the true logical outcome of that religious overstraining and overwroughtness that finally *liberty itself*, *absolute liberty*, was exalted into an ideal, and thus the nonsense of the impossible had to come glaringly

---

[1] *Verein.*   [2] *Vereinigung.*

to the light. — The union will assuredly offer a greater measure of liberty, as well as (and especially because by it one escapes all the coercion peculiar to State and society life) admit of being considered as 'a new liberty'; but nevertheless it will still contain enough of constraint and involuntariness. For its object is not this — liberty (which on the contrary it sacrifices to ownness), but only *ownness*. Referred to this, the difference between State and union is great enough. The former is an enemy and murderer of *ownness*, the latter a son, a co-worker with it; the former a spirit that would be adored in spirit and in truth, the latter my work, my *product*; the State is the lord of my spirit, who demands faith and prescribes to me articles of faith, the creed of legality; it exerts moral influence, dominates my spirit, drives away my ego to put itself in its place as 'my true ego' — in short, the State is *sacred*, and as against me, the individual man, it is the true man, the spirit, the ghost; but the union is my own creation, my creature, not sacred, not a spiritual power above my spirit, as little as any association of whatever sort. As I am not willing to be a slave of my maxims, but lay them bare to my continual criticism without *any warrant*, and admit no bail at all for their persistence, so still less do I obligate myself to the union for my future and pledge my soul to it, as is said to be done with the devil, and is really the case with the State and all spiritual authority; but I am and remain *more* to myself than State, Church, God, and the like; consequently infinitely more than the union too.

(*Ego* 409–10)

But I would rather be referred to men's selfishness than to their 'kindnesses',[1] their mercy, pity, etc. The former demands *reciprocity* (as thou to me, so I to thee), does

[1] Literally, 'love-services'.

nothing 'gratis', and may be won and—*bought*. But with what shall I obtain the kindness? It is a matter of chance whether I am at the time having to do with a 'loving' person. The affectionate one's service can be had only by —*begging*, be it by my lamentable appearance, by my need of help, my misery, my—*suffering*. What can I offer him for his assistance? Nothing! I must accept it as a— present. Love is *unpayable*, or rather, love can assuredly be paid for, but only by counter-love ('One good turn deserves another').

(*Ego* 413)

Let us therefore not aspire to community, but to *one-sidedness*. Let us not seek the most comprehensive commune, 'human society', but let us seek in others only means and organs which we may use as our property! As we do not see our equals in the tree, the beast, so the presupposition that others are *our equals* springs from a hypocrisy. No one is *my equal*, but I regard him, equally with all other beings, as my property. In opposition to this I am told that I should be a man among 'fellow-men' (*Judenfrage*, p. 60);[1] I should 'respect' the fellow-man in them. For me no one is a person to be respected, not even the fellow-man, but solely, like other beings, an *object* in which I take an interest or else do not, an interesting or uninteresting object, a usable or unusable person.

And, if I can use him, I doubtless come to an understanding and make myself at one with him, in order, by the agreement, to strengthen *my power*, and by combined force to accomplish more than individual force could effect. In this combination I see nothing whatever but a multiplication of my force, and I retain it only so long as it is *my* multiplied force. But thus it is a—union.

---

[1] Bruno Bauer, *Die Judenfrage* (Braunschweig, 1843).

Neither a natural ligature nor a spiritual one holds the union together, and it is not a natural, not a spiritual league. It is not brought about by one *blood*, not by one *faith* (spirit). In a natural league—like a family, a tribe, a nation, yes, mankind—the individuals have only the value of *specimens* of the same species or genus; in a spiritual league—like a commune, a Church—the individual signifies only a *member* of the same spirit; what you are in both cases as a unique person must be—suppressed. Only in the union can you assert yourself as unique, because the union does not possess you, but you possess it or make it of use to you.

Property is recognized in the union, and only in the union, because one no longer holds what is his as a fief from any being. The communists are only consistently carrying further what had already been long present during religious evolution, and especially in the State: to wit, propertylessness, the feudal system.

The State exerts itself to tame the desirous man; in other words, it seeks to direct his desire to it alone, and to *content* that desire with what it offers. To sate the desire for the desirous man's sake does not come into the mind: on the contrary, it stigmatizes as an 'egoistic man' the man who breathes out unbridled desire, and the 'egoistic man' is its enemy. He is this for it because the capacity to agree with him is wanting to the State; the egoist is precisely what it cannot 'comprehend'. Since the State (as nothing else is possible) has concern only for itself, it does not care for my needs, but takes care only of how it is to ruin me, make out of me another ego, a good citizen. It takes measures for the 'improvement of morals'.—And with what does it win individuals for itself? With itself, with what is the State's, with *State property*. It will be unremittingly active in making all participants in its 'goods', providing all with the 'good things of culture'; it presents them its education, opens to them the access to its institutions of culture, capacitates them to come to property (as, to a fief) in the way of industry, etc. For all these *fiefs* it demands only the just rent of continual *thanks*. But the 'unthankful' forget to pay these thanks. — Now, neither can 'society' do essentially otherwise than the State.

You bring into a union your whole power, your competence, and *make yourself count*; in a society you are *employed*, with your working power; in the former you live egoistically, in the latter humanly, that is, religiously, as a 'member in the body of this Lord'; to a society you owe what you have, and are in duty bound to it, are — possessed by 'social duties'; a union you utilize, and give it up undutifully and unfaithfully when you see no way to use it further. If a society is more than you, then it is more to you than yourself; a union is only your instrument, or the sword with which you sharpen and increase your natural force; the union exists for you and through you, the society conversely lays claim to you for itself and exists even without you; in short, the society is *sacred*, the union your *own*; the society consumes *you*, *you* consume the union.

Nevertheless people will not be backward with the objection that the agreement which has been concluded may again become burdensome to us and limit our freedom; they will say, we too would at last come to this, that 'everyone must sacrifice a part of his freedom for the sake of the generality'. But the sacrifice would not be made for the 'generality's' sake a bit, as little as I concluded the agreement for the 'generality's' or even for any other man's sake; rather I came into it only for the sake of my own benefit, from selfishness.[1] But, as regards the sacrificing,

[1] Literally, 'own-benefit'.

surely I 'sacrifice' only that which does not stand in my power, that is, I 'sacrifice' nothing at all.

$(Ego\ 414-17)$

Liberalism wants to give me what is mine, but it thinks to procure it for me not under the title of mine, but under that of the 'human'. As if it were attainable under this mask! The rights of man, the precious work of the Revolution, have the meaning that the Man in me *entitles* me to this and that; I as individual, as this man, am not entitled, but Man has the right and entitles me. Hence as man I may well be entitled; but, as I am more than man, to wit, a *special* man, it may be refused to this very me, the special one. If on the other hand you insist on the *value* of your gifts, keep up their price, do not let yourselves be forced to sell out below price, do not let yourselves be talked into the idea that your wares are not worth their price, do not make yourself ridiculous by a 'ridiculous price', but imitate the brave man who says, I will *sell* my life (property) dear, the enemy shall not have it at a cheap *bargain*; then you have recognized the reverse of communism as the correct thing, and the word then is not 'Give up your property!' but *'Realize* your property!'

Over the portal of our time stands not that Apollonian 'Know Yourself' but *'Realize Yourself!'*[1]

Proudhon calls property 'robbery' (*le vol*). But alien property—and he is talking of this alone—is not less existent by renunciation, cession, and humility; it is a *present.* Why so sentimentally call for compassion as a poor victim of robbery, when one is just a foolish, cowardly

---

[1] *'Verwerte Dich!'* which Byington translates as 'Get the value out of thyself!' (*werten*, to value), hence sacrificing half of the powerful meaning of the more conventional English equivalent, 'Realize Yourself!'—'Make Yourself *real* by getting the value out of yourself!' Cf. Nietzsche's *'Werde was du bist!'*—'Become what you are!'

giver of presents? Why here again put the fault on others as if they were robbing us, while we ourselves do bear the fault in leaving the others unrobbed? The poor are to blame for there being rich men.

Universally, no one grows indignant at *his*, but at *alien* property. They do not in truth attack property, but the alienation of property. They want to be able to call *more*, not less, *theirs*; they want to call everything *theirs*. They are fighting, therefore, against *alienness*, or, to form a word similar to property, against aliency. And how do they help themselves therein? Instead of transforming the alien into own, they play impartial and ask only that all property be left to a third party, such as human society. They revindicate the alien not in their own name but in a third party's. Now the 'egoistic' colouring is wiped off, and everything is so clean and—human!

Propertylessness, or ragamuffinism, this then is the 'essence of Christianity', as it is the essence of all religiousness (godliness, morality, humanity), and only announced itself most clearly, and, as glad tidings, became a gospel capable of development, in the 'absolute religion'.[1]

(*Ego* 418–20)

*   *   *

[1] In a lighthearted section of his reply to Moses Hess's critique of his book Stirner offered some examples of the Union:

Perhaps at this moment children are running together under his window in the comradeship of their play; let him look at them, and he will perceive merry egoistic unions. Perhaps Hess has a friend, a sweetheart; then he may know how heart joins itself to heart, how two of them unite egoistically in order to have the enjoyment of each other, and how neither 'gets the worse of the bargain'. Perhaps he meets a couple of close acquaintances on the street and is invited to accompany them to a wine-shop; does he go with them in order to do them an act of kindness, or does he 'unite' with them because he promises himself enjoyment from it? Do they have to give him their best thanks for his 'self-sacrifice', or do they know that for an hour they formed an 'egoistic union' together?

(*K.S.* 396)

REVOLUTION AND INSURRECTION

Revolution and insurrection must not be looked upon as synonymous. The former consists in an overturning of conditions, of the established condition or *status*, the State or society, and is accordingly a *political* or *social* act; the latter has indeed for its unavoidable consequence a transformation of circumstances, yet does not start from it but from men's discontent with themselves, is not an armed rising, but a rising of individuals, a getting up, without regard to the arrangements that spring from it. The Revolution aimed at new *arrangements*; insurrection leads us no longer to *let* ourselves be arranged, but to arrange ourselves, and sets no glittering hopes on 'institutions'. It is not a fight against the established, since, if it prospers, the established collapses of itself; it is only a working forth of me out of the established. If I leave the established, it is dead and passes into decay. Now, as my object is not the overthrow of an established order but my elevation above it, my purpose and deed are not a political or social but (as directed towards myself and my ownness alone) an *egoistic* purpose and deed.

The revolution commands one to make *arrangements*, the insurrection[1] demands that he *rise or exalt himself*.[2] What *constitution* was to be chosen, this question busied the revolutionary heads, and the whole political period foams with constitutional fights and constitutional questions, as the social talents too were uncommonly inventive in societary arrangements (phalansteries[3] and

---

[1] *Empörung*, literally 'up-rising'.
[2] *sich auf- oder emporzurichten*.
[3] A reference to Charles Fourier's ideal community, the 'phalanstery'. In fact Fourier with his acute psychological insights and his 'immoralist'

the like). The insurgent* strives to become constitutionless.

While, to get greater clarity, I am thinking up a comparison, the founding of Christianity comes unexpectedly into my mind. On the liberal side it is noted as a bad point in the first Christians that they preached obedience to the established heathen civil order, enjoined recognition of the heathen authorities, and confidently delivered a command, 'Give to the emperor that which is the emperor's.' Yet how much disturbance arose at the same time against the Roman supremacy, how mutinous did the Jews and even the Romans show themselves against their own temporal government! In short, how popular was 'political discontent'! Those Christians would hear nothing of it; would not side with the 'liberal tendencies'. The time was politically so agitated that, as is said in the gospels, people thought they could not accuse the founder of Christianity more successfully than if they arraigned him for 'political intrigue', and yet the same gospels report that he was precisely the one who took least part in these political doings. But why was he not a revolutionary, not a demagogue, as the Jews would gladly have seen him?

---

hatred of convention is the one plausible precursor of Stirner's psychological anarchism. Unfortunately, the vital chapter in the intellectual history of the nineteenth century, on Fourier and his influence, particularly in post-Hegelian Germany, has yet to be written. Stirner probably only knew of his work vaguely and indirectly, as Marx did, through the writings of Wilhelm Weitling. He did not shy away from the work of any of the other men who had made a strong impression upon him; indeed, he went to great pains to refute them. It is unlikely that he would have made an exception of a man so kindred as Fourier—moreover, there is much in Fourier that he would have been quick to criticize.

* To secure myself against a criminal charge I superfluously make the express remark that I choose the word 'insurrection' on account of its *etymological sense*, and therefore am not using it in the limited sense which is disallowed by the penal code. (This footnote is a precautionary effort of Stirner's to avoid running foul of the Saxon State press censorship laws.)

Why was he not a liberal? Because he expected no salvation from a change of *conditions*, and this whole business was indifferent to him. He was not a revolutionary, like Caesar, but an insurgent; not a State-overturner, but one who straightened *himself* up.[1] That was why it was for him only a matter of 'Be ye wise as serpents,' which expresses the same sense as, in the special case, that 'Give to the emperor that which is the emperor's'; for he was not carrying on any liberal or political fight against the established authorities, but wanted to walk his *own* way, untroubled about, and undisturbed by, these authorities. Not less indifferent to him than the government were its enemies, for neither understood what he wanted, and he had only to keep them off from him with the wisdom of the serpent. But, even though not a ringleader of popular mutiny, not a demagogue or revolutionary, he (and every one of the ancient Christians) was so much the more an *insurgent*, who lifted himself above everything that seemed sublime to the government and its opponents, and absolved himself from everything to which they remained bound, and who at the same time cut off the sources of life of the whole heathen world, so the established State must wither away as a matter of course; precisely because he put from him the upsetting of the established, he was its deadly enemy and real annihilator; for he walled it in, confidently and recklessly carrying up the building of *his* temple over it, without heeding the pains of the immured.

Now, will it happen to the Christian order of the world, as it did to the heathen? A revolution certainly does not

[1] Stirner obviously identified himself partially with his insurrectionary hero, Christ. The image is of 'Christ the tiger' as it is later to be found in the writing of such diverse figures as Nietzsche, Soloviev, Yeats and D. H. Lawrence. The creator of *The Ego and His Own* is not unlike the man on the Sabbath who goes to an impotent man crippled for thirty-eight years and tells him to 'Rise take, up thy bed, and walk.' (John v 1-9).

bring on the end if an insurrection is not consummated first!

My intercourse with the world, what does it aim at? I want to have the enjoyment of it, therefore it must be my property, and therefore I want to win it. I do not want the liberty of men, nor their equality; I want only *my* power over them, I want to make them my property, *material for enjoyment*. And, if I do not succeed in that, well, then I call even the power over life and death, which Church and State reserved to themselves—mine. Brand that officer's widow who, in the flight through Russia, after her leg has been shot away, takes the garter from it, strangles her child therewith, and then bleeds to death alongside the corpse—brand the memory of the—infanticide. Who knows, if this child had remained alive, how much it might have 'been of use to the world'! The mother murdered it because she wanted to die *satisfied* and at rest. Perhaps this case still appeals to your sentimentality, and you do not know how to read out of it anything further. Be it so; I on my part use it as an example for this, that *my* satisfaction decides about my relation to men, and that I do not renounce, from any access of humility, even the power over life and death.[1]

As regards 'social duties' in general, another does not give me my position towards others, therefore neither God nor humanity prescribes to me my relation to men, but I

[1] Stirner here gives birth to the idea that was both to fascinate and to terrify Dostoevsky—the man who makes himself God takes the power to kill and to save into his own hands. The currents of feeling that sustain *Crime and Punishment* with such intensity emanate from Dostoevsky's own impassioned brooding over the implications of a man setting out to prove himself a superior being through the calculated murder of a miserly old woman, whom he *reasons* to be worthless. It is typical of Stirner that he throws out an idea of astonishing significance, then moves on without developing it. (C.f. page 154 above for Stirner's stark and prophetic exaltation of *crime* as the most valid form of self-expression in a repressive society.)

give myself this position. This is more strikingly said thus: I have no *duty* to others, as I have a duty even to myself (that of self-preservation, and therefore not suicide) only so long as I distinguish myself from myself (my immortal soul from my earthly existence, etc.).

I no longer *humble* myself before any power, and I recognize that all powers are only my power, which I have to subject at once when they threaten to become a power *against* or *above* me; each of them must be only one of *my means* to carry my point, as a hound is our power against game, but is killed if it should fall upon us ourselves. All powers that dominate me I then reduce to serving me. The idols exist through me; I need only refrain from creating them anew, then they exist no longer: 'higher powers' exist only through my exalting them and abasing myself.

Consequently my relation to the world is this: I no longer do anything for it 'for God's sake', I do nothing 'for man's sake', but what I do I do 'for my sake'. Thus alone does the world satisfy me, while it is characteristic of the religious standpoint, in which I include the moral and humane also, that from it everything remains a pious wish (*pium desiderium*), an other-world matter, something unattained. Thus the general salvation of men, the moral world of a general love, eternal peace, the cessation of egoism, etc. 'Nothing in this world is perfect.' With this miserable phrase the good part from it, and take flight into their closet to God, or into their proud 'self-consciousness'. But we remain in this 'imperfect' world, because even so we can use it for our—self-enjoyment.

My intercourse with the world consists in my enjoying it, and so consuming it for my self-enjoyment. *Intercourse* is the *enjoyment of the world*, and belongs to my—self-enjoyment.

C.—MY SELF-ENJOYMENT

We stand at the boundary of a period. The world hitherto took thought for nothing but the gain of life, took care for —*life*. For whether all activity is put on the stretch for the life of this world or of the other, for the temporal or for the eternal, whether one hankers for 'daily bread' ('Give us our daily bread') or for 'holy bread' ('the true bread from heaven'; 'the bread of God, that comes from heaven and *gives life* to the world'; 'the bread of life'—John vi), whether one takes care for 'dear life' or for 'life to eternity' —this does not change the object of the strain and care, which in the one case as in the other shows itself to be *life*. Do the modern tendencies announce themselves otherwise? People now want nobody to be embarrassed for the most indispensable necessaries of life, but want every one to feel secure as to these; and on the other hand they teach that man has this life to attend to and the real world to adapt himself to, without vain care for another.

Let us take up the same thing from another side. When one is anxious only to live, he easily, in this solicitude, forgets the enjoyment of life. If his only concern is for life, and he thinks 'if I only have my dear life', he does not apply his full strength to using, that is, enjoying, life. But how does one use life? In using it up, like the candle, which one uses in burning it up. One uses life, and consequently himself the living one, in *consuming* it and himself. *Enjoyment of life* is using life up.

Now—we are in search of the *enjoyment* of life! And what did the religious world do? It went in search of life. Wherein consists the true life, the blessed life, etc.? How is it to be attained? What must man do and become in order to become a truly living man? How does he fulfil this calling?

These and similar questions indicate that the askers were still seeking for *themselves* — to wit, themselves in the true sense, in the sense of true living. 'What I am is foam and shadow; what I shall be is my true self.' To chase after this self, to produce it, to realize it, constitutes the hard task of mortals, who die only to *rise again*, live only to die, live only to find the true life.

Not till I am certain of myself, and no longer seeking for myself, am I really my property; I have myself, therefore I use and enjoy myself. On the other hand, I can never take comfort in myself as long as I think that I have still to find my true self and that it must come to this, that not I but Christ or some other spiritual, ghostly, self (the true man, the essence of man, and the like) lives in me.

A vast interval separates the two views. In the old I go towards myself, in the new I start from myself; in the former I long for myself, in the latter I have myself and do with myself as one does with any other property — I enjoy myself at my pleasure. I am no longer afraid for my life, but 'squander' it.

Henceforth, the question runs, not how one can acquire life, but how one can squander, enjoy it; or, not how one is to produce the true self in himself, but how one is to dissolve himself, to live himself out.[1]

---

[1] The hedonist-vitalist current is strong in Stirner. Life is like the eating of a ripe apple, it must be chewed right down to the bare core and forced to surrender all its hidden pleasures. His command to *squander* life, *consume* it, is directed entirely to the present moment; each passing moment is to be enjoyed in and for itself. The contrast to be marked is with the anti-hedonistic, puritanical ethos of capitalism as it reveals itself in the hoarding of money, the possessive retention of feelings and the compulsion to save time. Stirner's directive is to kindle one's life, possess it to the full, *real-ize* it — not to save but to squander. Here he anticipates the critiques of Thorstein Veblen (conspicuous consumption) and Sigmund Freud (libidinal repression), while at the same time doing what few social critics attempt — elaborating positive steps for overcoming the limiting situation.

What else should the ideal be but the sought for ever-distant self? One seeks for himself, consequently one does not yet have himself; one aspires towards what one *ought* to be, consequently one *is* not it. One lives in *longing* and has lived thousands of years in it, in *hope*. It is quite another thing to live in—*enjoyment*!

Does this perchance apply only to the so-called pious? No, it applies to all who belong to the closing period of history, even to its men of pleasure. For them too the workdays were followed by a Sunday, and the rush of the world by the dream of a better world, of a general happiness of humanity; in short, by an ideal. But philosophers especially are contrasted with the pious. Now, have they been thinking of anything else than the ideal, been planning for anything else than the absolute self? Longing and hope everywhere, and nothing but these. For me, call it romanticism.

If the *enjoyment of life* is to triumph over the *longing for life* or hope of life, it must vanquish this in its double significance, which Schiller introduces in his *Ideal and Life*; it must crush spiritual and secular poverty, exterminate the ideal and—the want of daily bread. He who must expend his life to prolong life cannot enjoy it, and he who is still seeking for his life does not have it and can as little enjoy it; both are poor, but 'blessed are the poor'.

(*Ego* 420–8)

The conservative tendency of Christianity does not permit thinking of death otherwise than with the purpose to take its sting from it and—live on and preserve oneself nicely. The Christian lets everything happen and come upon him if he—the arch-Jew—can only haggle and smuggle himself into heaven; he must not kill himself, he must only—preserve himself and work at the 'preparation of a future abode'. Conservatism or 'conquest of death' lies at his heart; 'the last enemy that is abolished is death'.* 'Christ has taken the power from death and brought life and *imperishable* being to light through the gospel.'† 'Imperishableness', stability.

(*Ego* 429–30)

Calling — destiny — task! —

What one can become he does become. A born poet may well be hindered by the disfavour of circumstances from standing on the high level of his time, and, after the great studies that are indispensable for this, producing *consummate* works of art; but he will make poetry, be he a ploughman or so lucky as to live at the court of Weimar. A born musician will make music, no matter whether on all instruments or only on an oaten pipe. A born philosophical head can give proof of itself as university philosopher or as village philosopher. Finally, a born dolt, who, as is very well compatible with this, may at the same time be a sly-boots, will always remain a blockhead (as probably every one who has visited schools is in a position to realize from the many instances of fellow-scholars), whether he was drilled and trained into the chief of a bureau, or served that same chief as bootblack. Certainly, the born shallow-pates indisputably form the most numerous class of men. And why, indeed, should not the same distinctions show themselves in the human species that are unmistakable in every species of beasts? The more gifted and the less gifted are to be found everywhere.

Only a few, however, are so imbecile that one could not get ideas into them. Hence, people usually consider all men capable of having religion. To a certain degree they

* 1 Cor. xv 26.   † 2 Tim. i 10.

may be trained to other ideas too, to some musical intelligence, even some philosophy. At this point then the priesthood of religion, of morality, of culture, of science, etc., takes its start, and the communists, for instance, want to make everything accessible to all by their 'public school'. There is heard a common assertion that this 'great mass' cannot get along without religion; the communists broaden it into the proposition that not only the 'great mass', but absolutely all, are called to everything.

Not enough that the great mass has been trained to religion, now it is actually to have to occupy itself with 'everything human'. Training is growing ever more general and more comprehensive.

You poor beings who could live so happily if you might skip according to your mind, you are to dance to the pipe of schoolmasters and bear-leaders, in order to perform tricks that you yourselves would never use yourselves for. And you do not even kick over the traces at last against being always taken otherwise than you want to give yourselves. No, you mechanically recite to yourselves the question that is recited to you: 'What am I called to? What *ought* I to do?' You need only ask thus, to have yourselves *told* what you ought to do and *ordered* to do it, to have your *calling* marked out for you, or else to order yourselves and impose it on yourselves according to the spirit's prescription. Then in reference to the will the word is, I will to do what I *ought*.

A man is 'called' to nothing, and has no 'calling', no 'destiny', as little as a plant or a beast has a 'calling'. The flower does not follow the calling to complete itself, but it spends all its forces to enjoy and consume the world as well as it can—it sucks in as much of the juices of the earth, as much air of the ether, as much light of the sun, as it can get and lodge. The bird lives up to no calling, but it uses its forces as much as is practicable; it catches beetles and sings to its heart's delight. But the forces of the flower and the bird are slight in comparison to those of a man, and a man who applies his forces will affect the world much more powerfully than flower and beast. A calling he has not, but he has forces that manifest themselves where they are because their being consists solely in their manifestation, and are as little able to abide inactive as life, which, if it 'stood still' only a second, would no longer be life. Now, one might call out to the man, 'use your force.' Yet to this imperative would be given the meaning that it was man's task to use his force. It is not so. Rather, each one really uses his force without first looking upon this as his calling: at all times every one uses as much force as he possesses. One does say of a beaten man that he ought to have exerted his force more; but one forgets that, if in the moment of succumbing he had had the force to exert his forces (bodily forces), he would not have failed to do it: even if it was only the discouragement of a minute, this was yet a — destitution of force, a minute long. Forces may assuredly be sharpened and redoubled, especially by hostile resistance or friendly assistance; but where one misses their application one may be sure of their absence too. One can strike fire out of a stone, but without the blow none comes out; in like manner a man too needs 'impact'.

Now, for this reason that forces always of themselves show themselves operative, the command to use them would be superfluous and senseless. To use his forces is not man's *calling* and task, but is his *act*, real and extant at all times. Force is only a simpler word for manifestation of force.

Now, as this rose is a true rose to begin with, this nightingale always a true nightingale, so I am not for the first time a true man when I fulfil my calling, live up to my destiny, but I am a 'true man' from the start. My first babble is the token of the life of a 'true man', the struggles of my life are the outpourings of his force, my last breath is the last exhalation of the force of the 'man'.

The true man does not lie in the future, an object of longing, but lies, existent and real, in the present. Whatever and whoever I may be, joyous and suffering, a child or a greybeard, in confidence or doubt, in sleep or in waking, I am it, I am the true man.

But, if I am Man, and have really found in myself him whom religious humanity designated as the distant goal, then everything 'truly human' is also *my own*. What was ascribed to the idea of humanity belongs to me. That freedom of trade, for example, which humanity has yet to attain—and which, like an enchanting dream, people remove to humanity's golden future—I take by anticipation as my property, and carry it on for the time in the form of smuggling. There may indeed be but few smugglers who have sufficient understanding to thus account to themselves for their doings, but the instinct of egoism replaces their consciousness. Above I have shown the same thing about freedom of the press.

(*Ego* 433–7)

* * *

ART AND RELIGION[1]

As soon as the presentiment awakens that man has a beyond in himself, i.e. that he is not content with his

---

[1] This section is taken from Stirner's 1842 article of the same name. He argues that the artist, through creating an object beyond himself, in a

animal and natural state, but must become *another*, (and
for the man *of the present*, the *other* person that he is to
become stands of course in the future, and must be
expected only beyond his present state of being—a man of
the *life to come*: thus for the boy, youth is the future and the
beyond into which he must first grow, and thus the
moral man is the beyond of the merely innocent child).
As soon as that presentiment awakens in man and he
presses forward to separate and divide himself into that
which he *is*, and that which he is to *become*, then he
ardently strives towards the latter, towards this second
and different man, and he does not rest until he sees
before him the *form* of this man of the beyond. For a long
time his inner self heaves to and fro; he can only feel that
a luminous figure is trying to rise up in the darkness of
his inner being, but is as yet lacking clear contours and a
fixed form. In relation to the people who are groping
around uncertainly in the darkness, the artistic genius
also gropes for a while seeking the form of their presentiment; but he succeeds in doing what none other can: he
gives form to the presentiment, he finds the shape, he
creates the—ideal. What is the perfect man, the most
proper destiny of man, of which all long to catch sight,
other than the ideal man, the ideal of man? The artist
has finally discovered the right word, the right image,
the right perception of that for which all were longing;
he proposes it: it is the *ideal*. 'Yes, that is right! That is
the form of the perfect one, the expression of our longing,
the good news (gospel), which is brought home by the

---

sense splits his self. There is a component of alienation in every artistic
creation by virtue of the simple fact that the external world is being
mediated through an independent form; it is no longer immediate. Moreover, Stirner adds, it is the artist who manages to transcend the state of
'religious' dread, of meaninglessness, and his work is likely to be idealized
as a signpost to salvation by those less creative.

explorers we sent out long ago, to answer the thirst-parched questions of our mind!' Thus the people cry out at the creation of the genius and fall—worshipping down.

Yes, *worshipping*! The burning urge in man which drives him not to single but to duplicate himself, not to be satisfied with himself as the natural man, but to seek the other, the spiritual man—this drive is satisfied through the work of the genius, and the splitting in two is completed. For the first time man breathes with relief, for his inner confusion is resolved, the disturbing presentiment is *thrown out as form*: man stands *facing* himself. What he faces is himself and yet not himself: it is his *beyond*, to which all his thoughts and feelings flow without quite reaching it, and it is *his* beyond, as it is wrapped in and inseparably interwoven with his present, on this side. It is the *God* of his inner world, but he is outside; consequently he cannot grasp nor understand it. He stretches forth his arms with desire, but what stands facing him cannot be reached; for if it could be reached, how would it still be *opposite* him? Where would the division be with all its pains and all its ecstasy. Where, and let us not fear to call this division by another name, where would *religion* be?—

Herein lie all the torments, all the struggles of centuries: for it is frightening *to be outside oneself*, and everyone is outside himself, who has himself as object, without being able to unite this object entirely with himself, and to destroy it as an object, as a substance, and as a resistant thing. The religious world lives in the joys and suffering which it experiences from this object, it lives in the division of itself, and its spiritual existence is not a rational[1] but an intellectual[2] one. Religion is an

---

[1] *vernünftiges.*   [2] *verständiges.*

INTELLECTUAL AFFAIR! The mind of the pietist is as inflexible in relation to this object, as this object itself is hard, so that none of his kind can win it entirely for himself, but must rather submit to it—and this mind is *intellect*. 'Cold intellect!?'—So you know nothing but that type of 'cold' intellect? you do not know that nothing is so ardently hot, so heroic, as intellect? *Censeo, Carthaginem esse delendam* [1] said Cato's intellect, and he abode by it undeviatingly. The earth moves round the sun, said Galileo's intellect, even while the weak old man abjured the truth on his knees, and when he stood up he repeated 'And yet it does move round the sun.' No power is great enough to upset our thinking that $2 \times 2 = 4$, and the intellect's eternal word remains this: 'Here I stand, I can do no other!' And the matter with which such intellect is concerned—an intellect which is only unshakeable because its object ($2 \times 2 = 4$, etc.) cannot be questioned—this matter is said to be religion?[2] Yes, it is religion. Religion also has an unassailable object, into whose power it has fallen. The artist has created it for religion's sake, only the artist could take it away from religion. For religion itself lacks genius. No man can be a religious genius, and no one will assert that one may distinguish in religion between the genius, the talented, and the untalented ... Only the founder of religion has genius, but he is also the creator of the ideal—a creation which renders impossible any further genius. Where the spirit is bound to an object and all measure of its activity is determined by this same object, where, I say, the spirit is

[1] 'I propose that Carthage be destroyed.'

[2] Dostoevsky, who is most unlikely to have read this article, uses $2 \times 2 = 4$ as the central metaphor in his attack on the coldness, the immured inflexibility, the inhumaneness of reason and the rationalist spirit in his *Notes from the Underground* (1864). The image of the broken mathematical certainty must have been 'in the air'; perhaps Stirner introduced it.

dependent on an object, which it seeks to explain, investi-
gate, feel, love, etc., then it is not free, and since freedom
is the condition for genius, it can also have no genius. (For
were the godly man to seek to surmount the insuper-
ability of this object by a consistent doubt about the
existence of God, then he would even cease therewith to
be godly, just as a man who believes in ghosts no longer
can be so qualified if he doubts consistently about the
existence of ghosts. The godly man only constructs
'proofs for the existence of God' for himself, since, spell-
bound (captivated) within the circle of belief in this
existence, he reserves for himself *within* this sphere a free
mobility of—mind and penetration). Godliness can as
little be co-opted with genius as can a linen-mill. Religion
remains accessible even to the dullest man, and every
unimaginative simpleton can and indeed will still have
his religion, since his lack of imagination does not prevent
him from living in dependence.

(K.S. 258–61)

*   *   *

And, as one stormily pursues his own self, the never-
attained, so one also despises shrewd people's rule to
take men as they are, and prefers to take them as they
should be; and, for this reason, hounds every one on after
his should-be self and 'endeavours to make all into equally
entitled, equally respectable, equally moral or rational
men'.*

Yes, 'if men were what they *should* be, *could* be, if all
men were rational, all loved each other as brothers',

* *Die Kommunisten in der Schweiz nach den bei Weitling vorgefunden Papieren*,
transcript from the report of a Zürich governmental commission, (Füssli,
Zürich, 1843), p. 24.

then it would be a paradisaical life.* — All right, men are as they should be, can be. What should they be? Surely not more than they can be! And what can they be? Not more, again, than they — can, than they have the competence, the force, to be. But this they really are, because what they are not they are *incapable* of being; for to be capable means — really to be. One is not capable for anything that one really is not; one is not capable of anything that one does not really do. Could a man blinded by cataract see? Oh yes, if he had his cataract successfully removed. But now he cannot see because he does not see. Possibility and reality always coincide. One can do nothing that one does not, as one does nothing that one cannot.[1]

The singularity of this assertion vanishes when one reflects that the words 'it is possible that ... ' almost never contain another meaning than 'I can imagine that ... ', for instance, it is possible for all men to live rationally; that is, I can imagine that all, etc. Now — since my thinking cannot, and accordingly does not, cause all men to live rationally, but this must still be left to the men themselves — general reason is for me only thinkable, a thinkableness, but as such in fact a *reality* that is called a possibility only in reference to what I *can* not bring to pass, to wit, the rationality of others. So far as depends

* Op. cit., p. 63.

[1] This passage seems at variance with Stirner's optimistic anti-deterministic, 'all-things-are-possible' philosophy. It seems partly intended as a defence against the criticism that he is just another Utopian dreamer. He did not want to be associated with an ethereal romanticism that seeks through impossible dreams to escape from painful reality. Nevertheless, his egoism, his confidence in the individual's capacity to define his own environment is undeniably romantic; the proviso remains that Stirner places his emphasis on the links between the dream and the reality, the former must be 'real-izable'. In the end he stays true to his Hegelian heritage: life is a dialectical process in which the boundlessly egoistic sprouts from finite determinations.

on you, all men might be rational, for you have nothing against it; nay, so far as your thinking reaches, you perhaps cannot discover any hindrance either, and accordingly nothing does stand in the way of the thing in your thinking; it is thinkable to you.

As men are not all rational, though, it is probable that they — cannot be so.

If something which one imagines to be easily possible is not, or does not happen, then one may be assured that something stands in the way of the thing, and that it is — impossible. Our time has its art, science, etc.; the art may be bad in all conscience; but may one say that we deserved to have a better, and 'could' have it if we only would? We have just as much art as we can have. Our art of today is the *only art possible*, and therefore real, at the time.

Even in the sense to which one might at last still reduce the word 'possible', that it should mean 'future', it retains the full force of the 'real'. If one says, 'It is possible that the sun will rise tomorrow' — this means only, 'for today tomorrow is the real future'; for I suppose there is hardly need of the suggestion that a future is real 'future' only when it has not yet appeared.

Yet wherefore this dignifying of a word? If the most prolific misunderstanding of thousands of years were not in ambush behind it, if this single concept of the little word 'possible' were not haunted by all the spooks of possessed men, its contemplation should trouble us little here.

The thought, it was just now shown, rules the possessed world. Well, then, possibility is nothing but thinkableness, and innumerable sacrifices have hitherto been made to hideous *thinkableness*. It was *thinkable* that men might become rational; thinkable, that they might know Christ;

thinkable, that they might become moral and enthusiastic for the good; thinkable, that they might all take refuge in the Church's lap; thinkable, that they might meditate, speak, and do, nothing dangerous to the State; thinkable, that they *might* be obedient subjects; but, because it was thinkable, it was—so ran the inference—possible, and further, because it was possible to men (right here lies the deceptive point; because it is thinkable to me, it is possible to *men*), therefore they *ought* to be so, it was their *calling*; and finally—one is to take men only according to this calling, only as *called* men, 'not as they are, but as they ought to be'.

(Ego 438–40)

Your nature is, once for all, a human one; you are human natures, human beings. But, just because you already are so, you do not still need to become so. Beasts too are 'trained', and a trained beast executes many unnatural things. But a trained dog is no better for itself than a natural one, and has no profit from it, even if it is more companionable for us.

(Ego 443)

It is different if you do not chase after an *ideal* as your 'destiny', but dissolve yourself as time dissolves everything. The dissolution is not your 'destiny', because it is present time.

Yet the *culture*, the religiousness, of men has assuredly made them free, but only free from one lord, to lead them to another. I have learned by religion to tame my appetite, I break the world's resistance by the cunning that is put in my hand by *science*; I even serve no man; 'I am no man's lackey'. But then it comes. You must obey God more than man. Just so I am indeed free from irrational determination by my impulses, but obedient to the master *Reason*. I have gained 'spiritual freedom', 'freedom of the spirit'. But with that I have then become subject to that very *spirit*. The spirit gives me orders, reason guides me, they are my leaders and commanders. The 'rational', the 'servants of the spirit', rule. But, if *I* am not flesh, I am in truth not spirit either. Freedom of the spirit is servitude of me, because I am more than spirit or flesh.

Without doubt culture has made me *powerful*. It has given me power over all *motives*, over the impulses of my nature as well as over the exactions and violences of the world. I know, and have gained the force for it by culture, that I need not let myself be coerced by any of my appetites, pleasures, emotions, etc.; I am their—*master*; in like manner I become, through the sciences and arts, the *master* of the refractory world, whom sea and earth obey, and to whom even the stars must give an account of themselves. The spirit has made me *master*. — But I have no power over the spirit itself. From religion (culture) I do learn the means for the 'vanquishing of the world', but not how I am to subdue *God* too and become master of him; for God 'is the spirit'. And this same spirit, of which I am unable to become master, may have the most manifold shapes; he may be called God or National Spirit, State, Family, Reason, also—Liberty, Humanity, Man.

I receive with thanks what the centuries of culture have acquired for me; I am not willing to throw away and give up anything of it: I have not lived in vain. The experience that I have *power* over my nature, and need not be the slave of my appetites, shall not be lost to me; the experience that I can subdue the world by culture's

means is too dear-bought for me to be able to forget it.
But I want still more.

(Ego 443-5)

*   *   *

KNOWLEDGE[1]

Only philosophers can die and find in death their true
self; with them dies the era of the Reformation, the age of
knowledge. Yes, thus it is that knowledge itself must die,
and in death blossom again as *will*; freedom of thought,
belief, and conscience, these glorious, three-hundred-year-
old flowers, will sink back into the womb of the earth in
order that a new freedom, that of will, can nourish itself
on her most precious sap. Knowledge, and its freedom,
was the ideal of that time, one that has finally been
reached on the heights of philosophy: here the hero
himself will build his own funeral pyre and, saving the
eternal part of himself, carry it off to Olympus. Philosophy
is the termination of our past, the philosophers being
the Raphaels of the thought-period, in whom the old
principle in a glittering display of colour, and, by
rejuvenation, is changed from temporal to eternal.
Henceforth, whoever wishes to preserve knowledge will
lose it; but whoever abandons it will gain it again.
Philosophers alone are called to this abandonment and

[1] This short section on epistemology is taken from Stirner's 1842 article
on education, *Das unwahre Prinzip unserer Erziehung*. He posits knowledge as
a dynamic process rather than a related series of static facts. He is close to
Schopenhauer, unknown at the time, with his credo that man creates himself by *will* alone. Stirner goes further: unless knowledge is subordinated
to the will, he argues, it becomes rigid and burdensome—the idea
becomes larger than its creator, an anticipation of Nietzsche's critique of
'truth' and its martyrs in *Beyond Good and Evil*.

to this gain: they stand before the blazing fire and, like the dying hero, they must cremate their mortal *frame*, if the immortal spirit is to be free.

As much as possible must be discussed more clearly. Herein, in fact, still lies the error of our day, that knowledge is not complete and brought to transparency, that it remains material and formal, a positive knowledge which does not rise to the absolute, so that it weighs upon us like a burden. Like the ancient hero one must seek forgetfulness, one must drink from the waters of Lethe, which bring happiness; otherwise one does not come to oneself. All that is great must know how to die, and through its death be transfigured; only the lamentable, like the stiff-limbed High Court, gathers act upon act, and plays, with the perpetual childishness of the Chinese, for a millennium with elegant porcelain figures. True knowledge fulfils itself when it ceases to be knowledge and becomes again a simple human drive—the will. So, for example, the man who for years has pondered his 'human calling', will find, in the instant that he discovers this calling, that all worries and pilgrimages undertaken in his search sink into the Lethe of one simple feeling, one drive which from that hour will gradually guide him on. The 'human calling', which this man traced on a thousand paths and tracks, bursts out, as soon as it is recognized, in the flame of the moral will, and glows through the breast of the man who is no longer confused by his searching, but has become fresh and *naïve* again.

> Arise, bathe, disciple, undismayed,
> Your mortal breast to the dawn.[1]

That is the end, and at the same time the permanence,

---

[1] *Faust*, i, 445–6.

the eternity of knowledge: knowledge that, having become
once again more simple and immediate, acting as will,
puts itself (as knowledge) in a new form and reveals itself
afresh in every action ... A knowledge, which has not so
refined and concentrated itself that it carries me away to
volition, or in other words a knowledge which merely
burdens me as possession and property, instead of having
matched itself totally with me, so that the mobile ego,
unhampered by any trailing chattels, can journey through
the world, his senses refreshed,—a knowledge, finally,
which has not become *personal*,—gives a miserable preparation for life.

(*K.S.* 247–9)

*   *   *

I elect for myself what I have a fancy for, and in
electing I show myself—arbitrary.

(*Ego* 449)

Free thinking and free science busy *me*—for it is not I that
am free, not *I* that busy myself, but thinking is free and
busies me—with heaven and the heavenly or 'divine';
that is, properly, with the world and the worldly, not
this world but 'another' world; it is only the reversing
and deranging of the world, a busying with the *essence*
of the world, therefore a *derangement*. The thinker is blind
to the immediateness of things, and incapable of master-
ing them: he does not eat, does not drink, does not enjoy;
for the eater and drinker is never the thinker, nay, the
latter forgets eating and drinking, his getting on in life,
the cares of nourishment, etc., over his thinking; he
forgets it as the praying man too forgets it. This is why he
appears to the forceful son of nature as a queer Dick, a

fool—even if he does look upon him as holy, just as lunatics appeared so to the ancients. Free thinking is lunacy, because it is *pure movement of the inwardness*, of the merely *inward man*, which guides and regulates the rest of the man.

(*Ego* 452–3)

The professionals, the privileged, brook no freedom of thought, no thoughts that do not come from the 'Giver of all good', be he called God, pope, Church, or whatever else. If anybody has such illegitimate thoughts, he must whisper them into his confessor's ear, and have himself chastised by him till the slave-whip becomes unendurable to the free thoughts. In other ways too the professional spirit takes care that free thoughts shall not come at all: first and foremost, by a wise education. He on whom the principles of morality have been duly inculcated never becomes free again from moralizing thoughts, and robbery, perjury, overreaching, and the like, remain to him fixed ideas against which no freedom of thought protects him. He has his thoughts 'from above', and gets no further.

It is different with the holders of concessions or patents. Everyone must be able to have and form thoughts as he will. If he has the patent, or the concession, of a capacity to think, he needs no special *privilege*. But, as 'all men are rational', it is free to everyone to put into his head any thoughts whatever, and, to the extent of the patent of his natural endowment, to have a greater or less wealth of thoughts. Now one hears the admonitions that one 'is to honour all opinions and convictions', that 'every conviction is authorized', that one must be 'tolerant to the views of others', etc.

But 'your thoughts are not my thoughts, and your ways are not my ways'. Or rather, I mean the reverse: Your thoughts are *my* thoughts, which I dispose of as I will, and which I strike down unmercifully; they are my property, which I annihilate as I wish. I do not wait for authorization from you first, to decompose and blow away your thoughts. It does not matter to me that you call these thoughts yours too, they remain mine nevertheless, and how I will proceed with them is *my affair*, not a usurpation. It may please me to leave you in your thoughts; then I keep still. Do you believe thoughts fly around free like birds, so that every one may get himself some which he may then make good against me as his inviolable property? What is flying around is all—*mine*.

Do you believe you have your thoughts for yourselves and need answer to no one for them, or as you do also say, you have to give an account of them to God only? No, your great and small thoughts belong to me, and I handle them at my pleasure.

The thought is my *own* only when I have no misgiving about bringing it in danger of death every moment, when I do not have to fear its loss as a *loss for me*, a loss of me. The thought is my own only when I can indeed subjugate it, but it never can subjugate me, never fanaticizes me, makes me the tool of its realization.

So freedom of thought exists when I can have all possible thoughts; but the thoughts become property only by not being able to become masters. In the time of freedom of thought, thoughts (ideas) *rule*; but, if I attain to property in thought, they stand as my creatures.

(*Ego* 455–7)

The thinker is distinguished from the believer only by believing much more than the latter, who on his part thinks of much less as signified by his faith (creed). The thinker has a thousand tenets of faith where the believer gets along with few; but the former brings *coherence* into his tenets, and takes the coherence in turn for the scale to estimate their worth by. If one or the other does not fit into his budget, he throws it out.

The thinkers run parallel to the believers in their pronouncements. Instead of 'If it is from God you will not root it out', the word is 'If it is from the *truth*, is true, etc.'; instead of 'Give God the glory' — 'Give truth the glory'. But it is very much the same to me whether God or the truth wins; first and foremost I want to win.

Apart from this, how is an 'unlimited freedom' to be thinkable inside of the State or society? The State may well protect one against another, but yet it must not let itself be endangered by an unmeasured freedom, a so-called unbridledness. Thus in 'freedom of instruction' the *State* declares only this — that it approves of everyone who instructs as the State (or, speaking more comprehensibly, the political power) would have it. The point for the competitors is this 'as the State would have it'. If the clergy, for example, does not will as the State does, then it itself excludes itself from *competition* (*vide* France). The limit that is necessarily drawn in the State for any and all competition is called 'the oversight and superintendence of the State'. In bidding freedom of instruction keep within the due bounds, the State at the same time fixes the scope of freedom of thought; because, as a rule, people do not think further than their teachers have thought.[1]

(*Ego* 458–9)

---

[1] Stirner throughout this section has placed a quite original emphasis on censorship of *thought*, the direct epiphenomenon of indoctrination, a much more effective repressive weapon than censorship of the written word. The choice that has not been dreamed of does not exist, and certainly poses no threat — Stirner in fact introduces a radically modern and original notion of false or deprived consciousness. The State, through limiting the horizons it allows its subjects to view by means of its education system, severely impedes their potentiality for 'ownership'.

A 'rational' freedom of teaching, which recognizes only the conscience of reason,* does not bring us to the goal; we require an *egoistic* freedom of teaching rather, a freedom of teaching for all ownness, wherein *I* become audible and can announce myself unchecked. That I make myself *'audible'*,[1] this alone is 'reason', be I ever so irrational; in my making myself heard, and so bearing myself, others as well as I myself enjoy me, and at the same time consume me.

(*Ego* 460–1)

If the point is to have myself understood and to make communications, then assuredly I can make use only of *human* means, which are at my command because I am at the same time man. And really I have thoughts only as *man*; as I, I am at the same time *thoughtless*.[2] He who cannot get rid of a thought is so far *only* man, is a slave of *language*, this human institution, this treasury of *human* thoughts. Language or 'the word' tyrannizes hardest over us, because it brings up against us a whole army of *fixed ideas*. Just observe yourself in the act of reflection, at this moment, and you will find how you make progress only by becoming thoughtless and speechless every moment. You are not thoughtless and speechless merely in sleep, but even in the deepest reflection; yes, precisely then most so. And only by this thoughtlessness, this unrecognized 'freedom of thought' or freedom from the thought, are you your own. Only from it do you arrive at putting language to use as your *property*.

If thinking is not *my* thinking, it is merely a spun-out thought; it is slave work, or the work of a 'servant

* *Anekdota zur neuesten Philosophie und Publicistik*, ed. A. Ruge (Verlag des literarischen Comptoirs, Zürich and Winterthur, 1843), vol. 1, p. 127.
[1] *vernehmbar*.
[2] Literally 'thought-rid'.

obedient to the word'. For not a thought, but I, am the beginning for my thinking, and therefore I am its goal too, even as its whole course is only a course of my self-enjoyment; for absolute or free thinking, on the other hand, thinking itself is the beginning, and it plagues itself with propounding this beginning as the extremest 'abstraction' (such as being). This very abstraction, or this thought, is then spun out further.

(*Ego* 461–2)

But all thinking that does not sin against the holy spirit is belief in spirits or ghosts.

(*Ego* 463)

Christianity took away from the things of this world only their irresistibleness, made us independent of them. In like manner I raise myself above truths and their power: as I am supersensual, so I am supertrue. *Before me* truths are as common and as indifferent as things; they do not carry me away, and do not inspire me with enthusiasm. There exists not even one truth, not right, not freedom, humanity, etc., that has stability before me, and to which I subject myself. They are *words*, nothing but words, as all things are to the Christian nothing but 'vain things'. In words and truths (every word is a truth, as Hegel asserts that one cannot *tell* a lie) there is no salvation for me, as little as there is for the Christian in things and vanities. As the riches of this world do not make me happy, so neither do its truths. It is now no longer Satan, but the spirit, that plays the story of the temptation; and he does not seduce by the things of this world, but by its thoughts, by the 'glitter of the idea'.

Along with worldly goods, all sacred goods too must be put away as no longer valuable.

Truths are phrases, ways of speaking, words (*logos*); brought into connection, or into an articulate series, they form logic, science, philosophy.

For thinking and speaking I need truths and words, as I do foods for eating; without them I cannot think nor speak. Truths are men's thoughts, set down in words and therefore just as extant as other things, although extant only for the mind or for thinking. They are human institutions and human creatures, and, even if they are given out for divine revelations, there still remains in them the quality of alienness for me; yes, as my own creatures they are already alienated from me after the act of creation.

The Christian man is the man with faith in thinking, who believes in the supreme dominion of thoughts and wants to bring thoughts, so-called 'principles', to dominion. Many a one does indeed test the thoughts, and chooses none of them for his master without criticism, but in this he is like the dog who sniffs at people to smell out 'his master'; he is always aiming at the *ruling* thought. The Christian may reform and revolt an infinite deal, may demolish the ruling concepts of centuries; he will always aspire to a new 'principle' or new master again, always set up a higher or 'deeper' truth again, always call forth a cult again, always proclaim a spirit called to dominion, lay down a *law* for all.

If there is even one truth only to which man has to devote his life and his powers because he is man, then he is subjected to a rule, dominion, law; he is a serving-man. It is supposed that man, humanity, liberty, etc., are such truths.

On the other hand, one can say thus: Whether you will further occupy yourself with thinking depends on you; only know that, *if* in your thinking you would like to

make out anything worthy of notice, many hard problems
are to be solved, without vanquishing which you cannot
get far. There exists, therefore, no duty and no calling
for you to meddle with thoughts (ideas, truths); but, if
you will do so, you will do well to utilize what the forces
of others have already achieved towards clearing up these
difficult subjects.[1]

(*Ego* 463-5)

If thinking began at all, instead of being begun, if thinking
were a subject, an acting personality of its own, as even
the plant is such, then indeed there would be no abandoning the principle that thinking must begin with itself.
But it is just the personification of thinking that brings
to pass those innumerable errors. In the Hegelian system
they always talk as if thinking or 'the thinking spirit' (that
is, personified thinking, thinking as a ghost) thought and
acted; in critical liberalism it is always said that
'criticism' does this and that, or else that 'self-consciousness' finds this and that. But, if thinking ranks as the
personal actor, thinking itself must be presupposed; if
criticism ranks as such, a thought must likewise stand in
front. Thinking and criticism could be active only starting
from themselves, would have to be themselves the presupposition of their activity, as without being they could
not be active. But thinking, as a thing presupposed, is a
fixed thought, a *dogma*; thinking and criticism, therefore,
can start only from a *dogma*, from a thought, a fixed idea, a
presupposition.

(*Ego* 468-9)

---

[1] Stirner was not the anti-intellectual he is often accused of being. While
he relentlessly criticizes philosophy which abstracts itself into systems of
ideas dissociated from the world of experience, we must remember that
philosophy was his own consuming passion.

With this we come back again to what was enunciated above, that Christianity consists in the development of a world of thoughts, or that it is the proper 'freedom of thought', the 'free thought', the 'free spirit'. The 'true' criticism, which I called 'servile', is therefore just as much 'free' criticism, for it is not *my own*.

The case stands otherwise when what is yours is not made into something that is of itself, not personified, not made independent as a 'spirit' to itself. *Your* thinking has for a presupposition not 'thinking', but *you*. But thus you do presuppose yourself after all? Yes, but not for myself, but for my thinking. Before my thinking, there is—I. From this it follows that my thinking is not preceded by a *thought*, or that my thinking is without a 'presupposition'. For the presupposition which I am for my thinking is not one *made by thinking*, not one *thought of*, but it is *posited* thinking *itself*, it is the *owner* of the thought, and proves only that thinking is nothing more than—*property*, that an 'independent' thinking, a 'thinking spirit', does not exist at all.

(Ego 469–70)

I on my part start from a presupposition in presupposing *myself*; but my presupposition does not struggle for its perfection like 'Man struggling for his perfection', but only serves me to enjoy it and consume it. I consume my presupposition, and nothing else, and exist only in consuming it. But that presupposition is therefore not a presupposition at all: for, as I am the Unique, I know nothing of the duality of a presupposing and a presupposed ego (an 'incomplete' and a 'complete' ego or man); but this, that I consume myself, means only that I am. I do not presuppose myself, because I am every moment just positing or creating myself, and am I only by being not presupposed but posited, and, again, posited only in the moment when I posit myself; that is, I am creator and creature in one.[1]

(*Ego* 199–200)

The truth, or 'truth in general', people are bound not to give up, but to seek for. What else is it but the *être suprême*, the highest essence? Even 'true criticism' would have to despair if it lost faith in the truth. And yet the truth is only a—*thought*; but it is not merely 'a' thought, but the thought that is above all thoughts, the irrefragable thought; it is *the* thought itself, which gives the first hallowing to all others; it is the consecration of thoughts, the 'absolute', the 'sacred' thought. The truth wears longer than all the gods; for it is only in the truth's service, and for love of it, that people have overthrown the gods and at last God himself. 'The truth' outlasts the downfall of the world of gods, for it is the immortal soul of this transitory world of gods, it is Deity itself.

I will answer Pilate's question, What is truth? Truth is the free thought, the free idea, the free spirit; truth is what is free from you, what is not your own, what is not in your power. But truth is also the completely dependent, impersonal, unreal, and incorporeal; truth cannot step forward as you do, cannot move, change, develop; truth awaits and receives everything from you, and itself is only through you; for it exists only—in your head. You concede that the truth is a thought, but say that not every thought is a true one, or, as you are also likely to express it, not every thought is really and truly a thought. And by what do you measure and recognize the thought?

---

[1] Certainly Stirner's existentialist affirmation, 'I am', is as dogmatic as Descartes's 'I think, therefore I am', but for him it is the only dogma which is not *alienating*, the one which does not make being other than itself.

By *your impotence*, to wit, by your being no longer able to make any successful assault on it! When it overpowers you, inspires you, and carries you away, then you hold it to be the true one. Its dominion over you certifies to you its truth; and, when it possesses you, and you are possessed by it, then you feel well with it, for then you have found your—*lord and master*. When you were seeking the truth, what did your heart then long for? For your master! You did not aspire to *your* might, but to a Mighty One, and wanted to exalt a Mighty One ('Exalt ye the Lord our God!'). The truth, my dear Pilate, is—the Lord, and all who seek the truth are seeking and praising the Lord. Where does the Lord exist? Where else but in your head? He is only spirit, and, wherever you believe you really see him, there he is a—ghost; for the Lord is merely something that is thought of, and it was only the Christian pains and agony to make the invisible visible, the spiritual corporeal, that generated the ghost and was the frightful misery of the belief in ghosts.

As long as you believe in the truth, you do not believe in yourself, and you are a—*servant*, a—*religious man*. You alone are the truth, or rather, you are more than the truth, which is nothing at all before you. You too do assuredly ask about the truth, you too do assuredly 'criticize', but you do not ask about a 'higher truth'—to wit, one that should be higher than you—nor criticize according to the criterion of such a truth. You address yourself to thoughts and notions, as you do to the appearances of things, only for the purpose of making them palatable to you, enjoyable to you, and your own: you want only to subdue them and become their *owner*, you want to orient yourself and feel at home in them, and you find them true, or see them in their true light, when they can no longer slip away from you, no longer have any unseized or uncomprehended place, or when they are *right for you*, when they are your *property*. If afterwards they become heavier again, if they wriggle themselves out of your power again, then that is just their untruth — to wit, your impotence. Your impotence is their power, your humility their exaltation. Their truth, therefore, is you, or is the nothing which you are for them and in which they dissolve: their truth is their *nothingness*.

Only as my property do the spirits, the truths, get to rest; and they then for the first time really are, when they have been deprived of their sorry existence and made a property of mine, when it is no longer said 'the truth develops itself, rules, asserts itself; history (also a concept) wins the victory', and the like. The truth never has won a victory, but was always my *means* to the victory, like the sword ('the sword of truth'). The truth is dead, a letter, a word, a material that I can use up. All truth by itself is dead, a corpse; it is alive only in the same way as my lungs are alive — to wit, in the measure of my own vitality. Truths are material, like vegetables and weeds; as to whether vegetable or weed, the decision lies in me.

(*Ego* 470–3)

They say, the idea of liberty realizes itself in the history of the world. The reverse is the case; this idea is real as a man thinks it, and it is real in the measure in which it is idea, that is, in which I think it or *have* it. It is not the idea of liberty that develops itself, but men develop themselves, and, of course, in this self-development develop their thinking too.[1]

In short, the critic is not yet *owner*, because he still fights with ideas as with powerful aliens — as the Christian is not owner of his 'bad desires' so long as he has to

---

[1] An attack on Hegel's belief in the progressive march of history.

combat them; for him who contends against vice, vice *exists.*[1]

(*Ego* 476)

Why, warfare of the priesthood with *egoism*, of the spiritually minded with the worldly minded, constitutes the substance of all Christian history. In the newest criticism this war only becomes all-embracing, fanaticism complete. Indeed, neither can it pass away till after it has lived and raged itself out.

*   *   *

Whether what I think and do is Christian, what do I care? Whether it is human, liberal, humane, whether inhuman or illiberal, what do I ask about that? If only it accomplishes what I want, if only I satisfy myself in it, then overlay it with predicates as you will; it is all alike to me.

Perhaps I too, in the very next moment, defend myself against my former thoughts; I too am likely to change suddenly my mode of action; but not on account of its not corresponding to Christianity, not on account of its running counter to the eternal rights of man, not on account of its affronting the idea of mankind, humanity, and humanitarianism, but—because I am no longer all in it, because it no longer furnishes me any full enjoyment, because I doubt the earlier thought or no longer please myself in the mode of action just now practised.

As the world as property has become a *material* with

---

[1] This short aphorism anticipates Freud's exploration of the unconscious. Stirner, delving behind the wall of motivations that the actor consciously attributes to his acts, sees that he who condemns vice in another is afraid that the very same vice exists repressed in himself. Fear of self is projected into hatred of the immoral other.

which I undertake what I will, so the spirit too as property must sink down into a *material* before which I no longer entertain any sacred dread. Then, firstly, I shall shudder no more before a thought, let it appear as presumptuous and 'devilish' as it will, because, if it threatens to become too inconvenient and unsatisfactory for *me*, its end lies in my power; but neither shall I recoil from any deed because there dwells in it a spirit of godlessness, immorality, wrongfulness, as little as St Boniface pleased to desist, through religious scrupulousness, from cutting down the sacred oak of the heathens. If the *things* of the world have once become vain, the *thoughts* of the spirit must also become vain.

(Ego 477–8)

The egoist, before whom the humane shudder, is a spook as much as the devil is: he exists only as a bogey and phantasm in their brain. If they were not unsophisticatedly drifting back and forth in the antediluvian opposition of good and evil, to which they have given the modern names of 'human' and 'egoistic', they would not have freshened up the hoary 'sinner' into an 'egoist' either, and put a new patch on an old garment. But they could not do otherwise, for they hold it for their task to be 'men'. They are rid of the Good One; good is left!

We are perfect altogether, and on the whole earth there is not one man who is a sinner! There are crazy people who imagine that they are God the Father, God the Son, or the man in the moon, and so too the world swarms with tools who seem to themselves to be sinners; but, as the former are not the man in the moon, so the latter are — not sinners. Their sin is imaginary.

Yet, it is insidiously objected, their craziness or their possessedness is at least their sin. Their possessedness is nothing but what they—could achieve, the result of their development, just as Luther's faith in the Bible was all that he was—competent to bring out. The one brings himself into the madhouse with his development, the other brings himself therewith into the Pantheon and at the expense of—Valhalla.

There is no sinner and no sinful egoism!

Get away from me with your 'philanthropy'! Creep in, you philanthropist, into the 'dens of vice', linger awhile in the throng of the great city: will you not everywhere find sin, and sin, and again sin? Will you not wail over corrupt humanity, not lament at the monstrous egoism? Will you see a rich man without finding him pitiless and 'egoistic'? Perhaps you already call yourself an atheist, but you remain true to the Christian feeling that a camel will sooner go through a needle's eye than a rich man not be 'inhuman'. How many do you see anyhow that you would not throw into the 'egoistic mass'? What, therefore, has your philanthropy (love of man) found? Nothing but unlovable men! And where do they all come from? From you, from your philanthropy! You brought the sinner with you in your head, therefore you found him, therefore you inserted him everywhere. Do not call men sinners, and they are not: you alone are the creator of sinners; you, who fancy that you love men, are the very one to throw them into the mire of sin, the very one to divide them into vicious and virtuous, into human and inhuman; the very one to befoul them with the slaver of your possessedness; for you love not *men*, but *man*. But I tell you, you have never seen a sinner, you have only— dreamed of him.

Self-enjoyment is embittered for me by my thinking I must serve another, by my fancying myself under obligation to him, by my holding myself called for 'self-sacrifice', 'resignation', 'enthusiasm'. All right: if I no longer serve any idea, any 'higher essence', then it is clear of itself that I no longer serve any man either, but—under all circumstances—*myself*. But thus I am not merely in fact or in being, but also for my consciousness, the—unique one.

There pertains to *you* more than the divine, the human, etc.; *yours* pertains to you.

Look upon yourself as more powerful than they give you out for, and you have more power; look upon yourself as more, and you have more.

You are then not merely *called* to everything divine, *entitled* to everything human, but *owner* of what is yours, that is, of all that you possess the force to make your own;[1] you are *appropriate*[2] and capacitated for everything that is yours.

People have always supposed that they must give me a destiny lying outside myself, so that at last they demanded that I should lay claim to the human because I am—man. This is the Christian magic circle. Fichte's ego too is the same essence outside me, for every one is ego; and, if only this ego has rights, then it is 'the ego', it is not I. But I am not an ego along with other egos, but the sole ego: I am unique. Hence my wants too are unique, and my deeds; in short, everything about me is unique. And it is only as this unique I that I take everything for my own, as I set myself to work, and develop myself, only as this. I do not develop men, nor as man, but, as I, I develop—myself.

This is the meaning of the—*unique one*.

(*Ego* 480–3)

---

[1] *eigen.*   [2] *geeignet.*

VI. THE UNIQUE ONE[1]

But the unique one is an *indeterminate* concept and cannot be made determinate through other concepts or receive a 'more precise content': he is not the 'principle of a concept-series', but a word or concept incapable of all development as a word or concept. The development of the unique one is your self-development and mine, a *completely unique* development, since your development is totally different from mine ...

The unique one is the sincere, undeniable, obvious — phrase; he is the keystone to our phrase-world, this world in whose 'beginning was the *word*'.

The unique one is a statement, which, it is conceded with all openness and honesty, — states nothing. Man, spirit, true individual, personality, etc., are statements or predicates which abound in a fullness of content, phrases of the highest matter. The unique one is, in contrast to those holy and sublime phrases, the empty, unpretentious, and thoroughly common phrase ...

Since the content of the unique one is not thought content, it is also unthinkable and unspeakable, and since it cannot be uttered, this perfect phrase is at the same time — *no phrase*.

Only when *nothing* is stated about you and you are only named, are you acknowledged as yourself. As long as something is stated about you, you are only acknowledged

---

[1] I have replaced the first part of this short final chapter by a section from Stirner's reply to his critics, the *Recensenten Stirners* (1845). It is directed against Feuerbach's argument that a self-predicating concept, such as the 'egoist', is vacuous and hence meaningless — Stirner, Feuerbach advanced, had merely introduced a new predicate. The Stirner response gives form, with unmatched clarity, to what Sartre defined as the hub of existentialist philosophy, the axiom that existence precedes essence.

as this something (man, mind, Christ, etc.). But the
unique one states nothing, since he is only a name he
merely says that you are you and nothing other than you,
that you are a unique you, or you yourself. Hereby you are
unpredicated, and at the same time without determination, vocation, law, etc.

Speculation was adjusted to find a predicate which
would be so *general* that it would comprehend *each one*.
Such a predicate however should certainly not express
what each *ought* to be, but rather what he *is*. Hence, if
this predicate were 'man', it must not be taken as what
each ought to become, for otherwise all those who have
not yet become this would be excluded, but rather as
what each is. But this *what* is indeed an expression of
the universal in each one, for *what* each has in common with
the other, but it is not an expression of the *each*, it does not
express *who* each is. Are you exhaustively described when
it is said that you are man? Does one thereby also express
who you are? Does every predicate 'man' accomplish the
task of the predicate, to express the subject *completely*,
or does it not on the contrary omit the very subjectivity
of the subject, not saying who, but merely what, the
subject is?

Hence, if the predicate is to comprehend *each one*, each
must therefore appear in it as subject, that is not merely
as *what* he is, but as *who* he is.

But how can you figure as he who you are if you do not
figure yourself? Are you a double or are you only once
there? You are nowhere outside yourself, you are not in
the world for the second time, you are — unique. You can
indeed figure, if you figure *bodily*.

'You are unique' — is that not a judgment? If *you* in
the judgment 'You are man' do not appear as he who you
are then do you really appear as yourself in the judg-

ment 'You are unique'? The judgment 'You are unique'
is none other than 'You are you', a judgment which the
logician deems nonsensical, because it judges *nothing*,
says nothing, because it is empty, or a judgment that is no
judgment.

What the logician treats contemptuously is certainly
illogical or only '*formally* logical'; but also, considered
from a *logical* point of view, it is still only a phrase; it is
logic perishing in the form of a phrase.

The unique one ought only to be the last, the dying
statement (predicate) of you and me, only that statement which is turned into meaning: a statement which
is no more, a statement which grows silent and is
mute.

You — unique one! What remains of a thought-content,
a content of judgment in this? Nothing! ...

You, imponderable and unpronounceable one, are the
content of the phrase, the owner of the phrase, the
phrase incarnate; *you* are the *who*, the *he* of the phrase.

(*K.S.* 346–9)

*   *   *

When the accent was at last laid on Man or mankind, it
was again the idea that they '*pronounced eternal*'. 'Man does
not die!' They thought they had now found the reality
of the idea: *Man* is the I of history, of the world's history;
it is he, this *ideal*, that really develops, *realizes*, himself.
He is the really real and corporeal one, for history is his
body, in which individuals are only members. Christ is
the I of the world's history, even of the pre-Christian; in
modern apprehension it is man, the figure of Christ has
developed into the *figure of man*: man as such, man
absolutely, is the 'central point' of history. In 'man' the

imaginary beginning returns again; for 'man' is as imaginary as Christ is. 'Man', as the I of the world's history, closes the cycle of Christian apprehensions.

Christianity's magic circle would be broken if the strained relation between existence and calling, that is, between me as I am and me as I should be, ceased; it persists only as the longing of the idea for its bodiliness, and vanishes with the relaxing separation of the two: only when the idea remains — idea, as man or mankind is indeed a bodiless idea, is Christianity still extant. The corporeal idea, the corporeal or 'completed' spirit, floats before the Christian as 'the end of the days' or as the 'goal of history'; it is not present time to him.

The individual can only have a part in the founding of the Kingdom of God, or, according to the modern notion of the same thing, in the development and history of humanity; and only so far as he has a part in it does a Christian, or according to the modern expression human, value pertain to him; for the rest he is dust and a worm-bag.

That the individual is of himself a world's history, and possesses his property in the rest of the world's history, goes beyond what is Christian. To the Christian the world's history is the higher thing, because it is the history of Christ or 'man'; to the egoist only *his* history has value, because he wants to develop only *himself* not the mankind-idea, not God's plan, not the purposes of Providence, not liberty, and the like. He does not look upon himself as a tool of the idea or a vessel of God, he recognizes no calling, he does not fancy that he exists for the further development of mankind and that he must contribute his mite to it, but he lives himself out, careless of how well or ill humanity may fare thereby. If it were not open to confusion with the idea that a state of nature

is to be praised, one might recall Lenau's *Three Gypsies*.[1]
What, am I in the world to realize ideas? To do my part
by my citizenship, say, towards the realization of the idea
'State', or by marriage, as husband and father, to bring
the idea of the family into an existence? What does such
a calling concern me! I live after a calling as little as the
flower grows and gives fragrance after a calling.

The ideal 'Man' is *realized* when the Christian apprehension turns about and becomes the proposition, 'I, this
unique one, am man.' The conceptual question, 'what is
man?'—has then changed into the personal question,
'who is man?' With 'what' the concept was sought for,
in order to realize it; with 'who' it is no longer any
question at all, but the answer is personally on hand at
once in the asker: the question answers itself.

They say of God, 'Names name thee not'. That holds
good of me: no *concept* expresses me, nothing that is
designated as my essence exhausts me; they are only
names. Likewise they say of God that he is perfect and
has no calling to strive after perfection. That too holds
good of me alone.

I am *owner* of my might, and I am so when I know
myself as *unique*. In the *unique one* the owner himself
returns into his creative nothing, of which he is born.
Every higher essence above me, be it God, be it man,
weakens the feeling of my uniqueness, and pales only
before the sun of this consciousness. If I found my affair
on myself, the unique one, then my concern rests on its
transitory, mortal creator, who consumes himself, and I
may say:

I have founded my affair on nothing.

(Ego 488–90)

---

[1] Nikolaus Lenau (1802–50), poet and writer of intensely romantic
short stories.

SELECTED BIBLIOGRAPHY

The Works of Max Stirner

Der Einzige und sein Eigenthum (Wigand, Leipzig: 1st edn 1845 (first copies late in 1844); 2nd edn 1882; Reclam edn 1893).

English translation by S. T. Byington, *The Ego and His Own* (1st American edn 1907; Fifield, London, 1912; most recent edn Libertarian Book Club, New York, 1963).

Die Geschichte der Reaction (2 vol.) (Allgemeine Deutsche Verlags-Anstalt, Berlin, 1852).

Kleinere Schriften (ed. John Henry Mackay) (Bernard Zack, Treptow, 2nd – extended – edn 1914).

Über Schulgesetze (1834) (ed. Rolf Engert) (Verlag des dritten Reiches, Dresden, 1920).

Edited by Max Stirner

Die National-Oekonomen der Franzosen und Engländer (selected and translated from the works of J. B. Say and Adam Smith) (Wigand, Leipzig, 1845–7).

Background Texts

BAUER, Bruno: *Die gute Sache der Freiheit und meine eigene Angelegenheit* (Verlag des literarischen Comptoirs, Zürich and Winterthur, 1842).

FEUERBACH, Ludwig: *The Essence of Christianity* (1841) (Harper and Row, New York, 1957).

HEGEL: *The Phenomenology of Mind* (1807) (Allen and Unwin, London, 1964).

HEGEL: *The Philosophy of Right* (1821) (O.U.P., 1967).

PROUDHON, P. J.: *De la Création de l'ordre dans l'humanité* (Librairie de Prévot, Paris, 1843).

PROUDHON, P. J.: *Qu'est-ce que la Propriété?* (Brocard, Paris, 1840).

General Critical Texts

ARVON, Henri: *Aux Sources de l'existentialisme: Max Stirner* (Presses Universitaires de France, Paris, 1954). Shows Stirner in relation to his German, Young Hegelian heritage.

BASCH, Victor: *L'Individualisme anarchiste. Max Stirner* (Félix Alcan, Paris, 1904). The first full-length critical work.

ENGERT, Rolf: *Das Bildnis Max Stirners* (Verlag des dritten Reiches, Dresden, 1921). Includes two pencil portraits of Stirner and Engels's sketch of *Die Freien*.

HELMS, Hans G.: *Die Ideologie der anonymen Gesellschaft* (M. Du Mont Schauberg, Köln, 1966). A Marxist interpretation of Stirner as the first formulator of middle-class ideology, a precursor of fascism. In spite of its savage misreading, this book is a formidable piece of research and includes a ninety-two-page bibliography of Stirner's writings and their influences.

MACKAY, John Henry: *Max Stirner. Sein Leben und sein Werk* (Schuster und Loeffler, Berlin, 1898).

PATERSON, R. W. K.: *The Nihilistic Egoist, Max Stirner* (Oxford University Press, London, 1971). The most comprehensive study of Stirner to date.

Stirner and Anarchism

GUÉRIN, Daniel: *L'Anarchisme* (Gallimard, Paris, 1965).

JOLL, James: *The Anarchists* (Eyre and Spottiswoode, London, 1964).

KRIMERMAN, Leonard I. and PERRY, Lewis (eds): *Patterns of Anarchy* (Anchor, New York, 1967).

MARTIN, James J.: *Men Against the State. The Expositors of Individualist Anarchism in America*, 1827–1908 (Adrian Allen Assoc., DeKalb (Illinois), 1953).

READ, Herbert: 'Pragmatic Anarchism', *Encounter*, vol. 32, no. 1 (January 1968).

WOODCOCK, George: *Anarchism* (Penguin Books, Harmondsworth, 1963).

Stirner and Marx

MARX, Karl and ENGELS, Frederick: *The German Ideology* (1845–6) (Lawrence and Wishart, London, 1965).

HOOK, Sidney: *From Hegel to Marx* (Humanities Press, New York, 1950).

MCLELLAN, David: *The Young Hegelians and Karl Marx* (Macmillan, London, 1969).

Stirner and Nietzsche

BERNOULLI, Carl Albrecht: *Franz Overbeck und Friedrich Nietzsche. Eine Freundschaft* (2 vol.) (Diederichs, Jena, 1908). Includes quotations from Overbeck's memoirs.

LÖWITH, Karl: *From Hegel to Nietzsche* (Constable, London, 1965).

Miscellaneous

ANNENKOV, Pavel V.: *The Extraordinary Decade* (University of Michigan Press, Chicago, 1968).

BERDYAEV, Nicolas: *Slavery and Freedom* (Geoffrey Bles, London, 1943).

BILLINGTON, James H.: *The Icon and the Axe* (Weidenfeld and Nicolson, London, 1966). Notes V. S. Pecherin's interest in Stirner.

BRAZILL, William J.: *The Young Hegelians* (Yale University Press, 1970).

BUBER, Martin: *Between Man and Man* (Fontana, London, 1961). Includes the essay, *The Question to the Single One*.

BÜLOW, Hans von (ed. Marie von Bülow): *Briefe und Schriften* (Breitkopf und Härtel, Leipzig, 1908). Includes the 1892 speech.

CAMUS, Albert: *L'Homme révolté* (Gallimard, Paris, 1951).

KOLAKOWSKI, Leszek: 'Vom Sinn der Tradition', *Merkur*, vol. 23, no. 12 (December 1969).

MASARYK, Thomas: *The Spirit of Russia* (Allen and Unwin, London, 1919).

MESSER, Max: *Max Stirner* (Bard Marquardt, Berlin, 1907). No. 24 in a series edited by George Brandes.

MUSSOLINI, Benito: *Opera Omnia* (La Fenice, Firenze, 1951–63), vol. 4, p. 258 and vol. 14, pp. 193–4.

READ, Herbert: *The Contrary Experience* (Faber and Faber, London, 1963).

READ, Herbert: *The Forms of Things Unknown* (Faber and Faber, London, 1960), chapter 11.

READ, Herbert: *The Tenth Muse* (Routledge and Kegan Paul, London, 1957). Includes the article written on the centenary of Stirner's book.

RUSSELL, John: *Max Ernst, Life and Work* (Thames & Hudson, London, 1967).

RUTHERFORD, H. C.: *The Sovereign Self through Max Stirner* (Third New Atlantis Foundation Lecture, 1956).

SIMMEL, Georg: 'Die beiden Formen des Individualismus', *Das freie Wort* (Frankfurt/Main), October 5th, 1901).

STEINER, Rudolf: *Naturwissenschaft und Seelekunde* (Philosophisch-Anthropos-ophischer Verlag, Dornach-Schweiz, 1958), vol. 5, sec. 24.

71 72 73 10 9 8 7 6 5 4 3 2 1